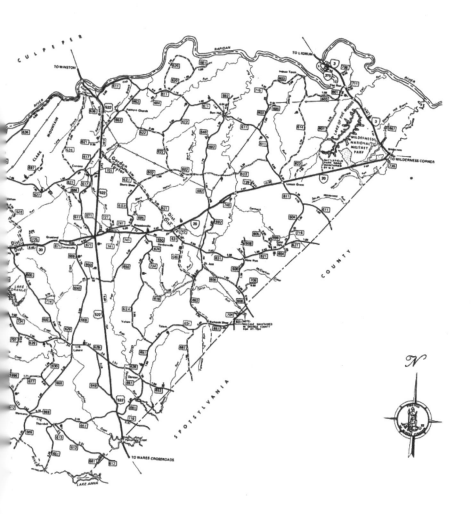

# Remembering:
## A History of Orange County, Virginia

# Remembering:
## A History of Orange County, Virginia

Frank S. Walker, Jr.

Orange County Historical Society
Orange, Virginia
2004

© 2004 by the Orange County Historical Society, Inc.
130 Caroline Street, Orange, VA 22960
All rights reserved.
Book and dust jacket design by Clara Colby.
Printed in the United States of America.
First published 2004.

3  5  7  9  8  6  4  2

Library of Congress Catalog Number: TX5-929-275

Walker, Frank S., Jr.
 Remembering: A History of Orange County, Virginia.
Includes bibliographical references and index.
ISBN: 1-932547-00-2

*To Bernice*
Wife and All-Around Best Friend
Whose untiring support, constructive suggestions, and hard work
have been a major part of every significant thing I have ever done,
including this book

# Contents

# *Foreword & Acknowledgments*

This work is "a" history of Orange County, not "the" history. The intent behind this particular writing is to provide a general overall history of the county while keeping it relatively short and readable. A glance across the stuffed filing cabinets, bulging map drawers, and packed book shelves at the Research Center of the Orange County Historical Society, however, makes it clear that many other Orange County-based histories await their authors. Histories of its churches, communities, educational systems, financial institutions — the list goes on and on.

You will see that the book is organized into seven main theme chapters with all but one having subchapters. Within the subchapters, major stories are more or less identified by paragraphs beginning with a capitalized line. There are other stories which are a significant part of several subchapters or major stories, and they are repeated in varying formats and with varying amounts of content where necessary. The effort is to create a book which can be read in stand-alone chapters, subchapters, and stories, if one so desires. I attempted to vary the re-presentations, and I hope they will be found helpful and not tedious.

Orange County's history is often made with reference to, or in response to, larger events taking place outside of its borders, and some explanation of those events is presented as an aid to understanding what occurred here. In lieu of space-consuming tables, statistical data is supplied as needed in the text. The index will be especially helpful in learning where a particular statistic is located.

The footnotes are more than a record of sources. There is oftentimes additional or related information on the item being noted. Short "tag line" references in the footnotes will lead you to the complete reference in the bibliography. The table of abbreviations will decipher the more cryptic references. Footnotes fully reference those sources whose contributions were too limited to warrant a listing in the bibliography.

THIS BOOK WAS GIVEN TO THE ORANGE COUNTY HISTORICAL SOCIETY because of the tremendous number of people who have helped in so many ways to create it. Indeed, as my eyesight and my ability to do research declined, I came to rely on others more and more to bring this book to publication. For me to take such wonderful assistance and then act as if this was all my doing would haunt me to my grave. My primary contribution, such as it is, has been one of organizing and relating a tremendous amount of information which exists in a vast number of sources. In that process, some new and expanded understandings may have evolved, and I do take such credit or blame as you wish to assign for that.

As I begin recognizing and thanking all the people who assisted, I keenly sense the dread of leaving someone out. If a contributor notes that his or her name is missing, please do forgive me and don't sulk. Kindly remind me, so proper credit can be given in a subsequent edition.

The first person to thank is my long-suffering wife, Bernice, and I have in fact dedicated this work to her. Her contributions were enormous, varied, and crucial. Without her, no book — and that's a fact.

When Joe Rowe was president of the Historical Society, he issued the call for someone to write a new history of Orange County. W.W. Scott's history ended with Reconstruction (1870), and both his interest areas and the information available to him at the time limited his presentation. Joe recognized that it was time for a re-do and update. As a tour guide and lifelong area resident, I had been toying with the idea of writing a new history of the county, but without Joe's insistence that it be done now, I suspect that the first word would remain unwritten. Thank you, Joe, for the jump start.

If Ann Miller wasn't so busy, she could have written this book and done it better. She almost did it anyway with *Antebellum Orange*. Ann has been the source of volumes of pertinent, valuable, and correct information, and a most careful and encouraging critic of my efforts to present it in an understandable manner. Steve Cushman, Pete Joyner, and Barbara Little, having also endured the publishing process, lent the wisdom of their experiences to good effect.

I owe much to the memory and writings of J. Randolph "Randy" Grymes, Jr., and William H. B. "Bill" Thomas. Randy's precision as a historian and a writer remains an awesome benchmark to be judged by. Bill's infectious enthusiasm made history come alive with sound and color. Both died without knowing I was contemplating this work, but their writings have been invaluable resources. Paul Slayton reminds me of Bill in some ways, and I have both profited from his research work product and enjoyed the opportunity to see the obvious pleasure he gets in sharing it.

Ken Clark is a combined historian, research librarian, and technical expert. He knows what I am trying to say I need, where it is, and how best to work with it. Jean McGann, Heather Isaak, and Marty Caldwell, whose work at the Research Center exposed them to more talk about "the book" and requests for assistance than anyone ought to have to endure, tolerated and assisted with good cheer.

A key to the development of this book was the work of the Historical Society Round Table, who read and discussed the early versions of each chapter, an exercise that took almost a year by the time it was over. The membership of the group is not rigidly established, and individuals came and went as their interests moved them. Ann Miller and Ken Clark were stalwarts, as well as Marty Caldwell, Rebecca Coleman, Carolyn French, Peg Harmon, Pete Joyner, Lynne Lewis, Jean McGann, and Lou Mittelman. Joe Rowe, Richard Sanford, Paul Slayton, and Atwell Somerville all read portions or all of the manuscript and offered helpful suggestions. I especially appreciate the Board of Directors of the Orange County African-American Historical Society reviewing and commenting on the chapter dealing with reconstruction and race. Ken Clark, Rebecca Coleman, Carolyn French, Mary Ann French, Gloria Gilmore, Lynne Lewis, Kate Longstreet, and Ann Miller of that body contributed much on this subject, one which I began to explore in detail just within the last few years. Duff Green, a walking Orange County history encyclopedia, lent both his knowledge and his vast photograph collection to the effort.

It would be hard to overstate the contributions of that group of capable and dedicated authors, historians, guides, and volunteers who staff the Fredericksburg and Spotsylvania National Military Park. Recently-retired Chief Historian Robert K. Krick set a standard that guaranteed excellent research and quality work product. Ray Castner, Hank Elliott, Janice Frye, Noel Harrison, John Hennessy, Elsa Lohman, Greg Mertz, Eric Mink, Don Pfanz, Sandy Rives, Frank O'Reilly, and Mac Wyckoff begin a very long list of very helpful Park personnel. They bring honor to the term "public servant." Tom Van Winkle and Carolyn Elstner of the Friends of Wilderness Battlefield and Keith Walters of the Friends of Mine Run have also exposed me to historic sites and information which significantly enhanced this work.

The Montpelier administrative staff, historians, archaeologists, guides, maintenance people, can all lay a claim to having contributed to this work. Lee Langston-Harrison, Pen Bowers, Mike Quinn, Matt Reeves, Bill Sage, Beth Taylor, Andy Washburn, Allison Enos, and the ubiquitous Ann Miller and Lynne Lewis — I will think of others as soon as the book goes to the printer.

The Memorial Foundation of the Germanna Colonies is populated with knowledgeable and helpful people. Thom Faircloth, Willie and Rose Marie Martin, John Pearce, and Doug Sanford are among those most often consulted. Ken Clark, in his role with the James Madison Museum, availed me of assistance from that quarter. Andy Daniel, Bettie Blue Omohundro, and Tim Burnett of Historic Gordonsville all assisted in various ways. Woodberry Forest's strong connection with Orange and Orange County drew that portion of Madison County into a number of stories, and I am grateful for the encouragement and assistance received from that quarter, particularly from Fred Jordan and Karen Culbertson.

In addition to the folks named above, I asked various other persons to also serve as advance readers for later drafts of the book. Barbara Bannar, Julie Blim, Joyce Clark, Steve Cushman, Thom Faircloth, Dan Holmes, George Jones, Fred Jordan, Gail Marshall, Tinsley Mack. John Moore, Barry Mountain, Hunter Rawlings, and Bob Shreve read some or all of the book in its later stages, and in so doing helped to make it better. Family members Bernice and Susan Walker, Austin and Pete Siebel, and Virginia St. Clair suffered through countless drafts and gave much helpful comment with barely a murmur of complaint. When it came to giving the almost-finished manuscript a strict and thorough editorial reading, the work of Bernice Walker and Lynne Lewis was nothing short of heroic.

As Ann Miller was to substance, Clara Colby was to presentation: thoroughly knowledgeable, highly competent, and indispensable. She took the manuscript, over which we had labored for so long, and brought it to life for the reader. Everything from chapter headings to cover design to illustration location was Clara's domain. And it wasn't all just artistry. Setting up the index cost her more than a little sleep. A special "thank you" to Clara.

Mike Remorenko and his staff at Design 3 Studio, Randy Beard and Martin Speer, contributed time and effort beyond their billings to prepare the illustrations, some of which tested their considerable expertise to make them attractive and useful.

While this work draws largely from local and regional sources, it could not have come into being without assistance from the Virginia Historical Society and the State Library of Virginia. Closer to home, the people and resources of the various Orange County court and governmental offices, the Chamber of Commerce, Office of Economic Development, and Public Library all had a hand in this effort.

Even with all these kind people and organizations helping me, I have most surely not been brought up short on all of the errors and omissions which can populate such writings. It's not their fault. They tried, but I am persistently human, and the blame lies with me.

Finally, I want to thank those generous contributors who have made the publication of this book possible. They are recognized and their names are preserved in a special section of the book, as well they should be. Without them, you would not be reading these words. In that regard, the work of the charmingly capable Peg Harmon as Publications Fund chairman was pivotal. The outpouring of support for this publication was both gratifying and a bit frightening. What if this history is not the work they

had expected it to be? My consolation, as it goes to press, is that I did what
I thought needed to be done, in the best way that I could do it. I trust that
you will find it worthy of your time and attention.

Frank S. Walker, Jr.

# With Deepest Appreciation

During an approximately six month period in 2002-2003, the Orange County Historical Society conducted a campaign to raise the funds needed to publish this book. The response was both broad-based and generous, and the Society wishes to recognize and memorialize the support of the individuals and organizations named below. Thank you. Thank you so very much.

## Patrons

The Kington Foundation
Mr. & Mrs. James H. T. McConnell, Jr.
May & Mike Saxton
Mr. & Mrs. Charles H. Seilheimer, Jr.

## Friends

Adra B. "Bee" Browning
Mr. & Mrs. Walter W. Craigie, Jr.
Mr. & Mrs. Joe Grills
Mr. & Mrs. O. Bruce Gupton
Mason Insurance Agency, Inc.
Mr. & Mrs. Carl E. Owens, Jr.
Mrs. A. Stuart Robertson, Jr.
Joseph Y. Rowe

Mr. Joseph T. Samuels, Jr.
Mrs. Elizabeth G. Schneider
Mr. & Mrs. Theodore G. Scott, Jr.
Mr. V. R. Shackelford, Jr.
Mr. & Mrs. John H. Snyder
Mr. Atwell W. Somerville
Mr. & Mrs. Frank S. Walker, Jr.

## Contributors

Mrs. John C. Barrow
Mr. William P. Boyer
Mr. & Mrs. H. Pendleton Bresee, Jr.
Mr. & Mrs. William A. Brockman, Jr.
Dorothy C. Browning
Mr. & Mrs. Henry Lee Carter
Susannah Chandler Chapter, D.A.R.
Isaiah & Rebecca Coleman
Stearns L. Coleman
Col. & Mrs. William H. Collier
Mr. & Mrs. Ralph E. Cook
Stephen P and Sandra Bain Cushman
Dr. A. C. Duffer
Mr. William H. Dunn
Faulconer Hardware, Inc.
Dr. & Mrs. David French

Friends of Mine Run
Friends of Wilderness Battlefield
Mr. & Mrs. James Gerock
Golden Horseshoe Chapter, D.A.R.
T. Mason Grasty
Mr. & Mrs. Angus M. Green
Dr. Maury L. Hanson, Jr.
Bob and Peg Harmon
Francis B. Hastings, Jr.
Patricia J. Hurst
Mr. & Mrs. John F. James
Mr. & Mrs. F. Claiborne Johnson, Jr.
Fred and Karen Jordan
Mr. & Mrs. U. P. Joyner, Jr.
Lynne G. Lewis & Paul J. Donohue
Gail S. Marshall

## Contributors (continued)

Ann L. Miller
James I. & Donna J. Mundy
Mr. & Mrs. Samuel S. Neale
Mr. & Mrs. William D. Newell
The Orange County African-American
    Historical Society
Mrs. Jo Sanford Perry
Woody and Frances Purcell
Gilbert K. Queitzsch
The Rapidan Foundation, Inc.
Doris B. Samuels
Richard L. and Thelma Sanford
Mr. Johnny Scott
Mr. & Mrs. Fred W. Sherman
Mr. & Mrs. W. A. Sherman

Dr. Walter & Audrey Shropshire
Austin & Pete Siebel, Virginia St. Clair
Mr. & Mrs. Roderic H. Slayton
A. Franklin Smith
Mr. & Mrs. Edward B. Sparks
Susan B. Strange
Barbara and Everette Tucker
Edward F. & Mildred Tyner
Mr. & Mrs. J. Nelson Tucker
Susan S. Walker
Joseph R. Wayner, Jr.
F. Beale Wilhoit
Woodberry Forest School History
    Department

# Table of Abbreviations

| | |
|---|---|
| ... | Called "ellipsis." A word or words have been eliminated from the material being quoted, the author having deemed them irrelevant. |
| *c.* | The reference is to an illustration caption at the page number given. |
| C.O. | Colonial Office. Repository of official communications between colonial governments and the Royal government. The Library of Congress is the primary source in America. |
| Ed. | (1) Editor of a work which was largely written by others. The editor's notes and organization of the material are often the key to making it understandable and useful.<br>(2) The edition of the work being referenced. |
| *Et seq.* | The specific reference material cited, plus that which follows it at the place cited. |
| *Hume Diary* | Two years of the diary of Fanny Page Hume have been edited and published: 1861 by James W. Cortada and 1862 by J. Randolph Grymes, Jr. |
| *Ibid.* | The matter referenced will be found in the same work and, if no page number is given, in the same place just cited in the preceding footnote. |
| *n.* | The reference is to a footnote at the page number given. |
| OCDB | Orange County Deed Book, in the county circuit court clerk's office. The number preceding it is the book number. The number following is the page number. |
| OCOB | Orange County Order Book, in the county circuit court clerk's office. The number preceding it is the book number. The number following is the page number. |

| | |
|---|---|
| OCWB | Orange County Will Books, in the county circuit court clerk's office. The number preceding it is the book number. The number following it is the page number. |
| *Op Cit.* | The matter referenced will be found in the same work just cited in the preceding footnote, at the location given. |
| O.R | *The War of the Rebellion: A Compilation of the Official Records of the Union and Confederate Armies.* Now widely and economically available on CD-ROM. |
| O.S., N.S. | Old Style calendar, New Style calendar. See the first footnote of Chapter I. |
| [sic] | Indicates that the word or phrase preceding it is reproduced exactly as it was written in the source document. |
| *Va. Mag. His/Bio.* | *Virginia Magazine of History and Biography*, a publication of the Virginia Historical Society. Copies are at the Orange County Historical Society Research Center. |
| WWI, WWII | World Wars I (Approx. 1914-18) and II (Approx. 1940-45). |

*Their Serene & Royal Highnesses*
*WILLIAM & ANN Prince & Princess of Orange & Nassau &c.&c.*

William and Anne, the Prince and Princess of Orange. This public image of the couple is at odds with a written description of their appearances. Artists painting wealthy or powerful patrons routinely, and wisely, flattered their subjects. Reproduced courtesy of the Library of Virginia, Richmond.

# CHAPTER I

# *Beginnings for a County & a Court House Town*

## A. "Orange County, be it Remembered ..."

On January 21, 1734, by the Old Style calendar,[1] certain freeholders (landowners) of St. Mark's Parish met to form a new Virginia county. The commission of William Gooch, the Lieutenant Governor of the colony, was read, appointing the Gentlemen Justices (judges) for the county's court. All but a few of the named appointees were present, and they swore to the several required oaths before attending to the housekeeping matters associated with starting up a new county. The words which begin line I, page 1, of Orange County Order Book 1, are those which title this subchapter.

The new county was being formed pursuant to an Act of Establishment adopted by the House of Burgesses at its August 1734 assembly,[2] an act which had subsequently received a favorable review from the Governor's Council and then was signed into law by Lieutenant Governor Gooch,[3] subject, as

---

[1] The New Style date for that same day is February 1, 1735. It is imperative to know that the Old Style/Julian calendar once existed. Under it, a year ended on March 24. The day after March 24, 1734, for example, was March 25, 1735. By the time the New Style/ Gregorian calendar was adopted retroactively for 1752, changing January 1, 1751 O.S. to January 1, 1752 N.S., the old calendar was also 11 days out of synch with sun time. That was corrected in the same year. One result: President James Madison, Jr., was born March 5, 1750(O.S.), which is also March 16, 1751 (N.S.)

[2] The Old Style calendar at work: January 1734 comes <u>after</u> August 1734.

[3] The actual Crown-appointed Governor of the Virginia colony at that time was the Earl of Orkney, a Scot Laird/Lord, who never set foot in the New World. His appointed "lieutenants" served in his name.

virtually everything else was, to review and final approval from England. The act recited that the new county "was to be called and known by the name of the County of Orange."[4] Dead for many years now was the much-beloved William of Orange, who, with his wife Mary, had ruled England after the Glorious Revolution of 1688. But in 1734, another William of Orange had married into British royalty and by so doing had become the reason for our "Orange" naming.

Our latter-day William had married Anne, Princess Royal, daughter of George II. The wedding had taken place just a few months prior to the convening of that August 1734 Virginia assembly, and the House of Burgesses was among those who had sent the new couple an address of congratulations and best wishes.[5] While the Act of Establishment for Orange County adopted by that body did not so specify, Governor Gooch in his dispatch to London of November 20, 1734, confirmed that the new county had been named in honor of the Prince of Orange and his bride.[6]

Additional information, little of it flattering, exists about Orange County's William and Anne. Evidently, details surrounding the union constituted fodder for the London gossip circles for a time. Anne was reportedly pockmarked as a result of an earlier illness and was also both very short and very stout. William, for his part, is supposed to have been small, deformed, and penniless. As Princess Royal, Anne desperately needed a consort, but suitors were not knocking down the castle door to deliver proposals of marriage. When William agreed to propose, King George was present with Anne for its announcement in open court. He advised his daughter that she could refuse the offer if she so desired. After briefly considering the past history and future possibilities of her love life, Anne announced, "I shall marry him were he a baboon." The story continues, but that is enough to give the flavor of the matter. Neither William nor Anne ascended to any of the several thrones available to their families, so neither earned a number to go after their names. William died in 1751, leaving Orange County, Virginia, as his only known legacy to history.[7]

---

[4] A good place to find a transcript of the Act is in Vol. 4 of *Hening's Statutes*, at page 450. Later references to such works will have a shorthand reference, such as: "4 *Hening's Statutes* 450." Check the bibliography for a more complete description of a referenced work.

[5] House of Burgesses *Journals,* 1727-1740, p. 230.

[6] The Gooch papers in the Library of Congress, C.O. 5: 1323/5, p. 299.

[7] Be regaled by the tale as recited in Baron John Hervey's *Memoirs*.

Among other things, the Act of Establishment recited the boundaries of the new county. The east boundary was to be "the dividing line" between the parish of St. George and the parish of St. Mark, that is, between today's Spotsylvania and Orange counties. The widow of Col. James Taylor II had received a payment in tobacco for the work of her late husband in surveying that line, and the Act does seem to be describing a line which exists. If, however, Col. Taylor, who died in 1729, ever marked the line or filed a survey plat, no one knows anything about it. As of this writing, the position of Orange and Spotsylvania County officials is that the line has never been established by a known survey and that the boundary being observed exists by virtue of established custom and general agreement. The boundary shown on maps of the area is usually the one drawn in the late 1920s by a United States Coast and Geodetic survey party, but that line is still only an informed estimate.

The southern boundary was with the line of Hanover County, which in those days meant that it extended roughly due west to the mountains. At that point, the Hanover line ended, and the Orange County line was understood to turn southwest into the wilds of what would someday become Kentucky. No one was about to claim that this line had ever been surveyed.

The northern boundary was "by the grant of the Lord Fairfax," a pronouncement that opened up a host of considerations. Through marriage and inheritance, the Fairfax family had been coming into the ownership of that Virginia land which originally had been granted by Charles II to his protectors, and which then had been acquired by members of the Culpeper family. With the death of Lady Margaret Culpeper in 1710, title to those vast holdings vested in her son, Thomas Fairfax, Sixth Baron of Cameron, the one Virginians know as "Lord Fairfax." Fairfax was looking to sell that land to repair the family's tattered finances, and he worked diligently to defend his title against all encroachers.

But exactly where was the southern boundary of the Fairfax land, the boundary which in turn was supposed to determine Orange County's northern border? That argument had started long before Orange County was formed, and the search for its northern boundary simply added fuel to the fire. Clearly, argued the colonial government, all Fairfax land lay north of the Rappahannock River. That was the assumption when St. Mark's parish had been set out in 1730, and nobody complained about it then. Fairfax protested that his southern boundary was the Rapidan River and that he had been complaining for years. It was not until 1745 that the Privy Council would side with Fairfax, ruling that he was the sole owner of 5,282,000 acres of Virginia land and that a portion of its southern boundary was the Rapidan. Orange County had already been formed by using the

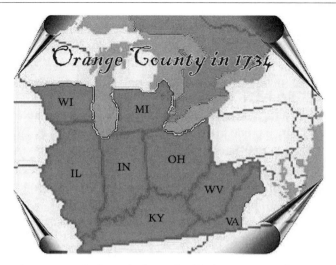

Orange County, per the boundaries recited in its 1734 Act of Establishment. Today's Orange County is in the "bump" along its right-hand edge. Extending British America to the Mississippi in the form of Orange County notified the French that their efforts to take over the lands along the Ohio and Mississippi rivers were going to be challenged, presaging the French and Indian War. Map designed by Kenneth M. Clark and reproduced with permission.

Rappahannock boundary, so the county wound up taking in a sizeable amount of Fairfax land.[8]

At the same time the southern boundary of the Fairfax lands was established, the Privy Council also determined that a line from the headspring of the Rapidan to the headspring of the Potomac would be the western boundary of the Fairfax holdings. That line, the "Fairfax Line," was finally surveyed in 1746.[9] Beyond the Fairfax Line, Orange County's northern boundary was understood to track generally along an extension of that line. In 1734, then, Orange County's northern boundary extended into the southern Great Lakes area.

Things were actually more settled when it came to determining the western boundary. "Westerly, by the utmost limits of Virginia," intones the

---

[8] To help get a favorable decision, Fairfax had agreed not to disturb existing colonial grants of his land and to forego various "regalities" that had been granted, such as the right to have his own courts and army.

[9] That line, N46°W, constitutes a part of the common boundary between today's Shenandoah and Rockingham Counties and continues on into West Virginia. It is easy to pick out on a state map.

Act, which sounds horribly vague. It was in fact generally understood that the western boundary would be the Mississippi River. Queen Elizabeth and Sir Walter Raleigh had in the 1580s named <u>all</u> of British North America "Virginia," and in 1606, a "Virginia Company" (not the Jamestown group) had tried to establish its colony in what is today's State of Maine. But by 1734 there were understood limits to what was "Virginia," even to the west. The French were already extending New France into the Ohio territory and were active all along the Mississippi. All the major colonial powers were jostling and squabbling for control of North America, a prelude to the Seven Year's War, but England was not ready to actively cross swords with France in 1734. Stepping on its toes by extending Orange County to the Mississippi would do for the moment, and that was accordingly done.

In sum, this newly-minted Orange County contained within its legally described boundaries all of the land areas which now comprise Ohio, Illinois, Indiana, Kentucky, and West Virginia, and the southernmost parts of Michigan and Wisconsin. Additionally and obviously, Orange County contained a large part of present-day Virginia. As settlers quickly moved west, however, the county just as quickly began to shrink.

All the lands west of the Blue Ridge were divided off in 1738. Gone with one stroke of a pen were the Valley, the Alleghenies, and the Northwest Territory. The lands were gone only from Orange County, however, not from Virginia. When the American Revolution started, one of the first things Governor Patrick Henry did was send George Rogers Clark into the Northwest Territory to defend Virginia's claim to it. After battles at Kaskakia, Cahokia, and Vincennes, Clark had the former Orange County lands safely under Virginia's control. Virginia would not agree to relinquish its claims to those western lands until the proposed new constitution was being considered in the 1780s.[10]

Culpeper County, constituting the Fairfax portion of the original Orange County east of the Blue Ridge, came into being in 1749. There was talk of splitting Orange County along the Rapidan almost from the time of the county's formation, and the act dividing St. Mark's Parish in that manner was adopted in May 1740.[11] There was, however, an extended hiatus before Culpeper County came into being. It was created after the Fairfax

---

[10] New York, Connecticut, and Massachusetts also made claims to various portions of those lands. Virginia did not actually cede its last claim (the Kentucky territory) to the United States until 1792.

[11] House of Burgesses *Journals*, p. 434. The petition for the division of the parish had been presented by Henry Willis, about whom more is to be said later. The county seat of Fairfax did not change its name to "Culpeper" until 1870.

ownership of that land had been confirmed, so a possible explanation might be that the delay was to await the decision of the Privy Council. In time, Rappahannock and Madison Counties were carved out of Culpeper.

The final dismemberment of Orange County came with the formation of Greene County in 1838. The proudly surviving remainder is a 355 square mile cradle of history, retaining the name of "Orange County," lying in the north-central Piedmont region of Virginia, some 17 miles wide by 37 miles long. The long axis of the county lies roughly on an east-northeast/west-southwest line, but in this work it will be considered as lying east-west.

AN INTERESTING STORY FROM THAT BRIEF TIME OF ORANGE COUNTY'S REIGN as one of the largest American counties ever formed involves a picture with an extended caption which appeared in a 1930s issue of the *Orange County Review*. The original source of the mini-story was Mr. J. G. Hempstead, who had lived in Chicago, Illinois, for a number of years before moving to central Virginia in 1920. He wound up buying a farm in Madison County, but he was very near the Orange County line, and he maintained an interest in what was going on with Orange.

When Orange County was gearing up for its bicentennial celebration, Mr. Hempstead advised its organizers that an Orange County courthouse stood in Chicago. Communications with the South Park Commission of Chicago produced confirmation and a photograph. The Park's documentation was to the effect that the building had originally been built by the French in the early 1700s to house their territorial government offices. After driving the French out of the area, the British began using that building for the same purposes. When that region of British America became Orange County, this public governmental structure stood within its borders. As the state of Illinois developed, the original physical location of the building wound up being in St. Clair County. In 1908, it was moved to Chicago, where the South Park staff exhibited it as the first courthouse for Orange County, Virginia. Since no designation of that Northwest Territory building as a court house exists in Orange County court records, that claim cannot be honored, but it does point out the almost immediate effect of the county's creation on places as far away as today's Illinois.

There is another provision of the act establishing Orange County which deserves mention: During the three-year period starting January 1, 1734, all inhabitants of the county living west of the "Sherrendo" (Shenandoah) river, and all who took up such residence were to be exempt from the payment of public, county, and parish levies. Rest assured that this incentive to move west was not overlooked by the settlers—nor by the French and Native Americans who would become their uneasy neighbors. For

Orange County's Chicago court house. This structure was built by the French and used as a government office when they occupied the Northwest Territory. The British made the same use of it when they took the region over, and it lay within the boundaries of the newly-formed Orange County. Chicago's Jackson Park guides pointed it out as Orange County's first court house. Pen and ink sketch of a much-copied newspaper photograph, drawn by Kevin Yowell. Reproduced with permission.

those of today's Virginia who thought that incentives to spur development were a modern phenomenon, be advised that what is going on today is only history repeating itself once again.

## B. A Union, Yea, a Marriage, of Church and State

By the time the County of Orange was to be established, there was an understood formula for such undertakings. First, an Anglican Church parish would be formed and the freeholders in that new parish called upon to elect the parish governing body, called a "vestry." If all seemed to be going well after a year or two, the political subdivision (county) would be established, having as a rule precisely the same boundaries as the parish. This pre-organization of counties by the church turns out to be only a part of a complicated, and in the estimation of many, conspiratorial interrelationship between the colony's religion and the colony's politics.

The Church of England, known as the "Anglican Church," exercised extensive power in pre-revolutionary Virginia. The charter that was granted to the Virginia Company of London by King James I included the provision that the Anglican Church would be the "state" church of the company's colony. In other words, the colony's government would be required to promote the organization and operation of Anglican parishes and see to it that the members of the colony supported their local parish churches. The Act of Toleration would be observed to the extent that a person could choose to be a "dissenter" (Presbyterian, Baptist, etc.). By law, though, he would still be a member of the local Anglican parish church, would still have to pay its parish levies and would be subject to a fine or ten lashes "well laid on" if he failed to attend that church. Church and state were thus interdependent in pre-revolutionary Virginia whether one liked it or not.[12]

Within the government of the Anglican Church, the Virginia colony was a part of the Diocese of London, under the direction and control of the Bishop of London. Like the Earl of Orkney with his lieutenant governors, the Bishop never graced the New World with his presence. Parish priests initially represented him in the wilds of Virginia, but once the colony was successfully established, he appointed a special representative, his "Commissary," to represent him. Probably the best known Commissary was the Reverend James Blair. Commissary Blair was the founder and first president of the College of William and Mary. He was also instrumental in the removal of several Virginia governors, among them Alexander Spotswood, about whom much remains to be told. Commissary Blair's power was not unlimited, however. His marriage in Williamsburg became the talk of the colony when it became known that the bride had refused to recite the word "obey" as a part of her marriage vows.

St. Mark's Parish, the Anglican version of Orange County, had been divided off from St. George's Parish (Spotsylvania County) in May 1730. The following January, the freeholders of the new parish met at Germanna, former Governor Spotswood's home town in what would become eastern Orange County. There they elected Vestrymen. A list of those good churchmen compared to a list of the first Gentlemen Justices subsequently appointed in 1734 is instructive.

---

[12] An example of the Anglican attitude is conveyed by a comment an Anglican priest is said to have made to one of his dissenting counterparts: "We are both doing God's work. You in your way; I in His."

| Vestrymen | Justices |
|---|---|
| Goodrich Lightfoot | Goodrich Lightfoot |
| James Barbour | James Barbour |
| Robert Slaughter | Robert Slaughter |
| Francis Slaughter | Francis Slaughter |
| Benjamin Cave | Benjamin Cave |
| Robert Green | Robert Green |
| John Finlason | John Finlason |
| Samuel Ball | Samuel Ball |
| Henry Field | Abraham Field |
| Francis Kirtley | Augustine Smith |
| William Peyton | John Taliaferro |
| Thomas Staunton | Benjamin Borden |
| | Thomas Chew |
| | Richard Mauldin |
| | Zachary Taylor |
| | John Lightfoot |
| | James Pollard |
| | Robert Eastham |
| | Charles Curtis |
| | Joist Hite |
| | Morgan Morgan |
| | John Smith |
| | George Hobson |

Fully one-third of the new county's judges had been vestrymen from the earliest days of the parish, a 1730s version of what is condemned today as interlocking directorates. Of the additional justices, several had been too young to be on the original vestry when it was formed, while others had not been parish residents in 1730. Also, the last four justices had settled in the Valley, too far away to serve as vestrymen of the county's mother church, but in a good position to administer the law in the western reaches of the county.

The vestry/justice interrelationship in Orange County was far from being an exception. In fact, it was understood that one of the main avenues to local political power lay through the parish vestries. A story which has circulated for years tells of an Anglican vestry in the Valley which was composed entirely of devout, but politically active, Presbyterians. While the story may be a stretch, the message as to the importance of vestry membership is accurate. One of the most severe charges leveled against

Lieutenant Governor Alexander Spotswood at the time the Earl of Orkney decided to relieve his lieutenant from further service was that Spotswood had meddled in the election of vestries.

With this interlocking church/civil power structure, it was not difficult for the vestry to "lay" levies on its parishioners, confident that the police power of the court, which it also controlled, could be called upon to collect them. With the proceeds of those levies, churches were built and ministers hired. Glebes, farms on which the ministers lived, plus the necessary farm buildings, equipment and livestock, were bought with levied funds. Part of a minister's upkeep was supposed to come from the operations of the glebe.[13] True, some of the funds went to support widows and orphans and to finance needy causes, but that could in no way mollify the dissenters. They wanted the Anglican boot off of their necks. When the revolution came, they revolted against both the King and his church.

A story demonstrates the ease and speed with which a parish levy could be laid and collected. It also demonstrates the sometimes less than brotherly dealings between vestries. The story involves the reaction of the vestry of St. George's Parish to the creation of our St. Mark's Parish. When it became known that the division creating a new parish was being authorized, the St. George's vestry promptly announced and collected a levy before the new parish could be formed. The levy was reportedly for the building of a St. George's glebe house. One of the first projects for the new St. Mark's vestry then was to seek the return of that portion of the St. George's levy raised from St. Mark's parishioners. St. George's flatly refused. Eventually higher authorities intervened, and 11,898 pounds of levied tobacco was grudgingly turned over to St. Mark's vestry.

Orange County does reflect one variation on the parish-to-county formula. As a prelude to the formation of Culpeper County, the expected division of St. Mark's Parish took place. For some reason, however, the existing county, Orange, did not keep the existing parish name of "St. Mark's." That name went with Culpeper, and the original Orange County parish was given a new name of "St. Thomas's."

---

[13] The glebe for St. Thomas' Parish was located just north of the Town of Orange. Glebeway subdivision, across Route 15 from the Holiday Inn, is on part of that land. For a part of its course to the Rapidan, Glebe Run flows alongside Route 634 (Woodberry Road).

## C. A "Top Man" Eyes the Bottom Line

One of the primary shakers and movers in the formation of Orange County was Colonel Henry Willis. Among his other holdings, Willis owned what is today called "Willis Hill," a portion of Marye's Heights in the Fredericksburg and Spotsylvania National Military Park. During the Colonel's lifetime, Marye's Heights was farmland, way out in the country. Now it's in deep, downtown Fredericksburg. William Byrd II, himself a "top man" in the Virginia colony, pronounced Col. Willis the "top man" in Fredericksburg, as indeed he was. Among his several public offices, Willis was a Spotsylvania County Justice, one of its representatives to the House of Burgesses, and a colonel in the county militia. In 1727, he was one of those appointed by the House of Burgesses to "lay off" the town of Fredericksburg. In 1728, he patented 10,000 acres of what was to be Orange County. A portion of that land is now occupied by the Town of Gordonsville. If anything important was happening in this part of the colony, he was in on it. The Willis home over time sounded to the footsteps of most of the rich, powerful, and ambitious of the colony, for a good word from him was almost certain to open many a door and pocketbook.

Col. Willis had been what we might today call a floor manager for Orange County's Act of Establishment, seeing to it that its passage was swift and uneventful. He was then present at the organizational meeting to assist and advise with the formation of the county. He was clearly intent on seeing that the new county got started on the right foot.

It is easy to say, however, that Col. Willis' concern for the organization of Orange County was more than just public-spirited charity. He had been appointed Clerk of the Orange County court, a salaried position. In addition, James Porteus, one of Willis' employees had been appointed Under Clerk, whose salaried position would relieve the colonel of much of the duty of paying him, while at the same time Porteus would continue to run the colonel's store. Finally, the new justices were going to rent a house Col. Willis owned on Black Walnut Run in the new county for use as court house until more suitable accommodations could be built. It was a clear case of "triple dipping," eighteenth-century style, into the treasury of the brand-new county. Also keep in mind that Willis had other paying positions in Spotsylvania County. It highlighted a reality for most of colonial Virginia's top men: they owned staggering amounts of property and were almost always desperately short of cash.

## D. The Court Houses of a Court House Town

It took some four or five years and several petitions to the Governor before a location for the Orange County court house was finally decided upon. The final directive of an exasperated Governor was to build it in an area between Somerville and Raccoon Fords, near the intersection of today's Routes 522 and 611. That, however, was only the starting point for the migrations of a county seat that wound up involving two of the best known taverns in the little crossroads settlement that came to be called Orange Court House.

Some folks had never been happy with the location of the first court house, and when Culpeper County was formed in 1749, others joined them in pointing out its remote location relative to the majority of the county's residents. The decision was made to relocate the county seat to the cross-roads settlement of Orange, holding court there in Timothy Crosthwait's tavern until more suitable facilities could be built. On November 24, 1749, court was accordingly convened for the first time in Orange, which back then was not much more than a wide spot in the road.[14]

Orange, however, was on one of the mountain roads connecting the deep water docks of the Rappahannock to the interior of north-central Virginia, and the settlement was probably well known throughout the region. Crosthwait's tavern was no doubt well known for the same reason, but its popularity with the local justices probably turned on their understanding that it was available for sale to the county. The County Fathers were confident enough on that point to build the new court facilities on Crosthwait's land long before they actually obtained title to it.[15]

On August 3, 1753, Crosthwait finally conveyed two acres of land to the county for forty shillings.[16] Already located on the land by then were a court house, a prison, a pillory, stocks, and a whipping post. While a ducking stool had been built at Raccoon Ford, one does not seem to have been built at Orange. Witches never appear to have been a local concern, and maybe the justices had settled on another way to control gossips and gen-

---

[14] Orange would not become an incorporated town until 1872, and it remained smaller than Gordonsville until the 1910 census.

[15] Crosthwait had appeared in court September 27, 1751, and acknowledged for the record his earlier promises to sell the county two acres for five shillings. 5 OCOB 325. By then, most of the new court facilities were already standing on the land.

[16] 12 OCDB 176. Crosthwait did use the time to talk the price up.

eral public nuisances.[17] In any case, the county was well into doing business at the new location.

The location of what we today call the "1752 court house" is believed to have been in the vicinity of the Orange police station on Chapman Street, with the "bounds" of the lot being roughly outlined by the connecting portions of Main Street, Short Street, Church Street, and Chapman Street. The court bounds were very important to some county prisoners of colonial times, such as debtors, people charged with minor offenses who couldn't make bond, and convicted persons serving time because they couldn't pay a fine. Such prisoners were often permitted by the court to have the "freedom of the bounds" during the day, thus allowing them some respite from the dark stench of the gaol. (Yes, pronounced "jail.") There was also a potential benefit for the county, since it afforded prisoners the opportunity to beseech passers-by to hire or bail them off the county's hands.

The 1752 court house served the county until 1803, when its replacement was built. The 1803 court house was also located on the old Crosthwait tavern lot, this time on a spot which is now across the tracks from today's railroad station/visitors' center. Problems with that site developed in 1854 when the Orange & Alexandria Railroad came to town. To entice the routing of the railroad through the county seat, the local leaders had offered a right-of-way through the public lot. The railroad proceeded to lay tracks almost at the door of the court house. That didn't cause much of an upset, however, since getting the railroad was a huge prize and the old court house had gotten, well, old. It was time to move again, and the William Bell tavern/Orange Hotel site was available. That location is the one where the historic court house stands today, and we need to take a moment to learn the story behind that particular site.[18]

ON FEBRUARY 2, 1800, MR. PAUL VERDIER ("VER-DEAR") BOUGHT 198 acres from the heirs of William Bell.[19] Bell had earlier gotten that land from Timothy Crosthwait, with the two acres less than an even 200 being

---

[17] 4 OCOB 378. The construction of the stool was ordered by the court of June 28, 1745, but no official use appears to have been made of it.

[18] For more detail on the evolution of the Town of Orange, including maps, see: Joyner, *The Village at Orange Courthouse*, a reference work on file at the Orange County Historical Society Research Center, also: Thomas, *Orange , Virginia, Story of a Court House Town.*.

[19] 21 OCDB 540.

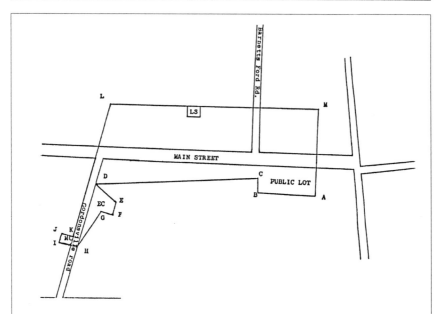

The "bounds" of the 1803 court house as surveyed in 1842. Prisoners having the "freedom of the bounds" could legally sit in the back pews of the Episcopal and Methodist churches (EC and MC), and go into the Lafayette Hotel stables (LH). The surveyors noted that the Orange Hotel stables were not included. When the railroad came, its tracks split the bounds area east of Barnett's Ford Road (Madison Road), putting the court house on the west edge of the tracks and the jail on the east edge. 38 OCDB 426.

conveyed reflecting Crosthwait's earlier sale of his tavern lot to the county. William Bell had also gone into the tavern business, and his establishment was just across the mountain road (today's Main Street) from Crosthwait's.

Verdier was something of a big thinker, and he began to expand and develop the Bell tavern facilities into what he started calling his "Orange Hotel." Even as late as 1819, however, the hotel was still only one of the uses for Verdier's collection of some half-dozen buildings on the site. One of the buildings housed a hat factory. At least a portion of another was Verdier's personal residence. A twentieth-century newspaper article reported that two of the outbuildings were stables able to accommodate 200 horses. Maintaining the "garage" in a separate building and at some distance was assuredly good hotel management in those days.

In 1819, Verdier moved his place of residence from the hotel lot to his new magnificent home "Montpeliso," the property we know today as "Peliso," the oldest standing residence in the Town of Orange. He also began selling building lots, with the Holladay House, Sparks Grocery, and Spring Garden (across from McDonald's) being original buildings built by the lot purchasers. Prosperity, however, must have bored Verdier. Skating along on the thin edge of financial ruin was where he seemed to find excitement, and it finally caught up with him.

By deed dated March 9, 1833, Verdier, in extreme financial distress, conveyed his hotel properties to Joseph Hiden, who in turn by deed dated May 18, 1833, conveyed it to Richard Rawlings.[20] Rawlings and Hiden together continued to develop and improve the hotel facilities. By the time Rawlings took out an insurance policy on the property in 1835, they had created a large three-story U- shaped structure whose wings bordered a spacious courtyard opening onto Main Street.[21]

To get an idea of the depth of the original hotel/court house lot, position yourself on the Main Street sidewalk across from the Belleview Avenue intersection. Look left to the Holladay House and imagine a large front porch, from which a set of steps sloped down to access the Main Street of the 1830s. (That's how the Holladay House was back then.) Now, figuring that the north edge of Main Street was a foot or so from the end of the last step, mentally carry that line down Main Street to the Court House lot. There was room for a grand and spacious court yard. To complete the exercise, mentally add a porch and steps to the Sparks' Grocery building, and you now have an idea of the width of Orange's Main Street of that era. Probably less than fifteen feet. It would be a narrow alley by today's standards, but a major thoroughfare for its day.

The Hiden/Rawlings Orange Hotel must have been quite something in its day. By the time the railroad had rendered the 1803 court house untenable, however, the hotel had already burned to the ground, and Rawlings was looking to do something else with the land. After much backing and filling, the county arranged to trade most of the old Crosthwait tavern/ court house lot for the Orange Hotel site. More time was then consumed with maneuverings on the design of the new court house, and it was not until 1858 that the then-popular Italianate design for the county's present

---

[20] 34 OCDB 332 and 34 OCDB 401 respectively. Verdier was down, not out. He already owned Tandy Collins' tavern some eleven miles east of Orange on the turnpike, and his operations there soon had everyone calling it Verdiersville.

[21] The floor plan drawn in that policy was reproduced in the October 30, 1980, edition of the *Orange County Review*. The Mutual Assurance Society of Richmond insured a number of local structures, and its records can be a valuable information source for researchers.

court house was selected. The building was quickly erected, and in 1859 the first court in Orange County's fourth court house was convened. As of this writing, work is underway to build a modern court complex on that same site which will incorporate and preserve the 1859 historic structure.

The fits and starts and maneuverings on the land swap were minor when compared to those associated with the design of the 1859 court house. A design committee which had been appointed in 1852 sought the advice of the Honorable Richard H. Field, Judge for the circuit containing Orange and a gentleman whose interest in court house architecture was well known. Judge Field, in turn, consulted with a professional architect on various technical questions. In six months the committee, in consultation with Judge Field, reported back a design for a brick structure with a portico and columns. It was, therefore, proposed as an addition to the large number of Jeffersonian, neoclassical structures in the county. As a part of the land trade deal, Mr. Hiden had even agreed to supply the brick (presumably salvaged from the ruins of the old hotel).

The committee's report was met with a pronouncement by the Court that consideration of a design would be suspended for three years. That was March 1853. When consideration was resumed in 1857, a new design committee was appointed.[22] That committee soon recommended the construction of an Italianate-style structure, which admittedly was a rather popular architectural style at the time. That recommendation was promptly approved, and construction of the building began without delay.

The reasons for the change in design have never seen the full light of day, but possibly Orange County just wanted to show its neighbors that it could build something that was not neoclassical.[23] One of the members of the second design committee was Benjamin Johnson Barbour, whose ancestral home, Barboursville, is as neoclassical as they get, having been actually designed by Jefferson. Mr. Barbour left no record of why he preferred an Italianate design, but it is understood that he was instrumental in securing the architect who produced it. Judge Field, for his part, was a son-in-law of another Barbour who had built Frascati, another grand neoclassical mansion on the Blue Ridge Turnpike. He had recommended the construction of a court house reminiscent of it; however, he apparently left

---

[22] The suspension order and the appointment of the new committee were by a judge other than Field.

[23] For a more detailed description of all that went on involving the 1859 court house, see Thomas' *Orange, Virginia: Story of a Courthouse Town*, pp. 30-35.

no record of objecting to the later, adopted design. What had happened? We don't exactly know.

## E. The Evolution of a County Government

The parish-to-county formula by which Orange County was formed was only one stage in the evolution of local governments in Virginia. A brief foray into the subject may help in understanding why the county is the way it is today.

At first, government, such as it was in the colony, was organized and operated by agents of the developer, the Virginia Company of London. The initial government was a form of communal living, a true "commonwealth." One rule for such a community, at least under the direction of the very capable Captain John Smith, was that those who did not labor did not eat. The return of Smith to England in 1609 led to the collapse of that experiment, and in 1610 a government under martial law was instituted. At the time, the colony was so small that there was no need for local governments apart from the overall colonial government.

Even after the Virginia Company's charter was revoked in 1624 and Virginia became a Crown Colony, it was still so small that political subdivisions were not deemed necessary. Individual Anglican parishes, however, were already electing representatives to the House of Burgesses, and with the growth of the colony accelerating, it wasn't going to be long before separate local governments would be needed.

In 1634 the Virginia colony was divided into eight shires, with the justices and parish vestries being responsible for such local government as was authorized. Within the shire, those men handled the duties associated with today's Circuit and District Courts, Board of Supervisors, Planning Commission, Board of Zoning Appeals, Virginia Department of Highways — everything.

The chief executive officer was the Shire Reeve, or Sheriff. The Sheriff wielded enormous power, for in addition to being the chief law enforcement and corrections officer, he was the collector of levies, for which he then served as treasurer, and as election judge, receiving and counting the shouted vote of each citizen as he came forward to announce his choice. Each shire also had a "Lieutenant," whose militia rank was colonel.[24] Each

---

[24] The term "Lieutenant" was a product of ancient custom and usage. The fact that such individuals routinely held the militia rank of colonel helps to explain the huge host of "colonels" which seemed to litter the countryside of Old Virginia.

colonel was responsible for the defense of his shire and for the performance of its militia. A Court Clerk was also appointed to handle the local government's official communications and to create and preserve its official records.

When more formal county governments came into being in the 1640s, the offices and the duties of the Sheriff, County Lieutenant, and Clerk of the Court remained essentially as they had been for the shires. Along with the Gentlemen Justices and vestries, they governed Virginia's counties. Over the years, the civil power of vestries was terminated, while some duties of the county's officers have been subdivided and others have been taken over by the state and federal governments. This process of evolution in creating local government for Virginia has given its counties a curious mixture of elected and appointed officials, all operating in a rather confusing legal and financial environment. There is no use in complaining that things might have been done differently. They just weren't.

Virginia is the only state in the union where incorporated cities and towns function as separate independent governments within their counties. While this may guarantee the residents of such jurisdictions that their voice will be heard, it also creates a fertile ground for controversy and power struggles. Real estate developers, for example, have become adept in manipulating the relationships between counties and their cities and towns in order to get permission to do what they want.

Another problem for local governments is the "Dillon Rule," or "Dillon's Rule," named for Iowa judge John F. Dillon. In the last half of the nineteenth century, Judge Dillon was considered one of America's foremost authorities on state/local governmental relations. In his decisions and writings, Dillon declared that local governments were "creatures of the state," nothing more, and that they had only those powers which the state had "expressly granted" to them, plus any other powers "necessarily or fairly implied" by those grants, or which were "absolutely indispensable" to the local governments in carrying out their state-mandated duties. The reality has been that where the Rule is rigidly enforced, localities exercise only expressly granted powers. Virginia adopted the Dillon Rule and is now one of the fewer than half-dozen states which enforce it rigidly.

About the same time Dillon's Rule was being formulated, the Home Rule movement began. Under Home Rule, a local government possesses all powers not specifically prohibited by the state and which are not in violation of the state or Federal constitutions or of the state's or Federal government's laws. A large majority of America's states follow some form of Home Rule.

There has long been a hue and cry in Virginia that Dillon's Rule is behind the urban sprawl gobbling up Virginia's landscape, plus a whole host of other problems.[25] There is some truth in that, and something needs to be done to give local governments more control of their destiny. Just switching to Home Rule, however, is not by itself the solution.

## F. A California Connection — Maybe

For the record, there are eight Orange counties in the United States.[26] In addition to Virginia's, there are Orange counties in California, Florida, Indiana, New York, North Carolina, Texas and Vermont. For years, local tradition held that Orange County, California, had been created and named by two former residents of Orange County, Virginia: Alfred Chapman and Andrew Glassell. Also, the right to name the new California county had supposedly been won in a poker game. All of that is great stuff, and some of it might actually be true.

One of the founders of Orange County, California, was indeed Andrew Glassell, whose family home was in Culpeper County, Virginia. His family descended from one of the many Scottish families to come to central Virginia, among them the Spotswoods, the Barbours, the Gordons, and the Pattons. Andrew Glassell had gone to California in the 1850s to practice law and had worked for a time in the U.S. Attorney General's office. Susan Glassell Patton, the grandmother of World War II general George Smith Patton, was Andrew's sister. Susan's husband was killed in the Civil War battle of Third Winchester, and her subsequent homeless refugeeing brought her to the old William Madison Residence at Woodberry Forest in Madison County for the winter of 1865-66. During that winter, Andrew sent money to Susan to finance her trip to California, away from war-torn Virginia. If the California Glassells needed any reminder of their Virginia roots, Susan and her family would have certainly provided it.[27]

---

[25] See: Richardson, *Sprawl in Virginia: Is Dillon the Villain?* Spring 2000 article downloaded from the internet and on file at the Orange County Historical Society. Jesse J. Richardson, Jr., is an attorney specializing in land use, zoning, and municipal law. He is also an assistant professor of urban affairs and planning at V.P.I. & S.U.

[26] There are also over 25 cities, towns, and communities with "Orange" in their name.

[27] Susan's grandson, WW II general George S. Patton, returned to his family's Virginia haunts and spent a year at V.M.I. before going on to West Point.

Another of the co-founders of the California county was indeed an Alfred Chapman, but this was not the brother of Reynolds Chapman, long-time Clerk of the Court of Orange County, Virginia. California's Alfred Beck Chapman had never been near Orange County, Virginia. He had been born in New Jersey into a family with strong Connecticut connections. His family moved to Alabama, and he went to West Point as an appointee from there. The approaching Civil War thus produced strongly mixed feelings for Chapman, and he resigned his military commission and moved to California to practice law. He and Andrew Glassell had attended the same school in Alabama, and the two reunited as California land developers.

In the early 1870s, Glassell and Chapman began a development which they initially called "Richlands." By then Andrew's brother, Capt. William Glassell, a Civil War veteran, had come to help with the development operations. When they finally decided to secure a post office for their new community, they learned that the name of Richlands had already been taken. Here, possibly, the Glassells' memories of old — and even then, historic — Orange County, Virginia, may have carried the day. Nobody in California recalls anything about a poker game. So much for a fabulous story, but it's a good one.

## G. The People's Choice?

Local elections tend to be a rich source of story material, and Orange County is no exception. For example, we have already learned that Alexander Spotswood was accused of having meddled in the election of Anglican vestries, a very serious charge for that time. We will learn in more detail later about James Madison receiving his only defeat at the polls as a result of his failure to ply voters with "bumbo," an alcoholic punch. Madison is a source of a couple of additional local election stories, both arising from the 1789 congressional elections, when he was pitted against his friend James Monroe for the seat in Congress that we now identify as representing the 7th Congressional District, "Madison's Seat," in the Federal government.

Both Madison and Monroe attempted to keep things on friendly terms, even though their friendship was severely tested by a series of face-to-face debates during the winter of 1788-89. On one particularly bitter cold day, the two appeared at Hebron Church for a scheduled debate. The leaders of that Lutheran congregation allowed the candidates to attend the service, but when it was time for debate, the two were informed that politics had no place inside the sanctuary. Madison and Monroe thus spent the final hours of that freezing day standing outside in the snow and cold, debating the merits of the just-adopted Constitution and similar topics. Riding home in the deepening winter night, Madison froze the end of his nose, and he claimed that he bore the scar of that event for the rest of his life.[28]

February 2, 1789, was election day, and Paul Jennings, Madison's body servant, reported on an event from that day involving his master. According to Jennings, there was a gentleman living some distance from the polling place who had no way of getting there. Madison dispatched a coach to pick up this surely-to-be-grateful voter and bring him to the polls. As the coach pulled up on its return, the gentleman, a Scot immigrant, leaned out of the coach window and shouted, "Put me down for Colonel Monroe, for he was the first man that took me by the hand in this country." Madison won the election handily, so he could chuckle about it.[29]

A less amusing election incident involved Madison's friend, neighbor, and former Virginia Governor, Mr. James Barbour. In 1830, the 55-year-old Barbour had decided to run for election to the Virginia House of Delegates, seeking what is known today as "Madison's Seat" in that chamber, representing the 30th Legislative District. Barbour had been a Virginia legislator from 1796 to 1812 before serving as governor and then going on to hold various national posts. Now, he sought to return to his political origins.[30]

Barbour's candidacy was opposed by one other person, but no record exists of the severity of the contest. Likewise, the voting was conducted with no report of irregularities. The voters included a much-aged James Madison, who came to town to cast a vote for his friend. The Sheriff announced that Mr. Barbour was the winner, and everyone retired to Blakey's Hotel to join in his victory celebration.

Some time after the cheering had died down, a complaint was filed with the Committee of Privileges and Elections of the House of Delegates, and the results of the election were reversed in favor of Barbour's opponent. There is no evidence of James Barbour having had a hand in irregularities, but it still had to be embarrassing to the veteran legislator.

---

[28] Ketcham, *James Madison*, p. 277. If the scarring was actually noticeable, portrait painters glossed over it — literally.

[29] Jennings, *A Colored Man's Reminiscences*, p. 7. The factual details somewhat corrected per Ketcham, *ibid.*

[30] Thomas, *Story of a Courthouse Town*, p. 20.

PROBABLY THE WILDEST ELECTION HELD IN ORANGE COUNTY INVOLVED THE vote taken November 20, 1741, for representatives to the House of Burgesses.[31] The polling place was the court house (in the Somerville Ford/ Raccoon Ford area at the time), and among the five candidates for the two seats were Messrs. Robert Slaughter and Henry Downs. When the polls opened at noon, a group of supposed voters poured into the court house and began creating such a disturbance that the Sheriff and the candidates fled the building until it could be cleared.

When the tumult finally died down, the Sheriff re-entered and posted Under-Sheriffs at each of the doors with drawn swords to control the flow of voters in and out. A John Rucker then appeared at one of the doors and demanded entrance. Upon gaining entrance, Rucker threw the Under-Sheriff out of the door, and a scuffle ensued, during which Rucker tried to take the Under-Sheriff's sword. A certain John Burke joined Rucker in "laying hands" upon the Under-Sheriff, who in turn was rescued by some of the bystanders.

In addition to engineering disturbances, Rucker, a vocal supporter of Robert Slaughter, had several large bowls of punch, whose contents he offered to anyone who stated an intent to vote for his man. (It turned out that Rucker had bet money on Slaughter being the top vote-getter.) The record doesn't state, but it would have been highly unlikely that Rucker was the only person dispensing alcohol at the polls that day. Suffice to say, the afternoon passed uneasily.

About nightfall, Jonathan Gibson, one of the Under-Sheriffs, quit his post at a door. Immediately "the People throng'd into the Court-house in a drunken riotous Manner, one of them jumping upon the Clerk's table, and dancing among the papers, so that the Sheriff was unable to clear the Bar, or the Clerks to take the Poll." Matters were clearly out of hand.

The candidates wanted the election postponed to the next day. The Sheriff refused to close the polls unless the candidates would post a bond protecting him from any sanctions he might incur for not completing the election on the appointed day. The candidates agreed, and the mob of voters started dispersing to find places to spend the night. At least two of the candidates then refused to sign the bond, and the Sheriff re-opened the polls. There was more loud confusion, evidently involving voters who supported the two non-signers and who had strategically not left when every-

---

[31] This incident was well researched and entertainingly reported by Ann Miller in the January/February 2001 Orange County Historical Society *Newsletter.* Summarized and presented here with her permission and my thanks.

body else did. At that point, the Sheriff announced that Robert Slaughter and Henry Downs had been duly elected, and he closed the polls amid howls of protest.

As you might suspect, that did not end the matter. Early in 1742, one of the losing candidates referred the whole mess to the House of Burgesses' Committee of Privileges and Elections. Not only did the committee find that Slaughter's election was improper, it also determined that Downs was a former indentured servant and sheep-stealing felon on the run from Maryland. He had been successfully posing as Virginia gentry, but he had finally overreached himself. Downs was summarily expelled from the House of Burgesses, and Slaughter's election was declared invalid.

A portion of Capt. John Smith's map showing detail from his 1608 exploration up the Rappahannock. Smith personally traveled as far as the cross (today's Fredericksburg), the area beyond was drawn based on Indian descriptions. Shackaconia is believed to be today's Indiantown in eastern Orange County. Stegara was in the vicinity of today's Somerset. An engraving of the map is in the Library of Congress.

A collection of Native American points found at a site in eastern Orange County and on exhibit at the Orange County Historical Society Research Center. The point in the upper left has been dated to 6,000 B.C. The two small points are arrowheads, the rest are spear points. Photo by Bernice Walker. Reproduced with permission.

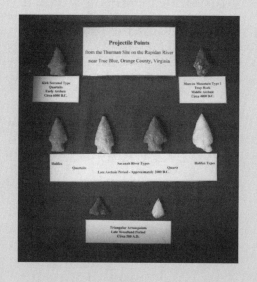

# CHAPTER II
# *Back to First Things*

## A. People and the Land

Before moving ahead with the history of Orange County after its formation, we need to go back in time and review its pre-formation history and natural characteristics, both of which were instrumental in producing much of what we know about the first decades of this new county's existence. Reading this chapter will not make one an expert in any of the sciences or professions involved because we don't need to get that deeply into those disciplines. What we do need to know is the story of the characteristics of this land, how we initially occupied and used it, and how we got along with others who were trying to do the same thing. That story is the sum and substance of Orange County's early history, and it was underway long before the county existed.

WHILE THE DUTCH AND FRENCH ALSO POKED AROUND IN THIS part of North America ahead of the English, it was the Spanish who left the earliest and most lasting impression of European colonization. After decades of exploring and sacking parts of Central and South America, the Spanish had begun to explore farther north. In 1570, they established a small Jesuit colony along one of the Chesapeake's tributaries, probably the York River.[1] That colony was in the midst of the Algonquian Indian territory, and before long most of the colonists had been massacred. The Spanish later returned and retaliated by executing inhabitants of a nearby Indian village. When the English arrived, then, they found themselves

---

[1] An item in Father Gregorio Bolivar's 1625 report to the Vatican. 110 *Va. Mag. His/Bio.* 74 (2002). The Spanish name for this region was "Ajacan." The Wicocomico Indian Nation, Inc., is preparing to publish a book which they say will chronicle an extended relationship of that tribe with the Spanish.

renewing a settler/Indian relationship which was already off on the wrong foot.[2]

A by-product of the Spanish venture into the Chesapeake, or as they named it, "Bahia de Santa Maria," was that they did some of the earliest mapping of the American coast. When Sir Walter Raleigh began his exploration and colonization efforts in 1585, then, he had some idea what to expect. Raleigh soon had even better maps. One of his party was John White, whose maps of the American coastline benefited explorers for years. The elbow in the barrier islands off the coast of today's North Carolina White noted as "Hatoraske," and the large bay into which the Virginia Company sailed in 1607, "Chesepioc."[3]

Raleigh's explorations and efforts at colonization did not uncover any great treasures in the ground or in the possession of its inhabitants. John Smith and his Jamestown settlers had no reason therefore to expect that the land under their feet would yield instant, easy wealth. That said, the land was not without value. It was just going to take time, intelligence, hard work, and usually some capital investment, to realize that value. By the time Orange County came into being, the Virginia colony was full of people who had learned those lessons and were ready to apply them to this part of Virginia.

## B. The Long Road to Germanna

It should come as no surprise to learn that the earliest of Virginia's major settlements away from the coast were on its great tidal rivers. Those streams offered relatively safe, convenient, and inexpensive routes into the interior. Where those rivers left the Coastal Plain and entered into the steeper Piedmont, they became narrower and shallower, with stretches of rapids. The first set of unnavigable rapids was commonly referred to by Tidewater folk as the "falls" of the river. At those falls, trading posts were set up, followed in time by docks and warehouses to serve the ships that could go

---

[2] The major Indian language groups for our area were: Algonquian (Powhatan confederation), Souian (Manahoac confederation), and Iroquoian (the Five, later the Six, Nations). See: Milanich, Jerald T., *Laboring in the Fields of the Lord: Spanish Missions and Southeast Indians*, Smithsonian Institution Press, Washington, 1999.

[3] White's wanderlust must have been catching. His daughter, Elynor White Dare, was the mother of Virginia Dare, the first English child born in America, mother and daughter later disappearing with the rest of the Lost Colony.

no farther upstream. Settlements then soon appeared, several of which grew into prominent Virginia towns and cities that survive to the present.

Fredericksburg, at the falls of the Rappahannock, began developing early into an internationally known port of entry for the Virginia colony. As an inland port, it offered convenient trade connections for the settlers of our region. By the time of the Act of 1727, which directed Col. Henry Willis and others to "lay off" that town, ocean-going ships from most trading nations in the world on friendly terms with England had already visited its docks. Goods were also moving briskly over the many other public and private docks along the Rappahannock, among them: Falmouth, Hobbs Hole (Tappahannock), Port Conway, and Port Royal. It would be another ten years before Rocketts Landing at the falls of the James would evolve into the inland port of Richmond, and it would be another dozen years after that before Bellhaven at the falls of the Potomac would become the bustling inland port of Alexandria.[4]

Commercial travel into the interior above the fall line would require that roads be hacked through the forest, then traveled with uncertainty as to what might be lying in wait alongside them. Those roads were also going to be horribly expensive to create and maintain. In any event the Virginia colony needed to grow and use up the land in the Tidewater before there would be a serious need to look to the interior. As it turned out, a little over a century would pass after the establishment of Jamestown before the Virginia colonists finally started building roads into the upland.

Those first inland roads continued the general east-west course originally charted by the rivers, and the colony developed along them. North-south roads soon followed, and by the time Orange County was formed, one had been found within its borders. It was called the "Carolina Road" but was more of an interrelated collection of game trails and Indian paths than a road. It was passable, however, and Europeans quickly took to using it. This particular Carolina Road ("Carolina Roads" and "Great Roads" appear in many places in Virginia) crossed the Rapidan into today's Orange County in the vicinity of Raccoon Ford.

The roads from the Rappahannock docks into the interior, and most particularly those from Fredericksburg, were the initial trading and development roads for this part of the colony. A number of the patrons of

---

[4] The fourth major coastal river, the York, divides into the Pamunkey and the Mattaponi before becoming unnavigable. No present-day major cities developed at their falls. The "fall line," an imaginary line connecting the falls of Virginia's eastern rivers, is recognized as the dividing line between the Tidewater and the Piedmont.

Fredericksburg's facilities lived on the north side of the Rappahannock, and getting goods to and from them presented the problem of crossing the Rappahannock. During dry spells there were any number of fords upstream from the town where a crossing was possible, but the best crossing was reached by traveling west, beyond the Great Fork where the Rapidan splits off from the Rappahannock. Above there, it might be necessary to ford both streams to reach a destination, but both by then were relatively small and usually easy to cross. It also made sense to keep going far enough west to avoid most of the low, swampy areas around Wilderness Run and the same type of terrain across the river in the Great Fork area.

If a wagoneer journeyed west as described above, and then turned north towards the Rapidan, he would be traveling in what was to become a commercial corridor in eastern Orange County, and he was headed towards an excellent natural ford at a place called Germanna. Today's Route 3 is the current version of that road, though the historic route to Germanna has occupied various roadbeds over time, generally farther to the east than Route 3.

In 1714, before any settlement of this part of Virginia had begun, Lieutenant Governor Alexander Spotswood established a colony of German indentured servants at Germanna. He built Fort Germanna on militarily defensible high ground overlooking the ford, its name combining the nationality of its inhabitants with that of Queen Anne, England's monarch from 1702 to 1714.[5] At the time Spotswood established Germanna, it was both the westernmost settlement in British America and the first in Virginia beyond the Tidewater.

By the mid-1700s, long trains of wagons were rumbling through the Rapidan shallows at Germanna on their way to and from the Fairfax lands. One destination was the settlement of Fairfax, which Culpeper County's first surveyor, seventeen year-old George Washington, would formally lay off in 1749. (In 1870, its name was changed to "Culpeper.") The Germanna of 1714 was located on the Orange County side of the Rapidan, just east of today's Route 3 bridge. The fort and its Germans have been gone for almost three centuries, but the commercial development of the Germanna Corridor has obviously taken on a life of its own.

---

[5] Before Queen Anne died in 1714, exploration of this area was under way, and "Anne" and "Anna" namings continued for a time. The fact that her successor, King George I, spoke only his native German and was not seen as English may have also motivated some nostalgic posthumous "Anna" namings.

Spotswood did not rely solely on the popularity of the ford at Germanna to put his settlement on the map of important places in British America. In 1720, when Spotsylvania County was being formed, he made sure that Germanna was its county seat. A few years later he completed his palatial Georgian home there, the structure which William Byrd II subsequently dubbed "the Enchanted Castle."[6]

Fort Germanna's five-sided palisade compound probably mimicked the design of the rebuilt fort of the Jamestown settlement, and it served as the gateway to the Virginia Piedmont, much as Fort James had served as the gateway to the Virginia Tidewater. The Germanna site remained popular long after a fort was no longer needed. Up on that knoll now are the remains of the Gordon house, a structure which was standing during the Civil War. One corner of the Gordon house intrudes onto the site of the remains of Spotswood's Enchanted Castle. Beneath a corner of the Enchanted Castle, archaeologists have found a palisade trench, a ditch in which split logs had been set, like fence posts, to make a wooden fort wall. Probably a wall of old Fort Germanna, but more digging is needed to be sure. Beneath the palisade trench are likely to be any number of Indian settlements. It is a fabulously rich archaeological site, awaiting workers— and lots and lots and lots of money.

Germanna was also the headquarters for Spotswood's iron mining and smelting operations. The settlement continued to support that industry after the removal of the Spotsylvania county seat to Fredericksburg and the formation of Orange County. The gold mining boom in the area during the first half of the nineteenth century also spurred Germanna's growth. Even after all that quieted down, Germanna was still a thriving rural commercial center, spread out on both sides of the Rapidan in the vicinity of the old ford. If a person had told Spotswood that his Germanna was destined to disappear from the face of the earth, he would have had every reason to refuse to believe it. Yet that is exactly what happened during the Civil War.[7]

---

[6] By 1732, Spotswood and Byrd were anything but friends. Byrd's naming of Spotswood's house was probably intended to deride its owner, but the positive meaning is the one that survives.

[7] The Memorial Foundation of the Germanna Colonies in Virginia, Inc., an association of the descendants of the original German settlers, along with the Department of Historic Preservation at Mary Washington College in Fredericksburg, are slowly getting Germanna back into public memory.

## C. To the Mountains

In the vicinity of Germanna is the lowest elevation in Orange County, some 170 feet above sea level. By ascending to the nearby high ground and finding an opening through the trees, an early explorer could see the "high mountains," the Blue Ridge, on the western skyline. He could also see some much lower mountains, also to the west, but very close by. The settlers called them the "little mountains," and many of them later built their homes on those slopes to escape the insects and stagnant air of the lowlands. We know those low ridge lines as the Southwest Mountains, the easternmost range of the Appalachian chain in Virginia.

The Southwest Mountains come into western Orange County just north of the town of Gordonsville, and as their name implies, they extend south-west-northeast, starting to fade out east of Rapidan. Clark Mountain with its 1,082 foot elevation is by no means the highest peak of the range in Orange County, but its location makes it a special place.[8] There is no higher elevation east of it in Virginia. Also, the land slopes away in a broad plain to the north, east and south as far as the eye can see. On a brilliantly clear day, the top of the Washington Monument is visible from there.

Route 15 from Orange to Gordonsville skirts along the edge of the easternmost ridge of the Southwest Mountains. Another ridge of those mountains forms much of the northern boundary of Orange County, the Rapidan River flowing along its base. During the Civil War, that particular ridge became the key to a Confederate defensive position known as the Rapidan Line, a position that was responsible for a great deal of the county's Civil War history.

The town of Orange is sitting at the juncture of several Southwest Mountain ridge lines, making it a town of hills. Orange also straddles one of the gaps in those ridges, a gap which brought the railroads through the town. Those railroads then produced a memorable commercial era for Orange. The location of Orange must have made more sense when it was a railroad town than it does now as a hilly automobile town.

Between the lowlands along the Rapidan and the highlands of the Southwest Mountains, lies a countryside which for the most part varies from gently to steeply rolling. At places along the Rapidan as well as along a number of the smaller streams in the county, the land broadens out into

---

[8] Other peaks in Orange County are Cowherd Mountain (1,197 feet), Merry Mountain (1,109 feet), Scott Mountain (973 feet), Gibson Mountain (960 feet), Hardwick Mountain (916 feet), and Chicken Mountain (Approx. 825 feet).

scenic floodplains. The topography is definitely not boring, and the combination of that with majestic views towards the Blue Ridge makes being in Orange County as much a pleasure for the resident as it is a delight to the visitor.

## D. Hot, Cold, Wet, Dry — We've Seen it All

Descriptions of the county's climate usually include the terms "temperate" or "modified continental," meaning for our purposes that it is generally pretty nice. A bare handful of hundred degree afternoons in the summer and a zero morning or two in the winter usually bracket extended periods of very tolerable weather. The survivors of that other Virginia Company, the one which got to the New World in 1606, had a much different story to tell about their weather. They had spent the winter freezing on the banks of a river in what is now the state of Maine, and that was more than enough. When the supply ships arrived in the spring, they got aboard and went back to England.

The worst snow storm is still believed to have been the Blizzard of 1857. On January 15, with the thermometer hovering near zero, a heavy snowfall began and continued for several days. Apparently no official depth was recorded, but county residents who ventured out after the last flakes fell reported drifts of eight feet and deeper. Quite a few residents coped by not stirring from their firesides for the next several weeks. Farmers with livestock to feed and water, however, had no choice but to get out in it and do what they could.

Probably the most suffering with cold weather that has ever taken place in Orange County came during the Civil War's Mine Run Campaign of late November-early December 1863. On the morning of November 30, the thermometer stood at zero, and, strung out along both sides of Mine Run, were some 150,000 shivering soldiers. Their misery was compounded by the fact that they had spent all of November 28 in a soaking winter rain, many without any wet weather gear. Most front-line units were under orders not to make fires, which would give away their positions. Observers on both sides reported on the intense and unrelieved suffering of the men, a number of whom died at their posts from the cold.

That touch of Orange County winter was enough for Federal General George Meade, who did not have his whole heart in the campaign from the start. He ordered his troops back to Culpeper County for the winter. While the Confederates were understrength and appeared vulnerable to Meade's superiors in Washington, General Lee, when reinforced by "General Winter," was much too strong to take on.

During summers, there are times when the humidity bears down like a hot, smothering blanket, but air conditioning has now reduced Orange County's "stewmidity" to a tolerable nuisance for most residents. Winter sports lovers usually have to drive to the mountains to find serious snow, but then they don't have to shovel all of it off their porches. Orange County is usually too far inland for the fall Atlantic storms to reach it with much zip left. The winds of Hazel (Oct. 15, 1954) and the rains of Camille (Aug. 20, 1969), however, head a list of definite exceptions.

Forty inches of rain per year is about average, with sixty percent of that falling during the frost-free growing season (roughly mid-April to late October). If one wants to see how much water we can get, go over to the Culpeper side of the Rapidan community and ask to have some of the high water marks pointed out on the buildings. It is awesome. In the spring of 1861, the Rapidan washed away the extensive facilities at Peyton's Mill, located a little over two miles downstream from the Route 15 bridge at Madison Mills.[9] The disappearance of their livelihood made it all the easier for the Peyton brothers to decide to organize an artillery unit and go fight for the Confederacy.[10]

It can also get very decidedly dry in Orange County. With the exception of the Everona limestone belt, estimating the groundwater available for plants is basically a function of knowing the water retaining capability of a particular soil type and the depth of that soil at a given location. There isn't any underground lake to tap. A general rule of thumb is that during the growing season, an inch of rain per week is needed. It doesn't make any difference how much fell last week, an inch will still be needed this week.

The drought of 1930 is the one to which all others are compared. That was before this writer was born, but I did not escape it. At some point in many of the summers during my farming days, we encountered dry spells. If I began to wail about how dry it was, some gray head would invariably turn, and I would find myself being fixed with a steady gaze and hearing, "You weren't here in 1930, were you, son?" Then I would get another 1930 story. I got so that I was certain I had lived through that summer.

In 1930 stretches of the "mighty Mississippi" were reduced to pool-dotted mud flats. Locally, Marsh Run at Somerset went dry, and because

---

[9] Cortada, *Hume Diary,* p. 26 (Entry for April 10, "The Rapidan is said to be higher than it has been for fifty years . . . .")

[10] The floods of 1937 and 1942 also did their full share of damage. Following the flood of 1995, Somerset farmers had to go out and get dead cows out of trees.

1930 was just one dry year in a cycle of dry years, it dried up at least briefly during the shorter dry spells of the next several summers. Wilderness Run also went dry. "Going dry" in country talk does not have to mean dust in the steam bed, but it usually means no flowing water. Without their stream "fence," cattle in adjacent pastures were sure to roam to find such pools of water as there were. Even those farmers who knew what was going on, considering their options, probably looked the other way for as long as they could.

The year 1930 was also hot. In nearby Charlottesville, there was a June high of 101 degrees and a July high of 107 degrees. Local observers remember everything being brown; the crop fields, pastures, lawns, gardens, all brown. Deeper-rooted trees remained green, and a few desperate farmers cut them down to let their cattle graze the leaves.

A couple of drought stories involve the Blue Ridge Mountains. Remember that until the Shenandoah National Park officially went into operation in 1936, there were a number of people living and farming on those slopes. The Blue Ridge Turnpike to New Market was also still open through that area. My father said that on still mornings during the summer of 1930, you could look toward the mountains and see a fragile lacework of dust columns rising above the trees, stirred up by wagons rolling through the rocky dust of the mountain roads.

Another story involves one of the farm families living up there that year. Some time in July, the father got all of the family members out into their various corn patches, and for several days they crawled up and down the rows, digging up the seed corn and putting it back in the bag. The seed hadn't sprouted, and it was now too late to make a crop, even if the rains started coming. One of those children in his later years worked for me, and he noted more than once that life in the mountains was independent, yes, but it could be hard, very hard.

A fascinating story was related by Mr. Hugh Gillum, one of the family of nine brothers who ran Madison Mills and related businesses in the Orange and Madison area. Mr. Hugh recalled that by the time farmers started coming in with such small grain as they had harvested in the early summer of 1930, the Rapidan was already so low that there wasn't enough water above the dam to drive even the small set of mill stones. The grain had to be put in storage. The situation was no better later in the summer when the slim corn harvest started trickling in. Then, in late September-early October, without any rainfall that could have possibly affected the river, the Rapidan began a slow rise. Before long, they could grind small grain and were able to do so for the rest of the year. It was 1931, however, before there was enough water behind the dam to routinely drive the big stones and permit the Gillums to grind corn.

Below the soil and weathered rock level (the "regolith"), and with the exception of the Everona limestone belt, water is stored in fractures—cracks in the bedrock—and bedding planes between rock layers. In some places in the county the bedrock is highly fractured, and it is easy to hit a number of them when drilling a well. In other areas, a well down 200-300 feet will not encounter enough water-storing fractures to support a household. As the county population grows, the necessity to find enough water to support it grows. The river-channeling floods of 1995 and 1996, coupled with ongoing upstream development and deforestation, are converting the Rapidan into more of a drainage ditch than a reliable, sustainable watercourse. An intensely dry 2002 coupled with the ever-increasing demand for water out of the Rapidan created a local water emergency which has added urgency to the search for additional sources.

It is not unusual to have an agricultural drought, when the soil is dry and the plants are suffering, but the wells, springs, and streams show almost no stress. More rare, but much more of a problem, are the hydrologic droughts, when the fractures in the bedrock start to go dry. Depending upon the time of year and the type of moisture reaching the soil surface, only 10-25% of it ever reaches the fracture zone. Recharging is slow at best. To date, no hydrologic study of the county, including a fracture zone analysis, has been done. While well drillers' reports are helpful, a comprehensive study is still needed. Also needed is a continuation of the region-wide water studies begun in the 1960s. That earlier planning had included the identification of possible surface impoundment sites to supplement groundwater supplies.

## E. Don't call it "DIRT!"

It is hard to overstate the importance of Orange County's soils to its early history. From the time the county was being settled and well up into the twentieth century, the health and wealth of its residents was determined largely by the productivity of the particular soil they were farming. This was clearly understood by most of the first settlers in Orange County, and they had developed an uncanny ability to judge soils by what they could see. Most of us today are largely ignorant on the subject, because our nutrition and our income are not dependent upon what we can grow, if we grow anything at all.

In the early days of Orange County, opportunities to earn a living away from the farm were almost nonexistent. It was farm or starve. If the soil was poor, it could very well be farm <u>and</u> starve. While farmland is still a significant asset of the county, only a small percentage of us now receive any direct income from farming. Indirectly, however, we all benefit from the county tax revenue generated by that asset and from the scenic vistas of well-tended fields.

Dirt over here is about the same as dirt over there, right? Wrong. A 1971 soil survey of Orange County revealed the presence of 16 different soil associations encompassing over 33 different soil types.[11] To map them out broadly, you need to draw a line from the traffic circle in Gordonsville, northeasterly through Madison Run to Everona (at the intersection of routes 617 and 627), then curve the line gradually to follow Mountain Run to the Rapidan. That line roughly traces the Everona limestone belt running through the county, a belt some one-half to three-quarters of a mile wide that has a particular geology and soils of its own. North and west of the belt, towards Barboursville and Orange, the soils are for the most part the ones having the highest natural fertility in the county. To the south and east are soils with comparatively lower natural fertility. This is not to say that many of the soils to the south and east will not reward good, knowledge-able management; however, that same management would earn even greater rewards if applied to the better soils. To put it another way, it takes a better farmer to make a living on the Nason-Tatum soils around Daniel than it does to make the same living on the Davidson and Rapidan soils around Montpelier Station.

The early arrivals to Orange County did not have access to sophisti-cated soils survey information, but they knew what they were doing when deciding where they wanted to settle. They understood clearly the old rule that "poor land makes poor people," and they had every intention of avoid-ing poverty.[12] But how did they go about picking their land?

First, one had to get on the land early. Knowing how to identify good soils was of no help if they had all been taken by the time you got to the region under development. For example, we know that Orange County was formed in 1734. How soon did you have to be in the area to get its best land? Answer: Long before 1728, because by that date virtually all of the good land of the future county had been taken.

---

[11] *Soil Survey of Orange County, Virginia*, U.S. Government Printing Office, 1971.

[12] Ann Miller's *Antebellum Orange*, a county history in itself, lists some 140 county homes still standing in Orange County that were built prior to 1860. Only 31 of them are east of Route 522. People farming poor land found it hard to justify the building or maintenance of substantial residences.

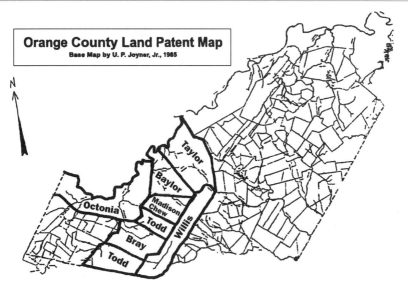

**Orange County Land Patent Map**
Base Map by U. P. Joyner, Jr., 1985

These patents, the last of which came six years before Orange County was formed, locked up almost all of the best soil in the area. The town of Orange is on the boundary between the Taylor (1722) and Baylor (1726) patents. The town of Gordonsville is in the lower right corner of the Willis (1728) patent. The Madison/Chew patent (1723) is the original Montpelier tract. The 24,000 acre Octonia patent (1722) extended beyond Stanardsville in today's Greene County. Base patent map prepared by U. P. Joyner, Jr., with specific patents highlighted by Barbara V. Little, Ann L. Miller, and Kenneth M. Clark. Reproduced with permission.

Scouting for the best Orange County land had begun early. We know that in 1704, Lt. Col. James Taylor II was petitioning the House of Burgesses for permission to mount an expedition into the uplands. There was much discussion and foot-dragging, and it isn't certain that the expedition was ever actually authorized. One has to suspect that Taylor and some of his friends slipped off into the uplands a time or two anyway.

In May 1713, Larkin Chew received a patent to 4,020 acres of land, which today is called "the Silver Mine Patent." That patent was located in the Burr Hill area of today's Orange County, stretching south along Mine Run and Black Walnut Run. While the patent's name indicates an interest in mining, the soils would have not been ignored. Chew elected not to develop his patent, and the land ultimately wound up belonging to that ever-acquisitive Colonel Henry Willis.

Spotswood was interested in the Virginia uplands almost from the day he arrived in 1710. He authorized an expedition to the Blue Ridge in the fall of his first year in office, and in 1714 he rode out at least as far as the foothills of the Blue Ridge. Spotswood's interest in the uplands translated into action with the establishment of Fort Germanna in 1714. In 1716 he led an expedition from Germanna to and over the Blue Ridge. Among the fifty or so guests on the Governor's trek were four county surveyors and some of the shrewdest land speculators in the Virginia colony, people who knew good land when they saw it. It should come as no surprise to learn that one of those "Knights of the Golden Horseshoe" was Col. James Taylor II.

In addition to the reported explorations and views of the uplands, there were surely innumerable undocumented ones. It is clear in any event that Orange County was extensively tramped over and inspected before any-one started driving corner stakes in the ground. What were the inspectors looking for? What did they find?

When the 1716 Knights arrived at the fork of the Rapidan and Robinson rivers, John Fontaine, for his part, observed that he saw "the largest timber, the finest and deepest mould [soil], and the best grass that I ever did see."[13] In commenting on Orange County's Davidson soil in 1927, a soil survey report noted that its forest trees are "noticeably larger and more vigorous" than those on other soils.[14] That characteristic of Davidson is today allow-ing a local nursery located on that soil to grow trees to a marketable size in one to two years less time than its competitors.

We can be sure that the inspectors were also looking for other types of vegetation, just as observers exhibited that ability at later times. During the Civil War, a soldier serving in another theater wrote home to report that he was camped in an area of Horse Chestnuts, which, as he reminded his readers, were a sure sign of poor soil. Had he been camped in eastern Orange County, he, like the colonial settlers before him, would have seen a lot of a relative of the Horse Chestnut, the Chinquapin (pronounced "chink-a-pin"), also an indicator of poor soil. The Great Fork area of Culpeper County in earlier times was often called "Chinquapin Neck," a hard place to make a living off the land.

This writer's grandfather was both a good farmer and located on Davidson soil, a spectacular combination. He was sometimes asked by neighbors to assess a piece of land which was for sale. I am told that Grand-

[13] Alexander, *Journal of John Fontaine*, p. 104.

[14] Hendrickson, *Soil Survey of Orange County*, p. 5.

father would ride onto the property being offered, hand his horse's reins to the seller, and say that he wanted the horse tied to a Black Walnut tree. If the seller had no such trees, Grandfather would get back on his horse and ride home. No use wasting time looking over land he couldn't recommend.

Ellwood in far eastern Orange County was recognized as a good farm. Such statistics as are available on Ellwood and its neighboring farms reveal that Ellwood consistently outproduced them. Good management? Certainly, but there was something else. Go to Ellwood and look at the trees in its lawn. There, south of the house, is an absolutely huge Black Walnut. Even though Ellwood is located in an area of generally poor soils, the farm itself occupies a fertile ridge. William Jones, the original developer of the Ellwood operation, knew how to pick land.

Some areas in eastern Orange county have soils so infertile and/or so physically unsuitable for farming that they became known as "the poison fields." (A similar area in Madison County is called "the desert.") The Lake of the Woods community on Flat Run is located for the most part on soils which are shallow and poorly drained, thwarting the developer's original intent to sell lots served by individual septic fields.

IN 1722, ALL THE LAND INSPECTIONS OF ORANGE COUNTY BEGAN PAYING off. Col. James Taylor II obtained a patent from King George I for 8,500 acres in the little mountain area and shortly thereafter began building Bloomsbury, which still stands just northwest of the Orange airport. Almost all of the land now occupied by the Town of Orange was once a part of that patent. Meadowfarm, located on that land at the southeastern edge of the town of Orange continues in the ownership of direct descendants of Col. Taylor. You would probably not be surprised to learn that Col. Taylor's patent contained almost all Davidson and closely related soils.

Also in 1722, eight investors patented 24,000 acres, a tract which became known as "The Octonia Grant."[15] Their property ran along the south bank of the Rapidan from Spicer's Mill, near the routes 633/674 intersection in Orange County, to beyond Stanardsville in today's Greene County. Again, good to excellent soils were involved. In 1726, Taylor's tidewater friend and neighbor, John Baylor, patented 6,500 acres, part of which is located between the Octonia grant and Taylor's Meadowfarm grant. In 1728, when Col. Henry Willis patented his 10,000 acres in what would become

---

[15] See Grymes, *The Octonia Grant,* for a detailed and interesting history of that grant. In doing the field work for his publication, Randy located in Greene County the only known surviving Octonia corner stone.

southwestern Orange County, his tract was just barely into the good soil. It was already starting to get scarce. A great deal of the Town of Gordonsville is on that former Willis land.

From a historical standpoint, probably the most significant patent of Orange County land was one in 1723 for 4,675 acres granted by King George I to Ambrose Madison and Capt. Thomas Chew. Madison and Chew had both recently married daughters of Col. James Taylor II. The 4,675 acres was Taylor's fee for surveying a tract for which a patent was being sought, and he arranged to have it granted directly to his two sons-in-law. The descendants of Ambrose Madison eventually bought the Chew portion, with the whole then constituting the original Montpelier tract. When you visit the Montpelier grounds, look at all those Black Walnut trees. It's Rapidan soil right there at the house, which is close to Davidson in natural fertility. As you would suspect, Montpelier also has a lot of Davidson.

An interesting, but academic, question is: If James Madison's family had been farming some of Orange County's poor soils, would we have ever heard of him? One answer is that he would have probably had to stay home and work, because there wouldn't have been enough farm income to permit buying slaves or hiring labor to allow him to leave. He surely would not have lived to age 85, as hard work and poor nutrition would have done him in much earlier. The reason the question is academic, however, is that the best answer is that Madison's family simply would not have settled on poor soils. People of wealth, power, and position in the Virginia colony knew the necessity of owning good land, and they either got to the developing areas early themselves or they had friends looking out for them. In Madison's case, it was Col. Taylor. Along with that old saying of "poor land makes poor people" goes another one: "Thems what has, gits more."

## F. Organizing the Land Grab

In the preceding subchapter, much was said about land being "patented." The patenting process was a major way in which settlers acquired title to land. Equally important, it was a process which required that the land be developed and contribute to the colony's economy. Patenting, however, was not used in the earliest days of the colony.[16]

Initially, the governing body of the Virginia Company held title to all of the land claimed by the colony, and the colonists were all tenants in common. By 1620, however, the headright system was in place, and in

---

[16] For more detail, consult Joyner, *Orange County Land Patents.*

another year or two the procedures for the granting of patents were established. In 1624, King James I revoked the charter of the badly managed
and nearly bankrupt Virginia Company, and the colony became a Crown
Colony, with the King then standing as the owner of all its lands. It was
from the King or his colonial representative, the governor, that patents to
Orange County's land were to be received.

For this discussion, the terms "grant" and "patent' are used interchange-
ably and sometimes together, such as in "granting a patent." If you find
yourself in a serious discussion with someone who knows colonial land
law, be advised that there are technical differences between a grant and a
patent and proceed humbly. Also, the headright system was extremely important in colonial Virginia's land ownership system.

The first efforts at headrights began shortly before 1620 in the form of
Virginia Company land "dividends" to shareholder/settlers and evolved
over time into outright grants of small acreages to incoming settlers.[17] To
receive a headright by the time Orange County was formed, a person appeared before the local court and proved to the justices' satisfaction that
the petitioner had paid his passage to the colony and was a free, independent individual. That person was then entitled to fifty acres of land, compliments of the county. If he had also brought over family members and
servants, he received an additional fifty acre headright for each such person. Probably one of the more significant individuals appearing in the Orange court to receive a headright was William Monroe, who at his death
left his rather considerable estate to trustees to pay for the education of the
poor.[18] Greene County's high school is named for him.

As you might suspect, the headright system was subject to some abuses.
One of the justices of the new Orange County was Joist Hite. (The first
name pronounced "yost.") When folks began checking on Hite's rather
considerable headright holdings, it was discovered that many of the named
individuals for whom Hite had received headrights were chickens, cows,
ducks, etc.

Individuals who wished to receive a patent had to petition the Crown
or the Royal Governor. What the petitioners were seeking was the exclusive right to develop a particular piece of land. Because the land had to be

---

[17] Consult Joyner, *The First Settlers,* pp. 51-53, for more detail on the origins of the
headright system.

[18] Monroe was granted a headright in 1749. The chapter in W. W. Scott's history of
Orange County entitled "The Orange Humane Society," recites the interesting story
of that education trust in detail.

described in some detail, surveys were almost always required. To protect the petitioner's interests while getting the survey and preparing the petition, a "warrant" could be issued, which was something like being given a number in a line. No one else could present a petition involving that same land until all prior warrants for it had expired.

Once a petition had been received, the King or the Governor would then hear evidence, if any was desired, as to the financial and managerial abilities of the petitioner to actually develop the subject property. Being in the good graces of the party being petitioned was almost always a necessity. If the petition was granted, the petitioner would receive a patent to the described tract of land. For a specified length of time thereafter, the government would recognize and protect an exclusive right in the land to the petitioner. For example, trespassers could be prosecuted in the King's Court. In return, the petitioner had to "seat and plant" the patent, that is clear and plant a certain amount of land, or populate it with livestock, or construct houses, mills, fences, etc., all adding value to the land. If the seating and planting requirement was not met, the patent "lapsed," and the land could then be regranted. Land speculators often tried to sell their patent tracts as quickly as possible. If they couldn't strike a quick sale, they might well let the patent lapse.

One of the larger patents of what was Orange County land at the time was the "Beverly Manor" patent of 118,491 acres of Valley land, granted in 1736. The patentees were William Beverly, John Randolph, Richard Randolph, and John Robinson. The City of Staunton ultimately grew out of the seating and planting of the Beverly Manor patent.

Probably one of the more spectacular abuses of the patent process involved a party who was building "patent houses" to seat and plant his patent, that is, building houses whose measurements met the minimums required by law.[19] So many acres were involved that ninety-two such houses had to be built. Not only that, the houses had to be occupied by settlers. The patentee got the houses built in time, but he had nowhere near that number of families to put in them. Not to worry. When the "genial inquisitor" arrived to verify that the seating and planting requirement had been met, he began a trek from house to house, greeting the occupant families and making a chalk mark on his hat for each house visited. As he left each house, the patentee's servants seen at that house rushed ahead along back trails to appear as "family" at some house farther up the road. One servant

---

[19] The Argelon Price house on display in the James Madison Museum is a patent house from the Clark Mountain area.

girl got so caught up in the spirit of the thing that she appeared at five or six different houses, at one dressed as a boy.[20]

## G. Rocks are Not Boring

This subchapter will not be a comprehensive course on Orange County's geology, as interesting as that geology is. For example, at one time a mile or so of the west coast of Africa was heaped up over this land we call Orange County. Also, the Southwest and Blue Ridge mountains are the result of the ongoing erosion of a slowly rising land mass. We are told that the ridges we see are the product of their having caps of weather-resistant rocks, particularly sandstone and Catoctin Greenstone. There is an extensive geologic history for the mid-Atlantic region, and geologists note that Virginia offers a buffet-like selection of almost every geologic event and geologic material known.

The geology presented here is intended to be that geology which directly affected the people who occupied and used this land. When we talked about the critical importance of soils, for example, we didn't say much about the underlying geology. Keep in mind, however, that upland soils are for the most part a weathered product of the rock under them. While that is an important indirect effect of the county's geology, sometimes the rocks themselves are what we need to talk about.

The latest, and probably final, major geologic "find" in Orange County involved the discovery of sizeable deposits of uranium ore in the northwestern area of the county. By 1980 a Canadian company had uranium leases on over 50,000 acres of Virginia land, some of it in the Somerset/Barboursville area of Orange County. The local battle to restrict, if not totally prohibit, the mining of that ore gave the county an early introduction into the world of conservation and preservation, an introduction which is paying dividends in scenic and historic preservation efforts today. Incidentally, the Canadians finally gave up and went away. The uranium is still here.

At the other end of the county from the uranium and over 200 years earlier in time, iron ore was mined and smelted. Naturally, Spotswood was in the middle of it. He began trying to get the Lords Board of Trade and Plantations to authorize him to do "manufacture," that is, smelt that ore, almost from the time he first established Fort Germanna in 1714. The gen-

---

[20] It was simply too good a scheme to keep under wraps. <u>Borden v. Culton, et al, 1806.</u>

eral rule, however, was that the colonies sold raw materials to manufacturers in England, from whom they then purchased their finished goods. Early settlers thus fit the economic definition of farmers; they were expected to sell wholesale and buy retail.

Spotswood finally received a nod to go ahead, and in the early 1720s his Tubal furnace on the Rappahannock began producing pig iron for export to England. Spotswood's "air furnace" at Massoponax in Spotsylvania County also produced some finished iron items for local sale. Firebacks were popular. They were large plates of cast iron set in the back of fireplaces that radiated additional heat. Three firebacks have been found in Orange County. A broken one owned by the Orange County Historical Society is on loan for exhibit to the James Madison Museum.[21]

The headquarters for Spotswood's iron operations was his Enchanted Castle at Germanna, and in 1732, William Byrd II paid a call there to learn what he could, with the idea of starting up his own operation. Byrd was not the only person interested in what was obviously an enormously profitable business. By 1750, there were six blast furnaces working the ore beds of the area.

Vast acreages of woodland were clear-cut to fuel the blast furnaces, woodland which had taken centuries to develop. That was because the underlying bedrock of the area gave rise to soils that were shallow, acidic, infertile, and poorly drained. Nothing grew well in them. Additional cutting over the years to build plank roads and to fuel gold mining machinery exhausted that "thin land" even further. The timber regrowth was slow, allowing virtually everything else which could grow in this part of Virginia to gain a crowded toehold and compete for sunlight, water, and nutrients. The result was a 70-square-mile temperate zone jungle, appropriately named "the Wilderness." Spell that with a capital "W." It was man-made. The Wilderness possessed a forbidding appearance and an ominous reputation, and it had already been around for almost a century before Civil War battles immortalized it in history.

In Orange County, the Wilderness began just east of Verdiersville (the routes 20/621 intersection) and continued unbroken into Spotsylvania and Culpeper counties. By the time of the Civil War, it was dotted here and there with small hard-scrabble farms and crisscrossed with a confusing lacework of roads, paths, and trails. Unless you stayed on an obviously major roadway, or had a guide, you could be risking your life to travel in the Wilderness.

---

[21] A short and interesting pamphlet on this subject is Meima's *Spotswood's Iron*.

The vegetation of the old Wilderness no longer exists. The trees today are at least twice as tall and the undergrowth less than half as dense as both were, even at the time of the Civil War. The surprisingly uneven terrain and the naturally infertile, shallow, poorly-drained, acidic soils remain. Modern farming practices are able to make them vastly more productive than they used to be, but it still isn't easy.

FOR SOME REASON, GOLD WAS NOT DISCOVERED IN THIS PART OF THE WORLD until the 1820s. Spotswood wrote about mining gold and silver, but it never seemed that he was talking about any discovered deposits. The Gold-Pyrite Belt running along the eastern Piedmont is now well recognized, but while Spotswood found and mined the iron ore which had evolved from the pyrite, he, and everybody else of his day, somehow missed the gold.

Gold mining began in eastern Orange County during the middle 1820s and continued strong until the mid-century California gold rush. Large scale commercial mining activity in the county finally ended in 1937. Most of the mining was confined to the area of the county east of Locust Grove, and the well-known Orange Grove mine, plus a handful of smaller operations, are now under the main lake of Lake of the Woods subdivision.

During the peak years, up to a dozen gold mines were operating in Orange County at any one time, and a total of 22 known mining ventures worked the county gold fields for at least some part of that time. It is commonly thought that the county's Mine Run got its name from the gold mines working in its watershed. Actually, Spotswood and his Knights named Mine Run in 1716 on the strength of Indian reports of silver deposits somewhere upstream. No silver was ever found, and one suspects that the Indians were telling the adventurers whatever they had to in order to keep the white men here and trade with them for guns, blankets, iron tools, jewelry, etc. Upon hearing this story, one of the author's tour clients exclaimed, somewhat uncharitably, "They were Orange County's first real estate agents."

GOLD AND IRON MINING WERE NOT THE ONLY NATURAL RESOURCE extraction businesses attempted in Orange County. For example, Payne Todd, James Madison's stepson, proposed to quarry marble in the Madison Run area near the family mill. He planned to use the profits of the marble operation to underwrite the construction of an elaborate plantation, which he had already christened "Toddsberth." By 1840, Todd had formed the Montpelier Marble Company and was soliciting investors. Toddsberth was indeed located on the Everona formation, and veins of white and colored marble do exist in it. Todd's particular quarry was located in the northeast corner of the intersection of today's Routes 15 and 639, with Toddsberth a few hundred yards east of the quarry, on the high ground on the south side of 639. In later years, a copper mine was also worked in that area.

Unfortunately, the marble Todd quarried was of unmarketable quality, and he lost everything, a fairly typical Payne Todd outcome. Keep in mind that Todd's addictions to alcohol and gambling did nothing to enhance the prospects of his enterprise from the start. Toddsberth was sold to pay creditors. Some folks are hard to dissuade, however, and there is a newspaper report of another group of investors organized to quarry marble in that same area in 1885. Their success, if any, did not make the papers.

The Everona formation gives Orange County some of its best road stone quarries. The geology is similar to that of the Valley of Virginia, with limestone being the predominant bedrock. A big difference, however, is that the Everona material is "metamorphic" rock, formed under high heat and pressure, and the Valley limestone is not. (Remember that the Everona was lying under a mile or two of the African continent.)

While we evidently do not have anything qualifying as a limestone cave in the Everona, local geologist Tinsley Mack did report that at a time when the old Superior Stone quarry at Gordonsville was pumped down, he observed several cave-like openings in the quarry walls. The largest was probably four feet in diameter. Streams of water were flowing from them into the quarry, which itself was quickly re-filling, and Mack had no problem quelling any instincts to go exploring. Maybe in a few million years we will have a full-sized Orange County cave.

Many of Orange County's better soils are some type of clay or clay loam. If you guessed that they might make good brick, you were right. The brick plant at Somerset routinely turns out over 600,000 brick per week. In earlier times, most large plantations had their own in-house brick making facilities, and the brick buildings on their land had been made from the land itself. In the Montpelier area, there are stories of a black female brick maker, apparently an independent contractor, at work during the colonial era.

At various times soapstone, talc, sandstone, greenstone, and various other construction materials have been mined in Orange County, but nothing of great or lasting import. George Jones, retired longtime Director of the Piedmont Research Station and a student of local geology, reported that in the Barboursville area there was a "mine" from which a graphite-like material had been obtained to grease wagon axles. In 1836 a single diamond was reported as having been found in the county. Well, maybe.

## H. The Life and Times of the County's First Citizens

This land was being occupied and used long before any Europeans arrived. The time-honored designation of "Indian" will be used most often for those people, even though the early explorers quickly determined that they had not landed on the east coast of India. "Native American" was the popular term coined during the last century, but we understand now that such folk were/are no more "native" than the Europeans who followed them to the New World. They just got here ahead of them. There had been even earlier Indian cultures which had evolved, flourished, and disappeared long before the evolution of those tribes who greeted the first European settlers.

The earliest evidence we have of Indians in Orange County comes from a Clovis spear point which was picked up on the Rapidan River bottoms north of Somerset. This point, named for a site in Clovis, New Mexico, where they were first found, has been dated to 9,000 B.C. Others have since been found in this area, confirming that date, which is around the end of the last ice age. This region would have had patches of scrub forest, with most of the land covered with low, tundra-like vegetation. It would have attracted migrating herds of large animals, such as elk, deer, and possibly woods bison.[22] The Indians themselves would have been representatives of the Paleo-Indian culture, who hunted the herd animals and moved with them. Winters here at that time were severe, and both the animals and the Indians probably made a point to be elsewhere by the time snow flew.[23]

As the climate warmed, the open plains disappeared into tall, dense forests, and the large herds stopped coming this far east. An Indian culture which could survive in that changed environment evolved. Features of that Archaic Indian culture, which existed from roughly 7,000 to 1,000 B.C, were semi-migratory family groups, hunting the resident large animals and smaller game of the woods and meadows. Traps and snares were used in addition to spears and clubs. They still moved often, and we find their flaked stone tools and axe heads everywhere in Orange County. As the years went by, more and more fishing and gathering of fruit, nuts, berries,

---

[22] Bovidae Bison Athabascae, the Canadian Woods Bison, as opposed to Bovidae Bison Bison, the North American Prairie Bison, popularly called the "Buffalo." Buffalo are not thought to have ranged east of the Blue Ridge Mountains.

[23] The recently-discovered Brook Run flint quarry in Culpeper County has also been dated to about 9,000 B.C.

roots, and other edible plant material was done by these people to supplement their game harvest.

By 1,000 B.C. the Woodland Indian culture had evolved, a culture which continued in our area until European settlement pressures forced it out. Multi-family tribal groups lived in semi-permanent villages, moving when the soil wore out or to avoid hostile neighbors. Confederations and alliances among tribal groups grew larger and more highly organized during this time.[24] The bow and arrow's contribution to hunting game came late in the period.[25] In addition to hunting and fishing for food, the Indians cultivated crops, such as corn and squash. Clay pottery, along with bone and shell tools and ornaments were in use, some of it polished and decorated. Trade-based commerce between friendly tribal groups existed. Because tribes of Woodland Indians were occupying the Orange County area at the time the settlers came, we know more about them than we do about their Paleo and Archaic predecessors, but still not as much as we would like.

THE TRIBES OCCUPYING THIS PART OF THE VIRGINIA PIEDMONT WHEN THE Virginia Company settlers arrived at Jamestown spoke the Siouan language and were generally divided into two large confederations. The Manahoac confederacy of tribes existed in our immediate area, with the Monacan territory beginning south of the Rivanna River. Eastward, between the Manahoacs and the Jamestown settlers were tribes speaking the Algonquian language, most of whom were members of the fearsome Powhatan confederation. Marking the approximate boundary between their territories in our region were the falls of the Rappahannock at today's Fredericksburg.

When news of the Jamestown settlement drifted inland, the Manahoacs saw no need to fight their way through the Algonquians just for a look at a group of white men. They might be killed off anyway, just as the Algonquians had dealt with the Spanish settlement earlier. If those people wanted to know who was living in the uplands, they could just come on up here and find out. That turned out to be exactly what those people did.

---

[24] At the 1787 Constitutional Convention, Benjamin Franklin exhorted the delegates to think creatively, citing as an example the very successful Iroquois Confederation, which had two basic rules: 1) only men held the positions of power and authority. They were elected to those positions, and the electorate could vote them out if they did not perform; 2) only women had the vote!

[25] Most of the stone points exhibited as "arrowheads," are actually spear points. Arrowheads are typically about the size of a thumbnail.

In August of 1608, Captain John Smith started sailing up the Rappahannock. The journey was a part of his explorations to supplement and expand upon his map of the Chesapeake Bay area. Part way upriver, they were joined by Mosco, an Algonquian whose tribe was part of a confederation that lived along the Potomac. Smith had gotten to know Mosco while exploring the northern reaches of the Chesapeake. The common language was almost surely Spanish. Sailing upstream, Smith and his party finally came to a rocky shallows and an island. The ship could go no further, and Smith, Mosco, and others went ashore. Welcome to Fredericksburg.

The party was soon attacked by Indians with bows and arrows. They responded with muskets. The uneven skirmish lasted about a half-hour, then the Indians withdrew, leaving one of their wounded behind. In that suffering captive, John Smith met his first Manahoac.

After a bit of food and drink, the Manahoac became rather chatty. Through Mosco, Smith learned something about the Manahoac people and their villages farther upriver. Out of this came the first crude map of what would become Orange County.

Fearing further attacks in this narrow section of the river, Smith ordered the ship to be sailed downriver to where the stream width could protect them. Sure enough, a large body of Manahoacs followed on shore, bouncing arrows off the ship and setting up a great yelling and hallooing every time an effort was made to talk with them.

Finally a conversation was established with the voices in the woods. After much talk, Indians appeared on a point of land that jutted out into the river. There was more talk, and they hung up their bows and quivers. Smith and a party then went ashore and returned the wounded captive to his people.

After much visiting and trading, it was time to go home. As his ship drifted downstream, Smith observed that they left "foure or five hundred of our merry Mannahocks, singing, dancing, and making merry."[26] It was the first and last time Europeans would see the Manahoacs as an organized society. In 1669 and again in 1670, a young German by the name of John Lederer came through the Orange-Madison-Culpeper area. On the second trip Lederer came through this immediate area, accompanied by Col. John Catlett of Port Royal and several guides. In a report which was published in 1672, Lederer stated that all the Manahoac villages had been long aban-

---

[26] This story of the encounter is condensed from: Bushnell, Jr., David I.; "The Manahoac Tribes in Virginia, 1608," 24 *Smithsonian Miscellaneous Papers* 8, p. 1 *et seq.*

doned and that the Indians were gone. It was a No Man's Land and had been for some time.[27] Possibly the combination of European-introduced diseases and tribal warfare had rendered this part of Virginia uninhabitable for the Manahoacs. All we know for sure is that they were gone.

At a later date, Lieutenant Governor Spotswood settled some Saponi Indians in the Orange County area to act as interpreters and guides, but they soon wore out their welcome. Complaints about those Indians burning the woods as a means of hunting — and of poaching the settlers' livestock — and of shots being fired near people put Spotswood on the defensive, and he eventually sent them home.

Then there is the story of Sawney, standing stark naked, drunk, and roaring in the main road through Germanna. In addition to being generally obnoxious, Sawney was trying to shoot people with a musket, into which one of the good ladies of the town had prudently poured water some time earlier.[28] In 1742 there was a group, among whom were Manicassa, Captain Tom, Blind Tom, Foolish Zack, and Little Zack, who wound up before the Orange County court, accused of terrorizing a citizen. They promised to behave and turned in their guns, which were returned upon their leaving the county.[29]

But those were only the echoes of a broken and dispersed society. A more substantial set of reminders exists. In addition to the spear points, arrowheads, tools, and ornaments which may be seen in various displays throughout the county, there are legacies on the land.

The Carolina Road was noted earlier in the chapter. As one of the earliest known north-south travel ways through this part of colonial Virginia, the settlers made extensive use of it. Where the Carolina Road crossed

---

[27] Governor Berkeley's charge to Lederer was to go to the high mountains and see what was beyond. Some argue that Lederer never got that far, but he definitely went through the Manahoac country. Ironically, Col. Catlett helped to determine that the Manahoacs were gone, only to return home and be killed by Algonquians. See: Fall, *Hidden Village*, p. 10.

[28] Spotsylvania County Order Book for 1724-1730, Page 1. "Sawney" had initially been a countrified name for a Shawnee Indian, but by our Sawney's time, it was just a name in general use. He was actually a Saponi.

[29] There was trouble in Surry County in 1728 with a "Captain Tom," who was identified as a Saponi. That Tom was threatening to form an alliance with the Catawabas and rise against the local English leaders. He might not be Orange County's Captain Tom, but he certainly sounds like him.(Letter report of Thomas Avent dated 27 Sept 1728, Document collection of the Virginia Historical Society).

into Orange County near Raccoon Ford, one of the county's first commercial settlements west of Germanna evolved.

Farther down the Rapidan, just before you get to the U-shaped bend that creates Culpeper County's Fox Neck, there is the Orange County community of Indiantown. It was the site of a Manahoac village and is believed to be the one described to John Smith in 1608 as Shackaconia, named for its chief. With the Manahoacs gone, Spotswood had used the site for his Saponis. When the Saponis were dismissed, European settlers moved onto the site. Home sites were already substantially cleared, a road and trail system accessing it was in place, and sources of water, sometimes a problem thereabouts, were already developed. The residents' use of the name Indiantown stands as a legacy to those who had come before them.

Still farther down the Rapidan is a fish trap, consisting of large stones set across the river shallows in a loose "vee" array, the point upstream. Swimming against the current, fish work their way from one flow-breaking stone to the next. All you would need this very day to complete the picture would be a Manahoac, hovering near his catch basket at the point of the trap.

Almost all the way in the opposite direction on the Rapidan in today's Orange County is an Indian burial mound on the river bank, actually now in the river bank. The mound is in the vicinity of another Manahoac village called Stegara, whose exact location is not known. There may be no connection between the village and the mound, but the mound is considered to be Manahoac. The river is slowly washing the mound away, but it was at least studied and reported on some years earlier.[30]

Maybe as time goes by we will discover and learn more about the people who were here in Orange County before us. Unfortunately for our county's history, but probably fortunately for them, they didn't wait for us to arrive.

---

[30] Holland, C.G., Speiden, Sandra D., van Rroijen, David; "The Rapidan Mound Revisited," Occasional Paper #4, Orange County Historical Society, 1982.

Lieutenant Governor Alexander Spotswood (1676-1740) and his wife Anne Butler Brayne Spotswood. Although officially untitled, the Spotswoods easily qualified as "colonial aristocracy," and over the years began to see Virginia, not England, as their true homeland. One of their Virginia homes was the Enchanted Castle at Germanna. Reproduced courtesy of the Virginia Historical Society, Richmond.

# CHAPTER III

## *Alexander Spotswood & the Settling of the Uplands*

On February 18, 1710 (O.S.), upon the petition of George Hamilton, Earl of Orkney, England's Queen Anne commissioned Alexander Spotswood to serve as the next Lieutenant Governor of the Virginia colony. In so doing, the Queen assigned a mission to a man who already had one of his own. He simply combined the two, and for the remainder of his life, in both his official and private endeavors, Spotswood strove to make: (a) the Virginia colony and (b) himself powerful and prosperous. The story of his success in those endeavors is part and parcel of the heritage of Orange County.

Spotswood had been born in Tangier (today's Morocco) late in 1676, at a time when in the Virginia colony Governor Berkeley was exacting retribution on the supporters of Nathaniel Bacon, whose rebellion had collapsed with his death. Spotswood's family could sympathize at least a little with the Baconites. At one time, they had been Scot nobility and are said to have sported the heathery surname of "Spottiswoode." Unfortunately, one ancestor had come out on the short end of a squabble between the Crown and Parliament, and he himself had then been shortened to the top of his shoulders. The family lost its title, but life goes on.

Young Spotswood received the majority of his education in England, and his initial career choice was for the military. In 1693, he was commissioned an Ensign in the Earl of Bath's regiment of foot posted in Flanders. In today's English, we would say he was made a second lieutenant in the color guard of an infantry regiment stationed in the Netherlands/Belgium region. This was a relatively quiet post at the time, and promotions came slowly. In 1696, Spotswood finally made First Lieutenant and was posted to Ireland for a time. Nothing really exciting was going on there either. Opportunities for an ambitious young man to make his mark and impress important people had been few and far between so far, but that was all about to change.

The death in 1700 of Charles II of Spain left that throne vacant with no clear successor. Charles himself had earlier nominated the grandson of French King Louis XIV, and now France thought it saw an opportunity to annex its rich and powerful neighbor. England and others were not about to let that happen. Before long, the War of Spanish Succession, also known as "Queen Anne's War," was underway, with Spotswood in the middle of it.

By 1702 Captain Spotswood was back in Flanders and serving as the Deputy Quartermaster General under John Churchill, the first Duke of Marlborough. He was placed in charge of supplying Churchill's army, a challenging assignment. Spotswood had a head for figures and a knack for getting things done, so the job suited him perfectly. Supplies flowed smoothly to Marlborough's troops, and promotions and recognition flowed to Spotswood.

But Alexander Spotswood was not about to serve as a rear-area staffer who never smelled gunpowder. It was his nature to get into the middle of whatever was happening, and that eventually caught up with him. In August 1704, during the Battle of Blenheim, in Bavaria, a mostly-spent French 4-pounder cannon ball thumped into the left shoulder of now Lieutenant Colonel Spotswood, breaking several bones. Broken only in body, not in spirit, Spotswood painfully made his way over to the offending missile and retrieved it. He then kept that cannon ball with him for most of the rest of his life.

Almost exactly three years later Spotswood was back in the field and participating in the Battle of Audenarde in Belgium. During that battle his horse was shot from under him, and he was captured. Marlborough personally undertook negotiations to arrange an exchange for his valuable staffer, and by May 1708, Spotswood was back supplying the troops. Upon his return to the army, Spotswood filed charges against the cavalry escort which had accompanied him at Audenarde, asserting that they had abandoned him in the field. Spotswood was ever sensitive to anything that smacked even slightly of a personal affront, and he wasn't about to let the matter drop. To his great indignation, the escort was found blameless.

Among the many persons whose attention Spotswood had by now attracted was George Hamilton, Earl of Orkney. Hamilton had been one of the Scots who supported the Act of Union, uniting England and Scotland to form Great Britain, and he had served on the first Parliament of the new union. He had also served as a general under Marlborough. Hamilton was clearly deserving of royal patronage, and he got it in the form of the governorship of the Virginia colony. At the onset, it was understood that the good Earl would not be going to Virginia, rather he would be appointing "lieutenants" to serve "in his [permanent] absence." Orkney's first appointee was a fellow Scot and good soldier, Alexander Spotswood.

At age 34, Spotswood was making a major career change. For whatever reason, the military had lost its allure, and he had made himself available to Orkney. Not only was he prepared to take the proposed office at half pay (he and Orkney would be splitting the governor's salary), Spotswood would be leaving the Mother Country, possibly forever. While history tells us that his decision was rewarded with an active and profitable career, all Spotswood had to count on at the time were his courage and self-confidence. History tells us that he never lacked for either.

Spotswood arrived in Virginia in June 1710 and assumed office.[1] He was the first Royal Governor Virginia had seen since Governor Nott's sudden death from a fever in 1706. The French had captured Nott's first replacement, Colonel Robert Hunter, en route to Virginia, and the delays occasioned by the war and the infrequent correspondence between Virginia and England had meant that Virginia's twelve-member Council had been running things pretty much to their satisfaction for some four years. Not infrequently in the years to come, Spotswood would find himself at odds with that confidently independent Council. He would also quickly come to learn that the various editions of the popularly elected House of Burgesses were no pushovers either. In November 1717, the House sitting at that time impeached him.[2] But initially, all was sweetness and light.

Virginia had been settled for 103 years by the time Spotswood arrived, but the colony had yet to extend its settled areas beyond the Tidewater. At one time that had made good sense, because initially the colony's great rivers offered the only convenient and safe ways to travel inland. Above the fall line those waterways lost those advantages. Also, on Good Friday 1622, the brothers of the deceased Algonquian chief Powhatan had staged a massacre that took the lives of between a quarter and a third of the Virginia colony's population, the most complete losses being among those who had tried to settle upriver. For quite a while, then, it just made sense to

---

[1] While we understand that Spotswood was actually a Lieutenant Governor, historic custom and usage, as well as literary economy, authorize our calling him "Governor."

[2] Admittedly, it had been a slow session of the House, and many of Spotswood's supporters had absented themselves. None of the eleven counts against him were sustained.

huddle together down in the Tidewater. There were now, however, good reasons to move west, not the least of which was the fact that one of Spotswood's instructions from London was to make that happen.

First, those enemies of long standing, the French and Spanish, were becoming more aggressive in their efforts to control the lands west of the English colonies. The French were particularly threatening with their extension of New France (part of today's Canada) into the Ohio country and their development of what they called their Louisiana territory along the Mississippi. The Spanish, who had been in the New World for a century before the English arrived, were also beginning to establish settlements to the south. If the English didn't start moving soon, they could find themselves with no way off the beach. Also, tobacco was already wearing out the Tidewater soils, and fresh land was needed for the colony's most important export.

Equally important, the Tidewater Algonquians had been pretty much subdued and the upland Manahoacs had moved away, significantly lessening Indian resistance to western migration. The disappearance of the Manahoacs was known as early as 1669 when the young German John Lederer began exploring into the future Orange/ Madison/ Culpeper area. Inertia is hard to overcome, though, and the thought of leaving everybody and everything and starting all over again in the uplands wasn't all that appealing. Such non-adventuresome thinking was of course foreign to Spotswood.

The Lords Commissioners of Trade and Plantations, known generally as the Board of Trade, was the body in London with primary oversight of Spotswood's governorship, and it was to them that most of his official correspondence was addressed. As early as December 15, 1710, Spotswood was reporting to the Board on "the discoveries which I have encouraged to be made this fall by a company of adventurers who found the mountains not above a hundred miles from our upper inhabitants and went up to the top of the highest mountain with their horses, though they had hitherto been thought to be unpassable, and they assured me that ye descent to the other side seemed to be as easy as that they had passed on this."[3] It sounded as if Spotswood would be blazing trails to the Blue Ridge the next summer, but it turned out that almost another four years would pass before serious settlement started in the uplands.

Instead of sponsoring new western settlements, Spotswood found himself having to concentrate on re-establishing the office of Governor. The

---

[3] From Brock, *The Official Letters of Alexander Spotswood*, Vol. 1, p. 40.

colonials had a huge backlog of matters that only a Royal Governor could deal with, but beyond that, they had gotten used to operating without one. Spotswood had to devote himself to plowing through a docket already waiting for him, while at the same time attempting to act on the instructions which accompanied him from London. As far as the Council and Burgesses were concerned, Spotswood's instructions were his problem, not theirs. Additionally, as Spotswood discovered, the Burgesses, through whom the money bills had to pass, were frugal to a fault. Underwriting western settlement was definitely not high on their agenda.[4]

The war with France and Spain imposed its own set of problems on Spotswood's plans. An English invasion of French Canada was undertaken in 1711, and Virginia was called upon to provide supplies. The Royal Navy guardships assigned to the Virginia colony were sent on the invasion, and the coast was open to French reprisals and Spanish raids. Spotswood had to devote considerable time to building a fort at Point Comfort at the mouth of the James River and to the military readiness of the colony generally.

Also, while the Indian threat in Virginia had abated considerably, periodic uprisings in neighboring colonies kept the Virginians edgy. To the north, the Five Nations of the Iroquois went on the warpath from time to time, terrorizing particularly the residents of the New York colony. At the southern end of the Great Iroquois War Trail, which ran along the eastern slope of the Blue Ridge, was another nation of the Iroquois, the Tuscarora. The territory they claimed included northeastern North Carolina. In September 1711, the Tuscarora arose and began killing settlers, a number of whom were Germans who had been brought to North Carolina by the Baron Christopher de Graffenried. While assisting with ending the uprising, Spotswood had an opportunity to confer with de Graffenried about bringing Germans to the Virginia colony. There's never an ill wind that doesn't blow some good.

The Tuscarora scare did help Spotswood get a bill past the Burgesses to fund the formation of several companies of Rangers. The Rangers were to patrol the lands west of the settled areas of the colony and monitor Indian activity. Presumably the Rangers would then be able to give an early warning of any trouble. Not incidentally, they would also be in an excellent position to learn about the trails to the mountains and of the passes through them. There was in fact already an active trade with the

---

[4] Spotswood did have a two shillings/hogshead tobacco tax which was his to spend as he saw fit, but major undertakings required the assistance of the tightfisted Burgesses.

Indian tribes to the west, using those trails and passes. By 1714 Spotswood had established something called the Virginia Indian Company to get himself into that business. Council member William Byrd II, like his father before him, had amassed a considerable fortune through the Indian trade, and he worked tirelessly to keep competitors from cutting in on it. Byrd had many friends on the other side of the Atlantic, and eventually Spotswood received an order from London to shut his Virginia Indian Company down.

Spotswood also had some pet building projects which probably interested him more than the need to plan for western settlement. He was one of the "gentlemen architects" of his day, and he found interesting things to do almost as soon as he set foot in the New World.[5]

In 1705 most of the College of William & Mary had burned, while in the same year, the Burgesses had authorized the expenditure of a small sum to begin building a Governor's "house." The replacement college building as well as the house remained largely unbuilt at the time Spotswood arrived. Spotswood proceeded to design much of what is today's Wren Building at the college, and his design changes for the Governor's "house" rendered it so much more grand and imposing — and expensive — that the disgruntled Burgesses began calling it the Governor's "Palace." The label stuck.[6] A couple of similar projects which received the Governor's attention were the design of the Powder Magazine, still standing at Williamsburg, plus a revision of the street plan for that town.

Another mark of Spotswood's governorship was the great lessening of the colonists' anxiety about those Indians who still lived among them. No doubt his dealings with the tribes involved more directness than diplomacy, and the growing strength of the colony required that the Governor be listened to. An example: There had been a small trust fund set up at William & Mary for the education of Indians. The college had seen itself as discharging its trust obligation by taking in a few Indian orphans and buying a few Indian slaves, then trying to teach them something. Spotswood changed the focus of the school by getting tribal leaders to send their sons there to learn the White Man's ways. The immediate result of that plan was to have a convenient collection of hostages at Williamsburg in the event of

---

[5] It would be another century before architecture would become a taught profession. Thomas Jefferson was probably the best known American gentleman architect, but Orange County's Alexander Spotswood and Jeremiah Morton were among the other very good ones.

[6] The Governor's Palace burned in 1781, and it was not accurately restored until the 1930s.

any Indian discontent. Negotiation, not massacre, was going to be the way problems would be handled. While governor, Spotswood also reorganized and relocated a number of Indian reservations and entered into several treaties favorable to the colony.

At the time of Spotswood's arrival, tobacco, Virginia's main money crop, was in trouble. Among the buyers' complaints was one that planters were routinely trying to fudge the grading system by packing stems and lugs in the middle of hogsheads and putting quality leaf on each end. Planters, for their part, charged that buyers often delayed buying tobacco of any quality, and consequently the planters were often penniless for large portions of each year, unable to pay levies, quit rents, etc. The situation was bad, getting worse. In 1711, Spotswood got a tobacco inspection and warehousing act passed. The act provided that planters could take their tobacco to government warehouses, where it would be inspected and a certificate issued which recited the amount and grade of the tobacco which the planter had submitted. The warehouses would then hold the tobacco until it was sold, at which time the certificate would be redeemed for cash. Buyers were to be thus assured of uniform quality, and planters could use the certificates as money. Spotswood has been credited with thereby creating the first paper money in the Virginia colony. Surely merchants and millers had earlier issued scrip that had some local, limited circulation, but possibly nothing had actually achieved the general acceptance and circulation of Spotswood's certificates.[7]

A glimpse at one of the less-than-appealing aspects of Spotswood's character, and then on to things involving Orange County: In 1718, a supposedly retired and reformed pirate living in North Carolina began preying on ships passing through the Virginia capes. The pirate's real name was Edward Teach, or maybe Edward Thatch. It didn't matter, because everybody knew him as Blackbeard. The Proprietors of the North Carolina colony seemed to be unable to corral Blackbeard. (There were those who said that he had the Proprietors in his pocket.) Spotswood secretly and personally commissioned two sloops of war and sent them into North Carolina waters after Blackbeard. They found and killed their quarry in Ocracoke inlet, bringing the head back to rot on a pike beside Hampton Roads. Spotswood received thanks and congratulations from almost everyone except the North Carolina Proprietors, who railed about the unauthorized

---

[7] The uses and abuses of the tobacco inspection and warehousing act are chronicled in Fall, *Hidden Village*, p. 18, *et seq.* The act was ultimately repealed as unworkable, but by 1730 Governor Gooch found it necessary to reinstitute a version of it.

and illegal invasion of their sovereignty. Spotswood didn't care a whit about what the Proprietors thought. He had decided what needed doing, and then he did it. It was an attitude, understandable though it might be in a Royal Governor with a military background, that created many problems for Spotswood. The phrase "able and imperious" has long been used to describe him, and it did fit. He accomplished much, but he used up friends and created enemies at an alarming rate.

In the spring of 1714, Christopher, Baron de Graffenried, sent Spotswood the first shipment of Germans, per their discussions at the time of the Tuscarora uprising. It consisted of twelve metalworkers from the Nassau-Siegen region, plus their families and a minister, some 40 souls in all.[8] Spotswood claimed to find their arrival unexpected, which might well have been the case. He definitely found the cost of their transport, payable by him, galling. Since they were already here, however, Spotswood suggested to the Council and Burgesses that good use be made of these people by putting them in an outpost far out into the uplands, where they could act as a buffer against Indian incursions. Specifically, he proposed settling the Germans in a fort on a piece of militarily defensible high ground in a bend of the river we now call the Rapidan, overlooking an excellent fording site.

Spotswood proposed to call the new settlement "Fort Germanna," combining the names of Queen Anne and of the nationality of its first occupants. Germanna is located at the juncture of today's Route 3 and the Rapidan River in eastern Orange County. At the time it was established, it was the westernmost settlement in British America. It was also the first Virginia settlement west of the fall line. Additional groups of Germans arrived in 1717 and 1719. Virginians, in the form of their German representatives, were finally getting off the beach.

Council was surely not fooled by Spotswood's innocent proposal. There weren't any Indians out there that the Rangers couldn't handle, and his plan would send experienced metalworkers into an area of known iron ore deposits. They played along, however, and authorized the building of that most basic of development features, a road, to Germanna.[9] With a road, Germanna would not be a wilderness outpost, it would be a colonial settle-

---

[8] Traditionally, the 1714 group have been called "miners," but the Germanna Foundation is now satisfied that they were metalworkers, which still meant that they knew a lot about furnace construction and iron smelting.

[9] III *Executive Journals* 371-372. Ordered built at public expense April 28, 1714.

ment connected to the commerce and society of the Tidewater and the world beyond. The planters would be coming before long.

The proposed Germanna settlement site was twelve miles west of the Great Fork, where the rivers we know today as the Rappahannock and the Rapidan join. It was nearly thirty miles beyond the established settlements of the colony, but it was not unknown.[10] In addition to the patrolling Rangers, other folks were becoming acquainted with the lands beyond the Tidewater.

In April 1704, Lt. Col. James Taylor II had petitioned the House of Burgesses for permission to mount an expedition into the uplands. He explained that he desired to check on the "strange Indians lately seen on our frontier." The Burgesses were not fooled. Taylor was already showing signs of the ambition which by 1720 would have him owning a string of properties stretching through six of today's Tidewater counties. They were sure that Taylor was just trying to get to the uplands ahead of them and look around for gold, silver, furs, good farm land, whatever.

The Burgesses dragged their feet for thirteen months and then referred Taylor's petition to Council, describing it as seeking "leave to go out on a discovery." Council was no less suspicious or jealous. More detail was sought.[11] Taylor's neighbor and friend John Baylor added his good name to the petition. Other important people were said to be interested in going. Guidelines for the activities of the expedition were proposed. The members offered to pay their own way. And so on. We don't know if the expedition was ever actually authorized, but one suspects that sooner or later Taylor and others slipped off into the uplands and looked around anyway.

In May 1713, Larkin Chew received a patent to 4,020 acres of land, which became known as "the Silver Mine Patent." When the courses and distances are plotted on the ground, it becomes apparent that this tract was in the Burr Hill area of today's Orange County, stretching south along Mine Run and Black Walnut Run for some distance. Chew was a friend of both James Taylor II and Spotswood. There had been talk of silver deposits in the area, and the Knights of the Golden Horseshoe named Mine Run based on Indian reports of some being along that stream. No silver was ever found. The patent went through several lapses and eventually wound

---

[10] What would become Fredericksburg was still a trading post in 1714, albeit a busy and growing one.

[11] A sample: "Ordered that the s$^d$ Coll° James Taylor give his Ex$^{ey}$ an acco$^t$ of the time he intends to set out on y$^e$ s$^d$ discovery and what force he intends to take along with him before he obtain any license for going out." III *Executive Journals* 6.

up in the hands of Colonel Henry Willis. By the time Spotswood's Germans arrived on the land, all the talk was of iron.

In 1716, Spotswood gave the development of the uplands a promotional boost. On August 29 (O.S.) he led an expedition from Germanna to and over the Blue Ridge. Among the fifty or so guests on the Governor's trek were four county surveyors and a collection of the most ambitious and aggressive land speculators in the colony. It should come as no surprise to learn that Col. James Taylor II was among them. By this time, Taylor was the Assistant County Surveyor for both King William and King and Queen Counties. When Spotsylvania County was formed, Taylor became one of its County Surveyors, with the area south of the Rapidan as his primary responsibility. That work would have him routinely scouting the area which would become Orange County.

Spotswood's party was escorted and guided by two companies of Rangers, plus several Indian guide/interpreters. The "Knights of the Golden Horseshoe," as his guests were eventually dubbed, were participating in an exciting and active, but orchestrated, outing — a junket, to put it in modern terms — to see the lands to the west.[12] The train of pack animals which followed them assured the company that they would eat well and drink even better. John Fontaine, a young man who accompanied Spotswood for a time and chronicled his activities, was also on this trip. A portion of Fontaine's entry for September 6, 1716, is instructive as to the spirit(s) of the expedition. The party had reached a river west of the mountains which they had over-romantically christened the "Euphrates." Thankfully, we know it today as the Shenandoah. This was the turning-back point for everyone but the Rangers, and the Knights were observing the occasion:

"We had a good dinner, and after it we got the men together, and loaded all their arms, and we drank the King's health in champagne, and fired a volley, the Princess's health in Burgundy, and fired a volley, and all the rest of the Royal Family in claret, and a volley. We drank the Governor's health and fired another volley. We had several sorts of liquors, viz; Virginia red wine and white wine, Irish usquebaugh, brandy shrub, two sorts of rum, champagne, canary, cherry punch, water, cider, etc."[13]

---

[12] Apparently all of the small (less than the size of a quarter) gold horseshoe mementoes that Spotswood gave his guests have disappeared. The last reported sighting of one was in a Richmond pawn shop in the 1940s, but even that item was not authenticated. The horseshoe was significant to the journey because most horses in the generally un-stony soils of the Tidewater were not shod.

[13] Alexander, *Journal of John Fontaine*, p. 106.

It has been generally accepted for over two centuries that Spotswood and his Knights followed the Rapidan, then briefly a tributary, and then crossed the Blue Ridge at Swift Run Gap. Such a trek would comport with Spotswood's mileage calculations and avoid the lands north of the Rapidan to which Lord Fairfax was already asserting title.[14] The earliest patents of land also generally follow that route. A 1737 map drawn by William Mayo shows a road to the mountains in the direction of Swift Run Gap with no other road or pass noted nearby. When Bishop Madison drew his map in 1805, he showed a road from Fredericksburg to the Valley via Swift Run Gap with no other nearby road or pass. It would seem that the route of the Knights had quickly become well-known and has remained a primary mountain crossing point into the present day.

There are some, however, who hold that the journey was actually up the Robinson River in today's Madison County.[15] To be honest, most of the latter camp is peopled by folks with Madison County connections, but what the heck. They're entitled to their opinion. The fact is that the precise route cannot be determined. Orange County historian W. W. Scott observed — dryly — that, "probably but for the frequent manifestations of loyalty by the party in drinking the healths of the royal family and themselves, a better idea could be formed of the route followed."[16] Enough said.

Then there is the story of Spotswood's knee buckle. A 1936 Federal Writers Project historian, making an inventory of the Bear family graveyard near Elkton, briefly ventured beyond his assignment to tell us that Spotswood lost a silver knee buckle encrusted with diamonds in that area during the 1716 ride. We also learn that upon his return to civilization, Spotswood is supposed to have advertised a generous reward for the return of that valuable item. Now, Spotswood was vain and didn't mind making himself the center of attention, but he was not stupid. He would not have worn such valuable jewelry on a rough ride (limbs tore the packs off horses on at least one occasion). In addition, there wasn't anyone "out there" to read such an ad and go look around. The ad, if there actually was one, sounds more like something Spotswood would have done to entice people to move west.

---

[14] See Kemper, "The Spotswood Mileage Accounts," III *William and Mary Quarterly* 171 (1923).

[15] A major argument for their position is the fact that the names for the rivers were still not entirely settled at the time. For more, see: Carpenter, 73 *Virginia Magazine of History and Biography* pp. 405-412 (1965).

[16] Scott, *History of Orange County*, p. 98.

It is fair to say that with the establishment of Fort Germanna and the journey of the Knights, interest in the uplands was high. Even so, money concerns remained a problem. The most vexing of those problems involved the costs of seating and planting any new patents and the various levies and quit rents that patentees would be called upon to pay. Anyone who patented land had a limited time within which to "seat and plant" the patent or it would be forfeited. Also, an annual "quit rent" of two shillings for every one hundred acres had to be paid to the Crown. Beyond that, persons holding land in a county were subject to various county, parish, and colonial levies. People were unsure of being able to make uplands patents profitable quickly enough to meet seating and planting costs while paying quit rents and levies at the same time. Development incentives were clearly in order.

In 1720, Spotswood and the Council hammered out some revisions to the land patenting procedures as they would apply to new western counties. They also excused patentees in such new counties from levies for a period of ten years. They further proposed that quit rent payments on those lands be suspended for that same period of time. Much of this was of course subject to London's approval. While waiting to hear, they proceeded to form Spotsylvania County out of the western ends of Essex, King William, and King and Queen counties. Germanna was selected as the seat of government for the new county, despite the fact that its most populous and prosperous settlements were in the Tidewater. Not only would Spotswood receive cash to build the county seat facilities, Germanna being the county seat would attract settlement to the area and create a need for the Tidewater types to travel west of the fall line and at least look around.

Spotsylvania County developed at a leisurely pace. The Act of Establishment was passed in 1720, but it was not until 1722 that its Sheriff was appointed, and it was another year after that before its Burgesses were seated in Williamsburg. The county's namesake also took his time building the court facilities next to Fort Germanna. He was mainly concerned with building himself a mansion at Germanna and with the construction of iron works some thirteen miles to the east along the Rappahannock. Then, almost suddenly, patenting of the uplands took off.

The 1722 Taylor and Octonia grants have been chronicled elsewhere in this work, and they were just a couple of the early ones for Orange County. Not surprisingly, one of the biggest land holders was Spotswood himself. His usual procedure was to grant land to an associate, who would then deed it over to him. By this process, Spotswood accumulated roughly 86,600 acres, which included an enormous portion of eastern Orange

County. His preference was clearly for those lands to which the new development incentives would apply.

1722 also marked another major turning point in Spotswood's life. He was replaced as Lieutenant Governor. The discontents and disagreements which accompanied the manner in which he discharged his office had finally worn down Orkney and the Board. Spotswood must have sensed that a change was in the air, and he did not appear to be all that surprised when it happened. Major, later Colonel, Hugh Drysdale was appointed Spotswood's successor on April 3, 1722, and he arrived at Williamsburg to take office on September 27. Spotswood, however, was not in town. He had gone to Albany, New York, to join in negotiations between the Five Nations and representatives of Virginia, Pennsylvania, and New York. The treaty which was agreed to at Albany represented a triumph for Virginia, and Spotswood returned to great acclaim.[17] He reported to the new Governor, Council, and the Burgesses, received their warm thanks, and made arrangements to leave Williamsburg for the peace and quiet of Germanna.

As early as 1721, Spotswood had a place to stay at Germanna, though it could not have been as fine a mansion as the one he ultimately built there. Wherever he was staying, his personal property there was entrusted to one Mary Peale, who turned out to be unworthy of that trust. Ultimately, Ms. Peale was sentenced to receive twenty lashes on her bare back for "wearing his cloaths, imbezelling his liquors & making his house at Germanna an ordinary."[18] Ms. Peale and her friends must have had quite a party out there on the banks of the Rapidan.

Problems, however, as always, followed Spotswood. Charges were soon raised over his land acquisition practices. In addition, he was called upon to show why title to most of those lands should not be revoked for his failure to pay quit rents. In 1724 Spotswood sailed for England to defend himself. He left behind a small, but thriving community at Germanna. His iron works on the Rappahannock, eventually dubbed the "Tubal Furnace," were in full production.[19] His fields and forests were being managed to

---

[17] Among other things, the Iroquois agreed to stay west of the Blue Ridge. (They had claimed the Manahoac territory after those tribes had moved away.) The way to western settlement was now wide open.

[18] Essex County court records.

[19] "Zillah also had a son, Tubal-Cain, who forged all kinds of tools out of bronze and iron." Genesis 4:22. "Cain" in Hebrew means "metalsmith." Spotswood's furnace was well named.

produce food, fiber, and trade goods. Things were going well, and he could only hope that they would continue.

Within months of his arrival in England, Spotswood married. His bride was Anne Butler Brayne, a daughter of well-connected parents and a god-daughter of the Duke of Ormond. In those days, all that meant a great deal. Spotswood had once written a cousin to the effect that his ongoing bach-elorhood was not out of dislike or disregard for marriage, but rather his feeling that marriage, if undertaken, needed to advance the family name. Miss Brayne was a valuable commodity in that regard, and while we must hope that the couple did indeed appreciate each other, Spotswood to some degree was just continuing to be Spotswood.

Also, Spotswood soon received good news from Virginia concerning his land holdings. Through his attorney he had requested that the improve-ments to his properties be viewed and appraised to determine whether enough had been done to satisfy the seating and planting requirements. The Spotsylvania County court ordered the appraisal on October 5, 1725, and the returns tell us something about how Spotswood got his land and what he did with it.[20]

We learn that the "Germanna Tract" of 3,229 acres was "granted to Wm. Robertson by patent last day of October 1716 and conveyed to Colo. Spotswood in November following." The "Iron Mine Tract" of 15,000 acres was "granted by patent the 20th February 1719 to Robert Beverly & Tho-mas Jones, which I have heard has since been sold to Colo. Spotswood." The reporter is Richard Hickman, who at the time was personally holding 28,000 acres as a trustee for Spotswood. All told, Spotswood is shown as owning 86,650 acres. Now, about the improvements:

On the Iron Mine Tract alone, Spotswood had houses, furnaces, dams, bridges, fenced enclosures and orchards valued at £7,187. He got addi-tional credit for having 164 cows and 45 horses on the property and for having cleared about 300 acres. His other tracts showed similar industry, and the improvements by law were sufficient to actually "save" 142,000 acres. The appraisers were Capt. Goodrich Lightfoot, Capt. Jeremiah Clowder, John Quarles and John Finleson, all known Spotswood cronies, but he had made it easy for them. "Lazy" is not one of the words you can use in describing Alexander Spotswood.

---

[20] The report filed with the county court was lost, but the copy sent to Spotswood in England survived. Cognets, *English Duplicates of Lost Virginia Records,* p. 116.

In 1729, Spotswood, still in England, was contacted by an acquaintance from the colonies who sought his help in regaining the Deputy Postmaster-General's post. The complaint was that he was being ousted for personal and political reasons, and he wanted Spotswood to whisper into the King's ear for him. It is hard to say exactly what went on, but when the dust cleared, Spotswood was the new Deputy Postmaster-General for British America.[21]

It took almost six years for Spotswood to clear up his land problems, but eventually it was decided that he could keep his many acres. It was time to go home, a seemingly strange idea for a British subject to have, but then Spotswood was becoming more and more of a colonial. Upon his arrival at Germanna in 1730, Spotswood's enemies must have groaned in dismay. Instead of returning disciplined and reduced in estate, Spotswood returned as the owner of all the properties he had claimed, as the Deputy Postmaster-General, and as a married family man. It must have been almost too much for some of them to bear.

Coming to Germanna with the Spotswoods were their two children (ultimately there would be four) and Anne Spotswood's sister, Dorothea Brayne, who became known to the locals as "Miss Thecky." The mansion, if not already habitable, was soon made so, and the Spotswoods settled in, ready to become Orange County's first First Family, as soon as there was an Orange County.

The Spotswood home in the Virginia Wilderness was a Georgian structure some eighty-five feet by thirty-five feet with a courtyard flanked by dependency wings. It was built on a man-made plateau with terraces down to the river. Archaeological excavation at the site evidences the presence of dressed stone columns and marble mantelpieces. A tree-lined walk led to a marble fountain near the river. All this at a time when a plain, story and a half structure less than twenty feet square was considered a substantial Virginia house. One has to suspect that Spotswood was the architect, but nothing has been found to date to confirm that.

For Germanna, 1732 brought two notable events. First, the county seat of Spotsylvania was moved to Fredericksburg. While on the surface that might be seen as a setback for Spotswood, he was probably delighted by the move, if in fact he did not actually author it. A new western county

---

[21] In 1732, Postmaster Spotswood reinstituted postal service from Philadelphia to Williamsburg. That service had earlier been rejected by Virginia. In 1737, Spotswood appointed Benjamin Franklin Postmaster for Philadelphia. For more on Spotswood as Postmaster, see Dodson, *Alexander Spotswood*, pp. 300-301.

The Enchanted Castle at Germanna. Built in the 1720s, Spotswood's huge Georgian house in the Wilderness burned following his death. An archaeological dig in its north wing in the mid-1990s uncovered this room whose uses have not yet been finally determined. A tunnel entrance and the trace remains of a wooden fort wall also await further investigation. Photograph by Bernice Walker.

would soon be forming, and Spotswood would naturally want Germanna to be in it. Quit rent relief, remember? Spotswood thought like that.[22]

The other 1732 event was the visit by William Byrd II, who at times was a Spotswood supporter and at other times one of his bitterest enemies. It seems certain that Byrd, along with the Reverend James Blair, the Bishop of London's colonial deputy, or "Commissary," were instrumental in having Spotswood replaced as governor. Now, here is Byrd, poking around Germanna and trying to learn the iron production business.

The intellectual William Byrd II had acquired one of the largest libraries in British America for his time. He was also the happy combination of a habitual journal-keeper and an excellent writer. History is the beneficiary of Spotswood not running Byrd out of Germanna, for through Byrd's observations and writings we are rewarded with a brief glimpse of life for the rich and powerful in the wilds of what is now eastern Orange County. Picking up in his journal where he arrives at the Spotswood home:

"Here I arrived about three o'clock and found only Mrs. Spotswood at home, who received her old acquaintance with many a gracious smile.[23] I

---

[22] Ultimately, London decided to give only partial quit rent relief to large landholders, but Spotswood and friends were assuming otherwise right up to the last moment.

[23] Byrd made periodic visits to England, and on at least one of them he had met Anne Brayne.

was carried into a room elegantly set off with a pair of pier glasses,[24] the largest of which came soon after to an odd misfortune. Amongst other favorite animals that cheered this lady's solitude, a brace of tame deer ran familiarly about the house, and one of them came to stare at me as a stranger. But unluckily, spying his own figure in the glass, he made a spring over the tea table that stood under it, and shattered the glass to pieces, and falling back upon the tea table, made a terrible fracas among the china. This exploit was so sudden, and accompanied with such a noise, that it surprised me and perfectly frightened Mrs. Spotswood. But it was worth all the damage to show the moderation and good humor with which she bore the disaster."[25]

It was Byrd on this same visit who labeled Spotswood's Germanna mansion the "Enchanted Castle." Byrd probably meant to be uncomplimentary, since many of his observations on Spotswood's endeavors during the visit were less than charitable. His name for the mansion, however, has both survived through the centuries and has also taken on its positive meaning.

Spotswood stayed out of the limelight when Orange County was formed, but his presence could not be ignored. During the formative days of the county, several of its founders went to "wait on Col. Spotswood" and see if he would assist with the securing of land for the court house and related county seat structures.[26] Also as noted earlier, the location of the eastern boundary of the new county assured that Germanna, along with much of Spotswood's other property, would be subject to such development incentives as that county might be granted. It is hard to see that as an accident.

It was from Germanna that Spotswood ran his iron smelting operations. Iron ore was known to exist in the western Spotsylvania/eastern Orange area long before Spotswood arrived in 1710.[27] Two problems had to be overcome, however, before the ore deposits could be exploited. First, London had to be convinced that colonial iron production would not be a

---

[24] Tall mirrors.

[25] From "A Progress to the Mines," in Byrd's *Writings*, pp. 356-370.

[26] Spotswood responded with an affidavit dated January 6, 1734/5, in which he agreed to give such land as would be needed and to allow timber and stone to be removed from his other lands for the building of the court facilities.

[27] When Lord de la Warr arrived in 1610 as the new Virginia Company Governor, one of his instructions was to explore and learn more about Virginia iron deposits, samples of which had arrived in London as early as 1608.

threat to the "home" iron industry. As England's woodlands began disappearing into blast furnaces at an alarming rate, the resistance of the Board of Trade to Spotswood's ongoing campaign to produce Virginia iron weakened.[28] The first call on English timber had to be for ships to defend the homeland and carry on trade. The ships could then be sent to find iron.

The second problem was, as always, money. Spotswood was positioned to find well-heeled partners, and he found them. One silent partner in many of his iron ventures was a Robert Cary, who like Orkney, never set foot on Virginia soil.

Naturally, Spotswood kept an eye out for additional sources of income. For a time, the British government was paying a bounty for "ships' stores" (tar, turpentine, oakum, etc.), so in addition to developing his iron business, Spotswood devoted a portion of his land and work force to reaping that bounty. Part of his land holdings in Culpeper County included large tracts of pine forests, from which the desired tar products could be extracted. He also brought in what today we call a consultant to teach his people how to grow the hemp necessary for producing some of the ships' stores. He stressed the need to turn out quality products, and he apparently assigned the group of Germans who arrived in 1717 to that particular duty.

Settlement quickly passed west of Germanna. By the time construction of the Enchanted Castle was started, the need for a fort had already disappeared. In fact, preliminary archaeological evidence suggests that Spotswood used a portion of the old Fort Germanna site as the location for his new house. One end of the castle structure sits on top of what appears to be a palisade trench for the old fort. Mills of various types were established along the Rapidan, substantial houses were built, and a ferry service supplemented the ford.[29] Germanna was becoming the name of a sizeable and busy community, not just the name of a fort or a grand mansion.

In the fall of 1739 and reciting an intent to leave Virginia, Spotswood advertised the Germanna properties and iron works for lease in the *Vir-*

---

[28] Upwards to two acres of woodland per day could be consumed by a furnace in full blast.

[29] Spotswood leased land to Orange County for the ferry operation, and in 1736, the actions of the ferry-keeper drove then-citizen Spotswood to appeal to the Justices for relief. Sample: "Moreover as the said Hawkings is perpetually drunk, he has carried his vulgar rudeness towards me to such an insufferable height as to come & insult me at y[e] door of my own dwelling . . . ." See the Nov/Dec 1998 *Newsletter* of the Orange County Historical Society for a more complete presentation on that incident.

*ginia Gazette.* He also advertised the sale of his personal property. Probably a visit to England was being planned by the Spotswoods. Anne Spotswood and her sister had not seen their family for nine years. It might also have had something to do with educating the children. We shall never know, for at almost the same time, England went back to war with Spain, and Spotswood's services were called for.[30] He was commissioned a general and authorized to raise Virginia troops for an invasion of Spanish possessions in South America. In 1740 Spotswood traveled to Annapolis on military business, and while there, contracted a fever which rapidly overwhelmed him. On June 7, 1740, Alexander Spotswood died at age 64. He was one of the greatest governors Virginia has ever known, and he was unquestionably the first First Citizen of Orange County.[31]

Following Spotswood's death, Anne Brayne Spotswood did not take her inheritance and flee to England. Like her husband, she had become more colonial than British, and the Wilderness which she had helped tame now held more attractions for her than Whitehall.[32] In 1742 she married the Reverend John Thompson of St. Mark's Parish/Culpeper. There had been some rumbling among the Spotswoods that such a marriage would lower Widow Spotswood's station in life. Reverend Thompson argued vigorously and successfully to the contrary, and shortly after the marriage he began building a mansion fully suited to his wife's station, albeit seemingly well beyond his. Possibly some Spotswood money wound up in that structure, which is called Salubria[33] and which still stands in Culpeper

---

[30] This one was called "The War of Jenkin's Ear," basically a trade war.

[31] Two related points: (a)Had Spotswood survived and gone on the expedition, he would have been serving with Admiral Vernon and would have met a young officer named Lawrence Washington. Washington would later build Mount Vernon on the Potomac. (b) Spotswood was the first, but not the only, Virginia Governor with connections to Orange County. Others are: James Barbour of Barboursville, 1812-14 (elected by the Virginia Legislature when Governor Smith died in a Richmond theater fire); James Lawson Kemper of Walnut Hills, 1874-78 (moved from Madison County); and J. Lindsay Almond, 1958-62 (raised in the Locust Grove area). A fifth Orange County resident, Hardin Burnley, served as Interim Governor for a few days in 1779.

[32] Sister Dorothea also stayed in Virginia, becoming the wife of a Spotsylvania planter.

[33] In 2001 Salubria was given to the Memorial Foundation of the Germanna Colonies in Virginia, Inc.

County near Route 3 and just north of Germanna. It is not certain, however, that Anne lived to occupy that grand residence, for she died in 1750.

Some years after Spotswood's death, the Enchanted Castle, apparently unoccupied at the time, burned. The site was eventually sold to members of the Gordon family (more Scots), and they built a home which actually intruded onto the southern end of the Enchanted Castle site. It is believed that the Gordons, as well as nearby neighbors, including possibly the Reverend Thompson, used some of the Castle's old building materials in their structures. Descendants of the Gordons continue to live in and around Orange County, with one, R. Lindsay Gordon, III, serving on the Orange County Board of Supervisors for 28 years, 19 of those as its Chairman.

In the years following Spotswood's death, Germanna evolved into a busy and prosperous rural commercial center, occupying both banks of the Rapidan in the vicinity of the ford. Gold mining, which got underway in the 1820s and peaked with the 1849 discovery of the more profitable deposits in California, surely gave the local economy a boost. In 1831, a Fredericksburg newspaper announced a lottery to raise funds to build a bridge across the Rapidan at Germanna.[34] Things were going well.

Spotswood's Germanna tract was eventually divided into large parcels and sold by his heirs. By 1793 the tract surrounding the town and Enchanted Castle was owned by Charles Urquhart, a Fredericksburg merchant. It was his son, Dr. Charles Urquhart, who attended John Wilkes Booth during that mortally wounded assassin's final hours. Dr. Urquhart is buried alongside his mother in their family cemetery a few hundred yards west of the Germanna Visitors' Center. Another interment of note in the vicinity took place in 2002, when the remains of John Spotswood, one of the Governor's two sons, were removed from their location near a Spotsylvania rock quarry and reinterred in the Memorial Garden at the visitors' center.

During the Civil War, Spotswood's Germanna disappeared. While the ford was recognized as an excellent river crossing, it was in a location that did not lend itself to being strongly defended. From a Confederate viewpoint, it was only the best of several isolated fords in that part of the Wilderness, all too far from either Fredericksburg or Orange to be incorporated into the Rappahannock or Rapidan defensive lines. Union forces also appeared to see no wisdom in trying to control the ford. Usually cavalry vedettes and infantry pickets monitored the area, and their resistance to

---

[34] It does not appear that a bridge was built at that time. One was in place by the time of the Civil War, but it was soon destroyed.

Civilian sketch artist Alfred Waud accompanied the Federal Army of the Potomac on the Mine Run Campaign. Here he portrays a portion of the V Corps on November 27, 1863, heading into Orange County via a pontoon bridge across the Rapidan at Germanna. The ruins of the bridge shown were about where the Route 3 bridge is today. The once-vibrant Germanna community has almost disappeared. Sketch prepared for *Harpers'* magazine. Reproduced with permission.

crossings was accordingly light. As armies tramped back and forth through Germanna, its commercial structures were soon destroyed. More and more residents "refugeed" away, and the abandoned buildings tended to wind up in campfires or as materials in military structures. Civil War illustrator Edwin Forbes' plate #289, entitled "Germanna on the Rapidan," gives a panorama of Germanna ford and the adjacent parts of Orange County as seen from the Culpeper side of the river. The ruins of a bridgehead stand on the Culpeper bank. The ruins of a couple of houses stand on the Orange County side. *Harper's Weekly* illustrator Alfred Waud did several Germanna sketches during the Mine Run Campaign. They show a couple of standing houses near the bridgehead on the Culpeper bank. That would have been around the first of December 1863. Those houses may well have been gone by the next spring.

Descendants of Governor Spotswood continued to live and own property in the Orange County area, and some can be found here today. Most of the post-war resettlement of Germanna as did take place, however, had little connection with the pre-war historic Germanna or its inhabitants. The earlier residents had long ago died or moved away, and such physical evidence of historic Germanna as remained rotted away or disappeared into what was probably the final regrowth of the Wilderness.

Not only did historic Germanna disappear as a physical place on the land, it also began to disappear from public memory. For nearly 100 years, a site as historic as any in Virginia survived only in the minds of those persons who committed themselves to remembering it. Those who did remember soon saw the need to organize their efforts to preserve that memory. In 1949, R. Brawdus Martin, a descendant of Germanna settler John Kemper, organized the first "Public Basket Picnic Party" which was held on the Enchanted Castle site. At about the same time Martin organized the Society of the Germanna Colonists and began to publish a Germanna newsletter. A related organization, the Society of the Knights of the Golden Horseshoe, was also formed. As the Enchanted Castle site disappeared into brush and bramble, they sought nearby places to gather.

In March 1956 the Memorial Foundation of the Germanna Colonies in Virginia, Inc., a charitable nonprofit corporation, was chartered, and over time assumed most of the programs and active members of the earlier societies. The regular membership of the Foundation today is composed of the descendants of the German colonists whose life as Americans began at Germanna, plus any interested organization or person who applies to join.

While the Foundation was initially headquartered in Culpeper, it has retained its focus on the Orange County portion of Germanna. In the same

Completed in 2000, the R. Brawdus Martin Germanna Visitors' Center sits on a portion of the Siegen Forest tract adjacent to the Germanna Community College's Germanna campus. The center houses the extensive records of the Memorial Foundation of the Germanna Colonies in Virginia, Inc. The pentagon-shaped building recalls the five-sided palisade walls of Fort Germanna, and the tower recalls the fort's tall central blockhouse. Picture by Bernice Walker. Reproduced with permission.

year in which it was chartered, the Foundation bought 270 acres in the southwest corner of the Route 3/Rapidan River intersection. That tract was named the "Siegen Forest," to commemorate a name from that region in Germany from which many of the 1714 settlers came. During the 1990s various contributions and grants were received, and in 2000 the Foundation completed the construction of a visitors' center on that land. It is appropriately named the R. Brawdus Martin Visitors' Center.

When the Virginia Community College System started up in the 1960s, there was considerable interest in establishing a campus to serve the Culpeper/Orange/Spotsylvania region. In 1969, the Germanna Foundation gave 100 acres of its Siegen Forest property to the Commonwealth of Virginia's State Board of Community Colleges for the purpose of establishing Germanna Community College. Shortly thereafter the Community College system announced its intent to build the first campus building at Germanna. Orange County historian J. Randolph "Randy" Grymes, Jr. promptly voiced his concern that since the location of the colonial Germanna community had not been definitely established, such construction might accidentally destroy whatever was left of it.

During a meeting at Germanna to review his concerns, Randy noted that in addition to looking over the college building site, the state archaeologists might wish to check out what was understood to be the Enchanted Castle site on an overgrown, apparently man-made plateau across Route 3. Colonial-era building materials were found on the plateau that afternoon, and the Virginia Historic Landmarks Commission was alerted to the find. The public memory of Germanna was being reawakened. By 1977, Commission archaeologists had confirmed the site of the Enchanted Castle as being across Route 3 from the Siegen Forest tract, and placement on the state and national historic registers followed, the latter in 1978. The threats to the survival of the Fort Germanna/Enchanted Castle sites were not over, however.

The owner of the land which included the Fort Germanna/Enchanted Castle sites platted the land as a large-lot subdivision, and by the 1980s he was selling those lots. It was determined that the historic sites lay under several adjoining lots, and protracted negotiations to buy them ensued. Eventually, Historic Gordonsville, Inc., the owner and operator of the Gordonsville Exchange Hotel Civil War Museum, was able to acquire the necessary $250,000.00 to buy the designated lots. Historic Gordonsville then conducted site development and archaeological work over the next several years, much of which was under the supervision of Orange County historian William H. B. "Bill" Thomas. Bill had been a founder of Historic Gordonsville and a prime mover in the efforts to purchase the property. A bachelor during the time he was working at Germanna, Bill enjoyed the company of Miss Katherine Russell, a cat with an historic name. The original Miss Russell had accompanied Spotswood to the New World in 1710, living wherever he lived and being introduced variously as his cousin or his housekeeper. When Spotswood married, Miss Russell dropped out of sight.

In 1990 Historic Gordonsville conveyed the Fort Germanna/Enchanted Castle lots to a corporate trust which is holding the property in trust for Mary Washington College of Fredericksburg. The Center for Historic Preservation at the college has been assigned responsibility for the management and development of the site. Over time additional surrounding property has been bought by friends of Germanna.

Taking a final look at Spotswood; it is difficult to determine how well all of his private ventures worked out. Numerous enterprises were undertaken and then modified or abandoned. Spotswood himself tossed out various assessments of his projects at various times, and it is hard to tell how much of a spin he was trying to put on the information at any particular time. When his cousin, John Graeme, ran the properties during the years Spotswood was in England, things apparently did slip, but Spotswood surely restored order upon his return. Governors subsequent to Spotswood tended to portray the colonial iron business as a struggling enterprise, presumably trying to keep the Board of Trade from shutting it down. On the other hand, Spotswood's financial agent and executor, the Reverend Robert Rose, made representations of enormous profitability following his client's death. Indirect evidence may be the most telling. Consider that:

(1) Spotswood was realizing enough profit in the Tubal iron works to buy out his partners in that operation and to induce him into becoming a partner in the Fredericksville furnace (now under Lake Anna). He also built an "air furnace" and deep water docks at Massaponax to service his iron business. He may have also had an interest in the Catharine furnace, whose ruins stand in the Chancellorsville battlefield. The profitability of iron production was generally recognized, and six furnaces were operating in the region by 1750, leading many to call it the birthplace of the American Industrial Revolution.

(2) At his death, the inventory of Spotswood's personal estate (that is, excluding land, mills, furnaces, houses, etc.) filled six foolscap pages and listed items having a total value of £1,139 17s 10d. His bedspread at Germanna was by itself worth more than the life savings of most men of his day. That particular item had gold and silver threads woven into it. Add in the real estate, and you have the holdings of one of the wealthiest men in British America for that time.

(3) Most importantly, Spotswood's estate was not subject to huge debts. He had to have been doing something right.

It is fair to say that Spotswood had accomplished his personal mission. But had he accomplished his public one? The consensus is that he did as much as conditions would permit. Consider the following two, albeit friendly, assessments from two very distant points in time:

A 1743 assessment by the Reverend Robert Rose: "He discharged his duty as Q$^r$ M$^r$ Gen$^l$ to the end of the year 1709 an office of immense fatigue and danger when He was constituted Lieutenant Gov$^r$ of Virginia a change which he never considered as a preferment. Here he remain$^d$ 12 years, and happy for the country which improved so much under his administration, that the people both with respect to their manner & fortunes made a very different appearance. In 1722 he was superceded for the same reason he was not advanced in the Army; He scorned to purchase any Great Mans favor, nor never sold his own."[35]

A 1990 assessment by historian Bruce Lenman: "Spotswood had many achievements and almost as many identities. He started as a successful soldier entrepreneur serving Queen Anne. From there he moved on to become an imperially minded bureaucrat and proconsul who tried to give order and cohesion to the Georgian British Empire. . . . He was one of the first who laid some of the foundation stones of America's future unity, and he played a seminal role in Manifest Destiny and the American Industrial Revolution. Not a bad record for one wandering Scot."[36]

As of this writing Alexander Spotswood and Germanna, his jewel in the Wilderness, are both starting to experience a revival in the consciousness of America. There is still a great deal which must happen, but Orange County may at long last be hosting the emergence of the last undeveloped major historic site in Virginia. While we await discoveries of the physical evidences of historic Germanna, we must continue to develop our understanding and appreciation of the role Spotswood and Germanna played during a significant era in the history of colonial Virginia, and consequently of the importance of this place here in Orange County to the history of our Nation.

---

[35] Rev. Rose to Andrew Anderson, Letter of July 25, 1743. 60 *Va. Mag. Of His/Bio.* 211.

[36] At the time of this quote, Bruce P. Lenman was professor of History at the University of St Andrews, Fife, Scotland, on sabbatical at the College of William and Mary. From his article "Alexander Spotswood and the Business of Empire," *Colonial Williamsburg*, Colonial Williamsburg Foundation, August 1990.

James Madison at age 32. In 1783, Charles Willson Peale captured this image of the victorious young rebel at the close of the Revolution. The portrait is a miniature, a popular size of the day, and it is in a frame which can be pinned to fabric. Courtesy of the Library of Congress, Rare Books and Special Collections Division.

# CHAPTER IV

# *The Rebellious Mr. Madison & His Home on the Hill*

## A. "When the Going Gets Tough . . ."[1]

By 1732, Alexander Spotswood and his family were back from England and comfortably established at Germanna. From his riverside retreat, the industrialist and former governor managed his various enterprises and monitored the results of his recently-concluded governorship of the Virginia colony. One of those results was a steady stream of settlers heading west beyond Germanna, looking to settle on land that was soon to become part of a new county. St. Mark's Parish had just been carved out of the western end of Spotsylvania County. Germanna was in the eastern end of the new parish, and the Spotsylvania County seat was being moved from Germanna to Fredericksburg.[2] It couldn't be much longer before the new parish would become a new county — Orange County as it turned out.

Among those 1732 migrants was Ambrose Madison and his family, heading towards a house waiting for them on the north slope of one of the Southwest Mountain ridges south of the Rapidan. That ridge was located in Madison's share of a 4,675 acre patent which had been given to him and Thomas Chew jointly in 1723 through the efforts of Colonel James Taylor II. Both Madison and Chew had married daughters of Colonel Taylor, Madison having married the eldest, Frances, in 1721. While Colonel Taylor had gone to live among the "little mountains" not long after he received a patent there in

---

[1] ". . ., The Tough Get Going." A slogan found on locker room walls everywhere.

[2] See Chapter I for additional detail on Orange County's formation. The county seat for Spotsylvania was later moved out of Fredericksburg to a rural area of the county.

1722, Madison delayed his arrival for almost another ten years. Property holdings and business ventures in the Tidewater required his presence, and he had dispatched a work party west to undertake the seating and planting of the new lands. Now at last, the Madisons were coming to live there.

Ambrose and his family could trace their American lineage to John Maddison, a ship's carpenter, who was awarded 600 acres of Virginia land via headright in 1653. Before he died some thirty years later, Maddison had accumulated nearly 2,000 acres, a testament to his industry and good business sense. The next generation built on that strong beginning. They also changed the spelling of the family surname, a not at all unusual practice during those times. Something that was unusual, however, was that Maddison's grandson, Ambrose Madison, did not retain his Tidewater properties when he moved to the Piedmont. For whatever reason, he was cutting his ties to the historic family lands and preparing to create a world of his own.

Traveling with Ambrose and Frances were their three children, two girls and a boy. The boy, James, was the eldest, born in 1723. This James would later become the father of President James Madison, Jr., and is referred to here and elsewhere as "James Madison, Senior," even though we all understand that the term "senior" was most likely never a part of his legal name and one for which he certainly had no need for the first 28 years of his life.

The destination for the Madisons was a house on his land which had probably been occupied by the resident overseer since its construction. It wasn't much, but it would do. The name given to the property was "Mount Pleasant," a name that would be in use for almost fifty years. Whether Ambrose envisioned another, better house for Mount Pleasant is not certain, but there was definitely a place for one.

There was a piece of ground higher up on the same ridge and a bit to the east of the present house that would have been a great site. That ridge was the northernmost one of the mountain chain in the area, and by getting up higher and clearing out some trees, one could secure a magnificent view all the way to the Blue Ridge. Even if there were ideas about another house, things were going to have to wait a while, for Ambrose first had to get his land into full production. New house plans in fact would wind up waiting longer that anyone might have imagined, because before the summer of 1732 was out, Ambrose Madison was dead.

Pompey, a slave from another plantation, was charged, tried, and executed as Ambrose Madison's murderer. The instrument of Madison's death was determined to be poison. Two Madison slaves who also had been found guilty as accomplices were whipped and returned to the brand-new widow and her family, to do with as they saw fit. Nothing has been found to date in the Mount Pleasant/Montpelier records to indicate that Frances Madison did anything but put the two back to work.[3]

One can speculate endlessly about motives for Ambrose Madison's demise, but without any other facts, such speculations are about as unhelpful as they are endless. A reality, however, is that in 1732 Frances Taylor Madison was a widow with three young children, living on a developing plantation in what was still more wilderness than it was civilization. What on earth was she going to do?

What Frances did was go to work, managing the plantation. Her father had died in 1729, but there was a vast network of Taylor relations and "connections" around. They rallied to help as much as they could, but it was Frances' grit and determination that made things run from day to day. And run they did. She maintained accounts in her own name, dealing with local merchants and London factors (agents) alike. Her husband's land holdings amounted to some 5,000 acres at the time of his death, and no one, not even Frances, could have survived without good overseers. She probably had help finding them, but then she was the one who had to work with them in resolving problems involving the land, the labor force (likely an uneasy mix of slave and free laborers), the crops, the livestock, you name it. Frances had to be more than just spunky. She needed to know how things ought to be done, and she apparently did. The Taylor family remains justifiably proud of their Frances.

Growing, working, and learning at his mother's side, was son James. As the sole male heir to his father's estate, he knew what the future held for him—a lot more of what he was already doing. The handing over of the farm keys was a time-honored way of appointing an owner or manager, and on James' eighteenth birthday in 1741, Frances probably did just that. It is unlikely, however, that, having successfully raised her son to legal majority, she then retired to a shade tree beside the Rapidan. The two were used to working together, and in addition James was having to give some of his time to off-farm duties. There were the demands made on any emerging community leader: church, court, and militia. He was also subject to

---

[3] The entire poisoning incident is chronicled in Miller, *The Short Life and Strange Death of Ambrose Madison*. The two Montpelier slaves were Turk and Dido. There is no record of them having been subsequently sold, and those names appear in later generations of Montpelier slaves, suggesting that they remained at Montpelier and raised families.

being called upon to make appraisals, settle estates, and the like. In addition, the family still had to look after business interests in the Tidewater, through which the plantation's commerce flowed. In time James developed a Tidewater interest of his very own. Her name was Nelly.

## B. Three Generations of Upland Madisons

In 1732, the same year that James and his family had moved west, Nelly Conway was born at, appropriately, Port Conway. That settlement was located some twenty miles downstream from Fredericksburg on the Northern Neck side of the Rappahannock, directly across the river from Port Royal. The site is in today's King George County, but no community exists there now. Little is known of Nelly's childhood and education, but the former was apparently satisfactory and the latter adequate. Some biographers have dubbed her "Eleanor Rose" Conway, just as others have nominated James Madison, Jr.'s, wife "Dorothea." In neither case are they correct. Who knew that, as babies, these girls needed romantic or aristocratic names to match their adult station in life? It was enough to love 'em, raise 'em, and pray that they didn't die young.

On September 15, 1749, James Madison, Sr., married Nelly Conway. On what would have been March 5, 1750, by the Old Style calendar, their first son, James Madison, Jr., was born at Port Conway.[4] That was right in the middle of the change-over from the Old Style to the New Style (today's) calendar. We observe the New Style date of March 16, 1751, as President Madison's birthday. At the time of James, Jr.'s, birth his future famous friend, Thomas Jefferson, was just a month away from his eighth birthday.

For the first child, Nelly Madison had gone back to her childhood home.[5] She had the next eleven at her own home in Orange County. Seven of the twelve survived to adulthood, reflecting a loss which was not terribly unusual for the time. Son Francis was born in 1753, Ambrose (there was usually at least one Ambrose in every generation) in 1755, Nelly in 1760, William in 1762, Sarah in 1764, and Frances in 1774. All the girls had middle names; none of the boys. Nelly's was "Conway," Sarah's was

---

[4] Remember, they had been married 18 months, not 6. An Old Style year ended March 24.

[5] Orange County was Madison's home, not his birthplace. Conversely, Orange County was the birthplace, but not the home, of U.S. President Zachary Taylor. Taylor was born 1784, with his family having already started their move to the Kentucky territory, producing ongoing confusion as to exactly where in Orange County that birth took place.

James Madison Sr., and Nelly Conway Madison (above); James Madison, Jr., and Dolley Payne Todd Madison (below). Two of the three generations of upland Madisons who lived at Montpelier. No likeness of Ambrose Madison and Frances Taylor Madison, the first generation, are known to exist. The lives of the Madisons were characterized by hard work at home and service to the community at large. The senior Madisons' likenesses courtesy of Belle Grove Plantation. The junior Madisons' courtesy of the Montpelier Foundation.

"Catlett," and Frances' was, appropriately, "Taylor." Her namesake grand-mother had died in 1761, living just long enough to see her son move into a new home that he had built nearby.

Between the births of William and Frances there had been four births in which none of the children survived to adulthood. James, vastly older and already a national figure by the time sister Frances got out of diapers, was more of a distant, uncle-like figure to her than a brother. William may also have seen himself as something of a family outsider. As a younger brother, he was subject to some management by James, a family role fairly typical for eldest sons of the day. Also, William chose an occupation (the military) generally not considered as respectable as the profession of farm-ing. Upon the death of their father in 1801, both William and Frances sued the estate, for which brother James was the executor. Following James' death in 1836, William proceeded to make money demands of Dolley, claim-ing old debts owed him by James. Eventually he sued the estate. In dis-missing the suit, the deciding judge observed that had the action not been brought by someone of the character of General Madison, it could have been deemed frivolous.[6]

As his family grew up around him, the senior James Madison contin-ued to grow in wealth and prominence. In the late 1750s, he decided that the family could afford a fine new home on their mountain. Construction started on a brick house. When completed, the Madison house was one of the most substantial of the small handful of brick residences built in Or-ange County during the eighteenth century. Not a bad way for the Madisons to let the world know that they had arrived.

Sometime around 1760, the family moved into their new home. Young James remembered helping to move some light furnishings and other items. The old house, probably back in use as general farm housing, soon burned. A survey made in 1844 shows a structure in that area identified as an overseer's house, but that was a later building which itself was soon gone. All of the other outbuildings also disappeared , and with the exception of the family cemetery, the old Mount Pleasant site became cropland. So thor-oughly were the traces of that site disturbed by farming that archaeologists have had quite a time trying to decide which of the structural remains discovered there might have been the main residence. After a false alarm or two, they discovered a basement for what was probably a moderate size

---

[6] Norfleet, *Woodberry Forest: The Extended View*, p. 191. Appendix III of that book, entitled:"About William Madison Himself," offers a good short biography of the general.

structure. This time they are reasonably certain that they have found the
Mount Pleasant house.

Near the Mount Pleasant house site is the area that evolved into the
family graveyard. Today's visitors to the Madison cemetery see a brick
walled enclosure with a number of tombstones and the two obelisks for
President James and wife Dolley. What they cannot see are evidences of
those who were buried there long before any walls were built or stones set.
That group includes James, Sr., and Nelly and probably Ambrose and
Frances. Documentary evidence indicates that they are there, but there are
no markers of any sort. In that respect, the elder Madisons share in death
something in common with the occupants of the African-American cemetery just a few hundred yards to the east. No tombstones. No markers,
except for an upturned stone at a grave here and there. Simply people who
had lived on and worked that land now resting together in it.[7]

A striking snow scene of the Montpelier African-American cemetery located
between the Madison family cemetery and the Montpelier mansion. Courtesy
of Matthew Reeves, Senior Archaeologist, Montpelier Foundation.

---

[7] There are five slave/freedmen/African-American cemeteries on land owned by
Montpelier, plus the Gilmore cemetery. The one nearest the Mount Pleasant site
may well contain some interments of freedmen, but it has been chosen as the site
to represent the buried slaves of Montpelier.

## C. The Training of a Powerful Mind

The senior James Madison recognized the value of a good education. He had managed to receive a reasonably decent one for his day, most of which probably came from his mother. Now it was time to do something as good or better for his children. Our special interest of course is son James and how it was that he came to be such a scholar. There was no real magic: he was an intelligent young man who worked very, very hard at developing and applying that intelligence. On occasion, too hard. After completing his course of study at the College of New Jersey (now Princeton), James asked his father for permission to stay another year to do special studies. Permission was granted, and James applied himself so diligently to his work that his health failed him. He returned home much debilitated, and it was some time before his strength and spirits recovered. James then suffered periodic recurrences of that condition for the rest of his life. A severe relapse occurred while he was serving as President, and for a brief time Dolley Madison feared for the life of her husband.[8]

If President Madison were among us today, he would probably protest at our wonder over his intelligence, and he would probably also argue that he was not the most intellectually competent man of his day. Thomas Jefferson, for example, knew many more languages than Madison, though few today would consider Madison's fluency in Latin and Greek, plus his working knowledge of French and Italian, a handicap. Madison also developed an understanding of constitutional law and of government in general that was unsurpassed by any of his peers. That was not by accident.

For five years, young James studied science and the classics under the Reverend Donald Robertson, a Scot minister whose excellent instruction in a broad range of subjects was remembered with appreciation by Madison for the rest of his life.[9] The school was near today's Spotsylvania/ Caroline County line, and Madison boarded there during school terms. For another two years, Madison studied at home in Orange County under the Reverend Thomas Martin, the Rector of St. Thomas', the local Anglican Parish Church. Martin was a graduate of the College of New Jersey at Princeton and had been strongly influenced by the faculty there. Chief among those was the Reverend John Witherspoon, whose thinking reflected

---

[8] Ketcham, *James Madison,*, p. 560. A three-week episode at a most critical time during the War of 1812.

[9] Madison did observe wryly that he had learned to speak French with a Scottish burr, which no doubt tended to amaze some of his listeners.

the Scottish Enlightenment and its thoughts on the rights of men in relation to their governments.

While Virginia planters' sons traditionally went to the thoroughly Anglican College of William and Mary for their higher education, that institution was in an academic and organizational decline at the time James was ready for that level of study. Reverend Martin strongly urged the College of New Jersey as the place for James, and he found a receptive audience in the Madison household.

The elder Madison did not march in perfect ideological lock step with his fellow Anglican neighbors anyway. Thanks in part to his efforts, "dissenting," that is, non-Anglican, religions were tolerated in Orange County with more charity than in surrounding counties. He may have also been swayed by the reputation for intellectual honesty attributed to Reverend Samuel Davies, at one time the Presbyterian minister at Hanover County's Pole Green Church, who had left Virginia to serve as the College of New Jersey's president. Whatever the reason(s), in the summer of 1769, James Madison, Jr., traveled to Princeton and enrolled at the college. He completed the three-year course of study in two, and then stayed on for that extra year. That concluded Madison's formal schooling, but in many ways his education had just begun.

Among the other things Madison had learned in his formal studies, he had acquired two of the most important skills a person can have: an understanding of how he learned (sometimes called "learning how to study"), and an ability to think analytically. He was prepared to teach himself. While there would always be others who would write or speak more brilliantly (Madison's soft speaking voice was forever a problem), no one was going to out-think him. The most widely-known example of Madison using his learning skills to put himself through a course of study involves his work leading up to the Federal Constitutional Convention of 1787.

## D. The Constitutional Scholar Emerges

The former British colonies of the Revolution had become independent states. While they called themselves "united" states, the fact of the matter was that great variations existed in what each state encouraged, controlled, or condemned. International and interstate commerce problems in particular were producing a national clamor for some sort of uniform, generally agreed-upon "rules of the game" for doing business. Any proposal to solve an interstate problem that went contrary to a particular state's interests, however, was almost certain to receive indifferent treatment within its borders. It didn't take someone with Madison's formal education to see that the present loose confederation of independent states was the basic problem. The way to get that problem solved, however, seemed to be eluding everyone.

There was no question that this new nation should have no form of government that could completely ignore state interests ("states' rights") or be able to govern without the consent of the people generally. America wanted nothing more to do with kings and the like. As big as America was likely to become, however, individual citizens could not be consulted on every national issue. A "town meeting" type of democracy could not work. They would need to speak through elected representatives. The government had to be a republic of some sort, and Madison went to work on creating one for America.

Thomas Jefferson had gone to Europe in 1784 to serve as one of three U. S. treaty commissioners (issues from the time of the Revolution remained unresolved), and upon Benjamin Franklin's retirement from the post of American Ambassador to France, Jefferson was appointed to replace him. Madison wrote Jefferson and asked that he be sent a full collection of works dealing with national and international history, politics, and commerce. Madison may have made the error of telling his liberally spending friend that cost was no object. Jefferson's response in any event was such a large shipment of books that Madison took to referring to it as his "literary cargo."

During the spring and summer of 1786, Madison applied himself with particular energy to the cargo. There was going to be a called convention in Annapolis in the fall to discuss trade problems, and he planned to be ready to discuss the larger problem of national government. He became an expert on virtually every form of federated republic which had been attempted in history and for which some written record existed. He learned how they had been formed, how they had operated—and why they had failed. As a way of setting his thoughts in order, he wrote himself a fairly lengthy book report entitled, "Of Ancient and Modern Confederacies." He also compiled specific lists and summaries on various subjects, such as raising revenue, financing and controlling the military, diplomatic relations, etc.

Madison's studies were far from finished when the August 1786 Annapolis Convention was supposed to take place, but as it turned out he was going to have more time. So many of the states had declined to send voting representatives that nothing could be done but issue a call for another convention, this one to be held the next May in Philadelphia. The Philadelphia convention would also go beyond trade issues and examine the larger subject of the "ills of the Union." That type of agenda was more to Madison's liking anyway, and he returned to his self-imposed course of study with redoubled energy. Fortunately, his health did not fail him at this time, obviously a tribute to his healthful Orange County surroundings.

By the time Madison arrived in Philadelphia in May 1787, he had designed a proposed form of government which went by the name of the "Virginia Plan." He had already discussed and reviewed his thinking extensively with friends and associates, and the existence and general content of the Plan were well known to many of the convention delegates. One result of all this was that Madison's reputation as an authority on constitutional government grew steadily. The delegates quickly adopted the Virginia Plan as a working draft for a new constitution, thus not only according great respect to what Madison had already done, but also giving him considerable influence over the decisions of what to do with the whole host of additions, deletions, substitutions, rewordings, etc., that were then proposed for the Plan. After that long summer ended, the delegates referred to Madison as the "Father of the Constitution," not because he had single-handedly written one. He hadn't. It was because he had so enlightened, instructed, and guided the delegates during the deliberations that they were able to make their own decisions about what should be in the proposed Constitution with understanding and confidence.

## E. The Making of a Rebel

Before there was a need for a Constitution, however, there had to be the Revolution, and for that, one must return to the days of a much younger Madison. Return in fact to the summer of 1772, when Madison was home in Orange County, just back from the College of New Jersey and recuperating from the breakdown in health attributed to his intense educational experience there. As he recuperated, Madison came to an interesting realization: As he saw it, he was unemployed. Not that there wasn't anything to do. His father had already given him a tract of land, and the various Madison enterprises could always use some help. For the present, however, Madison was content to allow the slaves and their overseers to tend his land without his active supervision, and the other family businesses did not attract him. He was strongly inclined to more intellectual pursuits, but he was not currently involved in any that promised some sort of a career.

The fact that an eldest son of a Virginia planter could be thinking of doing anything but coming home to farm tells us something more about the senior Madisons. Instead of demanding that son James assume the historic role for an eldest son, James and Nelly Madison seemed to be willing to allow him to consider pursuing some other occupation. Indeed, they may have taken pride in their son's intellectual abilities. This was heresy in a day when there was no more respectable, no higher calling, than farming. It did not hurt that son number three, Ambrose, was showing signs of becoming a skilled and dedicated farmer, but still the Madisons' neighbors must have been shaking their heads. First Princeton, and now this. Old Madison is going to regret not having sent that boy to William & Mary.

Young James studied some law, though not as a serious vocation, and he corresponded with a close college friend or two about choosing a life vocation. As quickly as his health permitted, Madison was back to studying, although he still probably felt himself at loose ends for most of 1773. In addition to his studies, Madison probably tutored his siblings and took care of assigned business matters for the plantation. Just because he wasn't going to be a farmer didn't mean that he had a license to loaf.

By the spring of 1774, it had been decided that brother William needed to attend a preparatory school at Princeton, one which met with his elder brother's approval. The two packed their belongings and headed north. Their trip to New Jersey took them through Philadelphia, which was absolutely a-boil. The Boston Tea Party of the previous year had not been overlooked by the British Parliament, and in retaliation, the port of Boston was being ordered closed.[10] The cry was for all states to unite in retaliating against that edict. All of Philadelphia was excitement and confusion.[11] There were calls for a Continental Congress to assemble there, with delegates from every colony. Madison was far from an unmoved observer, but he needed to get on to Princeton with brother Willey.

After depositing twelve-year-old William with the faculty of the Princeton preparatory school, Madison continued his travels as far north as New York. It is not known how many people he visited and conferred with as he moved through the country, but he clearly got the sense of the thinking in the other middle colonies. That thinking matched his own, and by the time he returned to Orange County, Madison had made up his mind: the colonies needed to be both united and free of British rule. James Madi-

---

[10] In December 1773, protesting a punitive tax on tea, a well-organized "mob" had boarded three tea ships in Boston harbor and had destroyed their cargoes by dumping the tea into the water. For a narrative history of that event, read "Tea" in Langguth, *Patriots*.

[11] By 1774, Philadelphia was the largest English speaking city in the world outside of London and was seen by many as the unofficial capital of the colonies.

son, Jr., had become a revolutionary, a patriot, or as the British saw it, a rebel.

The First Continental Congress did indeed convene in Philadelphia during that summer of 1774. Madison, still young and relatively unproven, was not one of the Virginia delegates. Among other things, the delegates there called for a ban on trade with England and called for the formation of local "Committees of Safety" to monitor compliance with the ban and to expose those not supporting it. Since the late 1760s there had been Committees of Correspondence throughout the colonies, whose function it was to report both locally and to the other colonies on British outrages and the responses to them. Now the considerably more activist Committees of Safety were about to join them.

During the years of Revolution several Committees of Safety wound up being the only form of government functioning in their localities. Orange County, however, maintained both an active court and a working Sheriff during that time. While there were militia companies and citizen patrols operating in the county from time to time, the Sheriff provided the ongoing law and order presence.

Madison did not lack for local kindred spirits with whom to share thoughts and make plans. His interest and knowledge did not go unnoticed. When the Orange County Committee of Safety was formed December 22, 1774, James Madison, Jr., was extended an invitation to join. His father and fourteen other local leaders made up the balance of the committee. The senior Madison was chairman, and the junior Madison was by more than ten years its youngest member.[12]

The Orange Committee of Safety did more than just monitor compliance with the trade ban. With the assistance of the local militia (James, senior, was its commander), pamphlets deemed seditious were seized from the Reverend Wingate, the then Rector of St. Thomas' Parish, and publicly burned. Keep in mind that the Anglican Church was the "state church" of the Virginia colony and had always benefited from special treatment at the hands of both the local and colonial governments. Now that Church was seen as a symbol of British oppression and as a hotbed of Tories and British spies, a not altogether incorrect view in fact. By the time the Revolution ended, the Anglican Church in Virginia lay in an organizational

---

[12] Appointed by the Legislature were: Thos. Barbour, Thos. Bell, Wm. Bell, Zacharia Burnley, Vivion Daniel, Jas. Madison (Chmn.), Jas. Madison, jun., Francis Moore, Wm. Moore, Wm. Pannill, John Scott, Lawrence Taliaferro, Francis Taylor (Clerk), James Taylor, and James Walker.

shambles, which was followed locally by the physical destruction of the Middle, or Brick, Church of St. Thomas' Parish.[13]

The Anglican Church eventually reorganized itself into the Episcopal Church of the United States, and its first Bishop in Virginia was the Reverend James Madison, a slightly older cousin of the President-to-be. Madison family members thus assisted with the disestablishment of the Church of their forefathers, and Madison family members then assisted with the establishment of its successor. But all that was for the future. The Madisons were initially occupied with getting a revolution started.

Young James drilled and practiced marksmanship with the Orange County militia, and by the end of the summer of 1775, he was made a colonel. Twice during the year the militia mustered and began marches on Williamsburg in response to Governor Dunmore's actions, but matters were resolved both times before they actually made it into the town. Some Orange County residents became members of the Culpeper Minute Men and helped defeat Dunmore at the Battle of Great Bridge, the first Revolutionary engagement on Virginia soil, but Madison was not with them.

It was generally understood that Madison's health would not permit field duty, and besides, his abilities could be better used elsewhere. His militia rank was more of a recognition of his patriotism than it was a demand that he lead troops in the field. Yet in 1815, President James Madison, Jr., would demonstrate a military character which could make one wonder if he had not been misjudged earlier.

## F. Learning the Legislative Ropes

In the spring of 1776, Madison was elected to represent Orange County in the Virginia House of Burgesses. Dunmore's ships had shelled Norfolk on New Year's Day 1776, leaving much of the city in flames. He then sailed away, abandoning Virginia, much to the satisfaction of the Burgesses. They were done with making laws which had to be approved by the crown. They were going to form a new revolutionary government for Virginia, work well suited to Madison's hand.

The Burgesses quickly voted an instruction to Virginia's delegation at the Continental Congress to move that body to declare the colonies free and independent of Great Britain. Virginia congressional delegate Thomas

---

[13] The Brick Church stood on the rise on the north side of Route 631 (Brick Church Road), just east of its intersection with Route 612. It had been built on land owned by Col James Taylor II.

Jefferson needed no more encouragement than that. On July 4, the Declaration of Independence, a product largely of his hand, was adopted. By then, the Virginia Burgesses were already focusing on producing a declaration of rights and a plan of government for their own state.

Madison found himself on the committee assigned the duty of formulating the declaration and plan, but he was far from being its dominant player. His legislative efforts to date had been local, limited jurisdiction stuff, carried out under the watchful gaze—and protection—of family.

At Williamsburg, Madison was entering the big leagues, and he knew it. As a junior legislator, he watched, listened, conferred with the major players during breaks, and made occasional small contributions. To him, and to most Burgesses, the unchallenged authority on republican governments was the wealthy, heavy-set, introverted George Mason of Gunston Hall. Much of what Mason proposed for the declaration and plan was accepted by the committee. Much of what Mason proposed was also absorbed by Madison and became a part of his education. Along with the thoughts of other constitutional scholars who influenced Madison, Mason's thinking was in the Virginia Plan that Madison took with him to Philadelphia in 1787. A modest Madison would continue to insist that Mason was the master of their shared discipline long after that crown had been publicly awarded him by his peers at the Constitutional Convention.

Comes 1777 and Madison was all ready to return to the House of Burgesses to continue the Revolution. What he got was a strong dose of reality. Confident that his one-year "record" as a Burgess, his family ties, and his personal standing in the community assured election, Madison decided to stand for election without serving "bumbo." Bumbo was the generic name given the various alcoholic punches doled out to voters at the polls by candidates for office. Its presence on election day was a given. Madison's decision to enact a one-man prohibition movement flew in the face of convention and ignored a politically cultivated thirst of long standing in Orange County. He was beaten out by Charles Porter, a local farmer, tavern keeper, and doler-out of bumbo, who went on to serve seven terms. A lesson in humility and human nature learned.

So Madison was at loose ends again, but not for long. By the summer of 1777, a vacancy had appeared in Governor Patrick Henry's Council of State, and Madison was elected by the Burgesses to fill it. The action of the Burgesses, as opposed to the action of the Orange County voters, highlights a characteristic of Madison which holds true to this day. He is respected almost to the point of veneration by constitutional scholars, legislators, historians, etc., while the general public understands that Madison did something really quite nice, but they have some trouble understanding precisely what it was. In any event, whatever he did wasn't all that sexy or headline-grabbing.

With his appointment to Council, Madison began to get out of touch with the day-to-day happenings in Orange County, though in truth things were fairly quiet on the home front for most of the Revolution. The county leaders laid in a supply of salt, necessary to preserve food, and a number of its men went off to war. It would be another four years before the war would reach central Virginia.[14]

At Williamsburg, Madison now found himself acting as the equivalent of a modern-day state senator. As opposed to the Royal Governor's Councils, whose members were usually appointed from the ranks of the Virginia aristocracy, the Virginia Council of State reflected more of a mixture of Virginia's Revolutionary leadership. They were used to working, and they had a lot of hard work to do, made doubly hard by the Revolution and the uneven fortunes of the colonial forces.

Madison got to see much of Patrick Henry, whose oratory could insert an iron backbone into the weakest patriot — and whose indifference to realities could sometimes be infuriating. From his Council service, Madison gained additional experience in practical government, plus an understanding that he and Henry disagreed on a number of points about what might constitute an effective government. He then enjoyed a brief period of service under his friend and new Governor, Thomas Jefferson, before higher duty called.

Back home in Orange County in early January 1779, the Saratoga "Convention" prisoners came through Orange on the way to their Charlottesville barracks.[15] These were what was left of British General Bourgoyne's army which he had surrendered at Saratoga, New York, in 1777. The word "Convention" was used to describe the arrangement worked out between Bourgoyne and the continental army commander, but to the Orange County citizens who lined the road to view the sick, starved, ragged procession, it

---

[14] Additional detail about that time in Orange County is provided by historian W. W. Scott in the chapter of his history of the county entitled, "Orange in the Revolution," pp. 63-76.

[15] In 1976, *The Daily Progress* newspaper in Charlottesville published a series of special inserts entitled, "The Revolution in Middle Virginia," with Volume II ("The Albemarle Barracks") describing the travels of the convention prisoners. The author is indebted to Miss Bettie Blue Omohundro of Gordonsville for making her saved copies of that series available.

was clearly "surrender." They were mostly Germans, and many of the Germans were Hessians.

In December 1779, Madison was appointed a delegate to the Continental Congress. He was now in the big Big Leagues, but there were questions about how much longer the colonies might be fielding a team. Every colonial military victory seemed to be offset by a defeat. The French were standoffish, apparently waiting to see which way things were going to wind up before seriously committing. Congress had no money. The states were bickering with Congress and with each other. Everybody was sick and tired of the war.

The confusion and bickering continued unabated into 1780. General Washington, however, managed somehow to keep an army in the field, and American resolve and performance were definitely improving. The year after that, 1781, the world turned upside down for the British at Yorktown, and America was left sitting on top.

In that last year of the Revolution, the war finally came to Orange County. Lord Cornwallis, in command of the British forces in the south, moved into Virginia in the late spring of 1781. The Marquis de Lafayette, in command of an elite, but small force of colonial troops, hurried from Maryland to do what he could to oppose Cornwallis. When the British began a push through central Virginia, Lafayette's grudging retreat infuriated Cornwallis, who is said to have begun referring to his opponent as "that boy." At 24 years of age, Lafayette was indeed the youngest Major General in the field, but he was no pushover.[16]

Lafayette finally pulled back across the Rapidan, using one or more fords in western Spotsylvania/eastern Orange, and he awaited reinforcements. When reinforcements, primarily in the form of troops commanded by Generals Wayne and Muhlenberg, were close enough to give support, Lafayette moved back across Orange County, seeking now to engage Cornwallis. The main body of his army crossed at Raccoon Ford and camped for the night of June 8-9, 1781, at Rhoadesville, which for years thereafter called itself "Lafayette."

The next day's march of Lafayette's army towards Louisa County used a road that the troops had cleared and widened. That road today is shown on county maps as the "Marquis Road" (Route 669). In the face of this

---

[16] At age 19, Lafayette was commissioned a Major General by act of the 1777 Continental Congress. He remains the youngest person to have held the permanent rank of Major General in the American military. (Custer was a Lieutenant Colonel when he died at Little Big Horn.)

strong force, Cornwallis ultimately elected to withdraw to Yorktown — and to defeat.

For a few days, at about the same time as Lafayette's march through the county, British cavalry raided the area around Antioch Church (on Route 660 near St. Just), terrifying the residents and pillaging their property. People were hiding their possessions and themselves wherever they could, and at least a few children were reported to have spent that time living in tobacco hogsheads in a swamp.[17] An unrelated but interesting note from this time deals with the identity of the jailer for Orange County. It was Mary Bell. The menfolk were off to war, and she had several young daughters who were not likely to go unnoticed by the soldiers passing through. Her position as jailer probably served the interests of both the county and Mrs. Bell.

When Lafayette returned to America in 1824-25, he came to Orange County and spent a week with the Madisons at Montpelier. He was wined and dined everywhere, and his Orange County stops included the Gordon Tavern at Gordonsville, Peliso at Orange, and Ellwood at Wilderness. In Charlottesville, Jefferson put on a banquet in Lafayette's honor, using the just-completed Rotunda building at the University of Virginia and inviting Madison as an additional honored guest. Madison was one of the original appointees to the Board of Visitors of the University, and following Jefferson's death, he succeeded his old friend as Rector of the University.[18]

## G. Towards a New Constitution

The end of the fighting still left Madison and his fellow congressmen with much to do and with virtually no resources or authority to get any of it done. The loose confederation of states was now even more of a hindrance to national unity without a common cause to rally around. It did not help that Britain, the loser in war, was trying to be the winner in peace. Much posturing, foot-dragging, and maneuvering to try to get America to make this or that concession ate up months of time. A draft of a proposed treaty finally reached America in the spring of 1783. The army had to be

---

[17] Additional detail on the raiding party and Lafayette's march through the county may be found in Thomas, *Patriots of the Upcountry*, pp. 66-72.

[18] Altogether Madison served the University from 1816 to 1834. Benjamin Johnson Barbour, another Orange County native, also served as Rector from 1866 to 1872. Barbour had inherited his father's Jefferson-designed Barboursville mansion, which burned Christmas Day 1884.

held together until it was certain there would be no more fighting, but there was no money to pay the troops. Some army units revolted and marched on Philadelphia. Congress soon had to flee Philadelphia and seek sanctuary in Madison's old haunts at Princeton.

The Princeton Congress adjourned in October 1783 following an announcement that the delegates would reconvene in Annapolis the following month. They reconvened without Madison, who correctly figured that nothing of value would be done by the few delegates who jeopardized their Christmas plans by actually appearing. He hurried home to the red hills of Orange County and Montpelier.

Montpelier? Yes, that was now the name of the plantation. About the time Madison left to serve in Congress that name started appearing. During Madison's four-year absence, it became the name of choice. He voiced no objection. One suspects that there were suggestions from his good friend, the Squire of Monticello, to the effect that all established properties of persons of wealth and wide learning were being given romantic continental names. By 1784, that particular Squire was on his way to Europe to try to tie up the loose ends left over from the peace treaty with Britain. He would soon thereafter ship the requested literary cargo to his good friend in Orange County.

From 1784 through 1786, Madison lived mostly at Montpelier. He was once again not involved with the type of work that he saw as his calling, but he was as busy as he had ever been. For one thing, he had to become reacquainted with the farming operations at Montpelier and the other business ventures of his father.[19] The elder Madison, now in his sixties, was starting to slow down, and son James recognized a need to pay closer attention to matters which had only somewhat interested him in years past. Now, with the Revolution over, he also hoped to be able to deal with those matters with a bit less to distract him.

It is hard to say when the bookish, intellectual Madison finally caught the farming bug that so completely engulfed him in his later years, but this could have been the beginning. It was not that he was a stranger to the natural world around him, his primary focus was simply on other things. In 1785 Madison was actually elected to the American Philosophical Society, whose closest counterpart today is probably the National Academy of Science. The membership roll of the Philosophical Society was studded

---

[19] In addition to his farming and ironworking enterprises, the elder Madison was a building contractor and acted as a "factor," or agent in dealing with foreign merchants on the behalf of others.

with the names of internationally known chemists, botanists, astronomers, etc., and Madison's contributions in meteorology, botany, and zoology, based primarily on work done at Montpelier, must have been seen as worthy.

Apparently somewhat less appealing to Madison were his father's iron operations. The main driveway of the time was a long, looping road whose ends connected to the road from Orange to Charlottesville. It passed across what is today the front lawn of the Montpelier mansion less than a hundred yards from the front door. Strung out along that driveway northeast of the house was a complex of blacksmith shops and other iron working facilities. The whole affair was undoubtedly smelly, dirty, and noisy. It also brought in cash money, something Montpelier always needed. A few years after his father's death, Madison relocated and scaled down the iron operations. In his later farming years, when he was bemoaning the difficulty of making any money, did Madison ever remember that in 1800, his father's iron operations had produced a significant portion of Montpelier's profit? If he did, he chose not to make much of it.

Madison's temporary retirement to Orange County did not remove him from the public eye. By the time his term in Congress was over, Madison was being recognized as one of the pre-eminent minds at work in the government of the new nation. He was also recognized as one of the leaders in the growing movement to reorganize that government. Visitors and letters followed him to Montpelier, and he did not turn them aside. He also traveled to meet and confer with like-minded people. And, of course, he studied and he wrote. And he wrote and he studied. Today's educators would instantly label it "continuing adult education."

Madison was also elected to represent Orange County in the Virginia legislature for the years 1784-87. He again found himself having to deal with Patrick Henry, whose leanings towards the re-institution of some sort of state-supported religion for Virginia flew in the face of Madison's strong commitment to religious liberty. In opposing Henry (successfully), Madison got to know Elder John Leland, a Massachusetts-born Orange County Baptist leader. Leland commanded a large following of Baptists—voters— in Orange County, and he and Madison would have a historic meeting involving them in 1788.

Continuing disagreements with Maryland over the ownership and use of the Potomac River had led Madison to get the Virginia legislature to appoint commissioners to meet with a similarly appointed Maryland delegation to resolve the problems. Madison had also let it be known that he would serve as a commissioner if desired. With the way before it so well prepared, the legislature did not take long in accommodating him. The meeting took place at Mount Vernon in March of 1785, and a great deal was accomplished, all in Madison's absence. For some reason, he did not get timely notice of the meeting.

A by-product of the Mount Vernon conference was a recognition that there was a need for uniform rules of commerce that involved more than just the states bordering the Potomac. It was agreed that all states would be asked to send commissioners to some future conference at which the general problems of trade would be considered. The Virginia legislature obligingly appointed Madison as a Virginia representative to that conference, which turned out to be the abortive Annapolis Convention of 1786. That convention was far from a complete failure, however, for from it came the call for what became the 1787 Constitutional Convention in Philadelphia.

The delegates to the Constitutional Convention in Philadelphia adopted a new United States Constitution on September 17, 1787. It should be noted in passing that only 75 years later to the day, along Antietam Creek, Maryland, more Americans died than in any other single day in history as a part of a severe test of that Constitution. That, however, was a concern for another time. The immediate concern was that this proposed new constitution now had to be ratified (confirmed) by at least nine of the thirteen states for it to go into effect. And there were plenty of people who stood in opposition to it.

Many opponents were simply against making changes. The problems with the old confederation were not ones which bothered them. Others were adamantly opposed to giving the central government so much power and control, though Madison's studies had showed the lack of such power and control to be the most common cause for the failure of republican governments. Rather than come home to Montpelier after the convention, Madison went to New York and joined Alexander Hamilton and John Jay in writing various portions of *The Federalist* papers, articles written to be published in support of the proposed constitution. Then, early in 1788, Madison received word from Orange County which soon had him on the road home.

Back in Orange County, the leaders and members of various religious groups had expressed great concern over the fact that the proposed new Constitution contained no freedom of religion language. Madison was routinely deflecting such arguments by pointing out that the central government would have only those powers granted to it by the states. No control over matters of religion was being granted, so the states would retain that power to themselves. Virginia, in particular, had excellent freedom of religion language in its statement of rights, so it was in good shape. "We're not so sure" was the tone of the response from Orange County.

While it was understood that Madison desired and expected to be elected by the Orange County voters as a representative to the Richmond convention which would consider ratifying the Constitution, the religious leaders in the county had other ideas. One of the strongest voices expressing concern was that of Madison's old acquaintance, Elder John Leland. Thomas Barbour was proposed as a competing candidate. Also, Charles Porter, the bumbo server, was standing for that election. Madison was in trouble at home, and some rapid fence mending was in order. Just days before the election of delegates to the Virginia ratification convention, Madison arrived in Fredericksburg and headed towards Orange. He sent word ahead that he wished to meet with Leland.

There is a small park on the side of Route 20, just west of Unionville, that commemorates the meeting between Madison and Leland. The actual place of the meeting is not known. It was March 1788, and it is unlikely that the elder Madisons were already "taking the waters" at Orange Springs in the southeastern end of the county. That would have otherwise been a logical meeting place. In any event, Madison and Leland met and discussed Leland's concerns. The two men knew each other from working together on state legislation, and it probably did not take long for each to make his points. The upshot was a promise by Madison that he would personally see to the adoption of amendments to the Constitution which would include freedom of religion language. That was enough for Leland. He advised his followers to vote for Madison, which was tantamount to election. Leland returned to his home near Rhoadesville,[20] and Madison went on to Montpelier to enjoy family and friends.

Madison was indeed elected an Orange County delegate to the ratification convention, and he set about finding out what kind of reception "his" constitution might receive. The results were not calculated to make him sleep well. Not only was Patrick Henry adamantly opposed (unfortunate, but to be expected of a strong states-rights advocate), but George Mason was also against ratification! Between them, those two formidable leaders could raise an opposition to the Constitution that would seal its doom in Virginia.

The delegates to the ratification convention assembled in Richmond on June 2, 1788. Madison and his supporters soon discerned that Mason's

---

[20] Leland's home is believed to have been somewhere along today's Route 742 (Strawberry Hill Road).

primary objections lay with the absence of what he saw as necessary amendments, and after those concerns were addressed, his opposition was considerably muted. Henry, however, was another case altogether. For over a week, he held the convention to the sole consideration of Article I, Paragraph 1.[21] As always, his speeches moved and molded the hearers, and he still almost single-handedly defeated ratification of the proposed Constitution in its "father's" home state. On June 25, however, the delegates voted 89-79 to ratify.

At the time of Virginia's vote, the delegates thought that it was the ninth state to ratify, thus putting the Constitution into effect for the United States. It was soon learned, however, that New Hampshire, who several months earlier had voted not to ratify, had reconsidered and ratified on June 21. Even so, Virginia's ratification was critical. At the time, Virginia was still the largest state in terms of land area, contained the largest number of U.S. citizens, and was enjoying significant prosperity. It would have been a crippling blow to the new nation not to have had Virginia's support and active involvement.

It was now time to create the legislatures for the new government. (There had never been any question about Washington being the first President.) Henry exacted some revenge on Madison by making sure that he was not made a senator, but in 1789, Madison was elected to the House of Delegates, the office which he apparently preferred anyway. The first session of the first Congress was largely devoted to getting the government up and running, but late in the session and true to his word, Madison proposed a package of seventeen amendments to the new Constitution. Twelve were adopted and forwarded to the states for ratification. The package of amendments was already being referred to as the "Bill of Rights." By December 15, 1791, enough states had ratified ten of the amendments to make them apply to the Constitution.[22]

Carrying out the Revolution and forming the new government had been very hard work, but no one could say that the anxieties and frustrations of those times were not accompanied by great excitement. Now it was just hard work, a whole lot of hard work. For a while, it looked as if America would go to war with France (much to Britain's satisfaction). Then there was trouble out west involving Britain and Spain, forcing Kentucky to

---

[21] Over 200 years later, it will still make the hair on your neck crawl when you read chapter 14, "Rocking Cradles in Virginia," in Miller, *The Business of May Next.*

[22] Proposed amendment #1 was never ratified. Proposed amendment #2 was ratified in 1992 as the 27th amendment.

consider secession. The Federalists, who wanted an extremely strong central government, seemed ready to take over the country. They were opposed by the Democratic Republicans, with whom Madison allied, and bitter, partisan politics became the order of the day. Every time a state didn't like what the central government was doing, it would threaten to secede. And everybody in the world seemed to want to pick on the new kid on the international block. A unified America was probably already too big and strong to physically overwhelm, but unity appeared to be a sometime thing. Also, the economic life could still be sucked out of it unless good trade relations were established and enforced in a world of shifting alliances. Trying to organize and operate a government in this environment was hard, HARD work.

## H. A Respite, Then Back to Work

Madison stuck with it until 1797, then he came home to Montpelier. He hoped it was forever. He was tired of what to him had already become Big Government. His always delicate health was invariably better at Montpelier, and his love for that piece of red Orange County land was steadily growing. His father's stamina and health, at age 74, wasn't what it used to be. There was family living throughout the region. Good friends and neighbors abounded. And Madison was a happily married man.

On September 15, 1794, Madison had married the Quaker widow Dolley Payne Todd. At age 43, Madison was seventeen years her senior, but Dolley was far from inexperienced in the world, with not all of those experiences being pleasant ones. Her father's finances and his relationship with the Quaker community both came to ruin late in his life. Early in 1790, at age 21, she had married John Todd, a Philadelphia lawyer, and by 1793 had two children. The yellow fever epidemic which hit Philadelphia that year killed her husband, her husband's parents, and her younger child.

Dolley had no choice but to pick up the pieces and move on. In those days young widows tended to remarry quickly, and she was no exception. Aaron Burr brought word that Madison would like to meet her, and the Philadelphia gossip circles went to work.[23] Madison had been a national figure for some time, and Dolley unquestionably knew a great deal about him. Madison for his part probably made it a point to learn a great deal

---

[23] A hurried note from Dolley to her best friend, Eliza Collins: "Thou must come to me. Aaron Burr says that the great little Madison has asked to be brought to see me this evening." Fritz, *The Great Little Madison*, p. 72.

Montpelier in 2003. Extensive changes will be made over the next several years to return the mansion to its Madison-era exterior appearance and interior room arrangement. Photo courtesy of the Montpelier Foundation.

about Dolley as quickly as he could. The courtship went smoothly, and a commitment by the couple to marry came quickly. That marriage as it turned out produced one of the most devoted presidential couples to ever grace the White House.

Before marriage, however, Dolley had one last piece of business to complete. Even with all she knew, she still had a lawyer friend check out her prospective husband. The attorney reported back that if he personally could not be her choice, then Madison was very suitable.[24] Dolley was pretty and charmingly sociable. She was also a careful and accurate judge of people, and, with the notable exception of Payne Todd, her surviving child from the first marriage, she was usually able to impress them.

Age was not the only significant difference between the newlyweds. Madison was short. His detractors said 5'4"or thereabouts; his supporters strained to add an inch or two. He was spare of frame and habitually wore black. He was a witty conversationalist in small groups, but silent and

---

[24] William Wilkins remained a friend and confidant. He was among the very few who called Dolley by a private name of "Julia." A transcript of his letter report to Dolley is at p. 29 of Mattern, Shulman, *Selected Letters*.

almost invisible in large ones. Dolley started out at least as tall as her spouse and then, in the fashion of the day, often wore turbans with feathers sticking in them. To say that she loomed over Madison is no exaggeration. In contrast to her husband's garb, Dolley wore dresses in the colors of the time. She was also a large framed woman. Again, detractors claimed "stout." She could be disarmingly talkative in any size assembly.

The Montpelier house the junior Madisons came to in 1797 was a version of the two-story, central hall with side rooms, design that dotted Piedmont Virginia at the time. The fact that the house was of brick did make it rather unusual. The arrival of the new couple now signaled the need to create more living space. Between 1797 and 1800, Madison added on to the house and reorganized the interior, eventually creating two adjacent, but mutually exclusive sets of living quarters, a "duplex" in the words of today's Montpelier guides. The senior Madisons lived in one side; the junior Madisons in the other. The living units even had separate kitchens located in their basements.

From 1797 to 1801, Madison lived at Montpelier, the longest unbroken stay since the boyhood years prior to his departure in 1762 for Donald Robertson's school. He built on the house and farmed the land with much enjoyment. The farming part was particularly important, because of the senior Madison's declining health and the fact that brother Ambrose, the farming brother, was dead.

The Madisons had bought up the Chew part of the original Montpelier patent, and in 1781, father James had given a portion of that land to son Ambrose. It lies on the opposite side of the same Southwest Mountain ridge on which the Montpelier house stands. Today's Route 15 south of Orange cuts through that property. Within a few years, Ambrose began building a home on his land, calling his place "Woodley Vale," or simply "Woodley." It stands today as the connecting portion between the two large wings built sometime around 1840 by his daughter Nelly Madison Willis.

Ambrose was the son who stayed home to farm, and he was a great help to his father in running Montpelier. In 1793, however, he died, leaving a void that was never completely filled during the remainder of the senior Madison's life. Ambrose's wife died just five years later, and "Uncle James" became their Nelly's guardian. Fortunately Nelly was a great favorite of her childless uncle, and the two always got along handsomely. Nelly and Paul Jennings were the only people with Madison when he died.

Before Madison made his return to public service, death claimed two more of the immediate family. Brother Francis died in 1800, and just a few weeks into 1801, he was followed in death by his father. A bitter loss was being followed by the end of an era. The eldest sister, Nelly Conway Madison Hite, was also in declining health. Death finally claimed sister Nelly in 1802. Going strong, however, was mother Nelly Conway Madison. As it turned out, she would come to within seven years of living as long as her famous son.

In 1777, Madison, Sr., purchased 2,301 acres, just across the Rapidan River at Barnett's Ford (today's Route 15 crossing). Francis was soon given 1,000 acres of that land, and within a few years, he built his home, "Prospect Hill." Now called "Greenway," that house stands on the first high ridge on the Madison County side of the Rapidan. Unfortunately, Francis' life and work went largely undocumented, and very little is known about him. Madison County Court records do show that in 1793 he was granted authority to build a dam for a milling operation near his home, and in 1795, Francis conveyed a 16.5 acre mill tract to father James, brother James, brother William, and himself. The mill operation was then run under the business name of "William Madison & Co., mercantile partnership."

In 1791, William Madison had bought 40 acres from Francis, and by 1793 he had built his home, "Woodberry Forest." Correspondence between Jefferson and Madison reveals that Jefferson was enticed into supplying the general design for the house. Madison knew how to make the architectural juices flow in his Albemarle County friend, and he got results beyond his expectations. With the senior Madison's death, William inherited another 1,300 acres around his house site. That death, coupled with Francis', also brought the Madison ownership of the mill to an end. By 1808, the property had been sold to settle the estates. A friend of the Madison family bought the property, and he decided to retain the Madison family name for it. Today we still know the settlement of which Greenway is a part by the name of Madison Mills.

## I. Serving in High Offices

By 1800, Madison was deep into farming and family. He probably knew that those days were numbered as soon as it was announced that Jefferson had been elected President. Jefferson was almost certain to call on him for help, and he could not refuse. Sure enough, the call came: Jefferson wanted him to be Secretary of State.

At least Madison's journey was going to be a short one. The seat of government was now the new city of Washington on the Potomac. The choice of that site had been in large measure the result of a grudging compromise the Madison-led Republicans had brokered with the Hamilton-led Federalists involving the assumption of state debts incurred in financing the Revolution.[25] The location of the Federal City therefore was no source of surprise or delight for Madison. He was even late getting there. He had to bury his father and attend to some estate matters before taking to the road.

A highlight of Madison's secretaryship had to be the Louisiana Purchase. Early in 1803, the Jefferson administration had inquired of the French emperor/dictator Napoleon Bonaparte as to the possibility of America buying the port of New Orleans, which the French had recently obtained from the Spanish. The response was that all French holdings in North America were for sale! Jefferson and Madison jumped at the deal. In one transaction, the size of the United States was more than doubled. Over time, Jefferson and Madison said that they had figured out how to square the way they handled that piece of business with the provisions of the Constitution. Some people still don't agree.

A long, agonizing low point had to be the embargo. By 1805 the almost-defenseless American merchant navy was being preyed upon unmercifully. England and France were at war, and neither recognized America as a neutral trading nation. The situation steadily worsened, and in 1807 the Jefferson administration persuaded Congress to declare an embargo, stopping all American shipping. As the embargo dragged on with no end in sight, New England began agitating to secede from the Union.[26] As Britain's aggressiveness towards America took on the aspect of forcing the new nation back into some version of its colonial dependency, war became inevitable. It would be "Mr. Madison's War," the War of 1812.[27]

Madison took every opportunity he could find to get back to Orange County, but the opportunities seemed few and far between. Then in 1808, he was elected President.

Madison's inauguration on Saturday March 4, 1809, probably did not figure as one of the highlights of his Presidency. He had too many things to think about that were less than pleasant. He was assuming the leading role

---

[25] A readable summary of those events is presented in Chapter 2 ("The Dinner") of Ellis' *Founding Brothers.*

[26] New England began muttering about secession as early as Jefferson's first term. By the time the New England states representatives met in Hartford CT in 1814, cooler heads had prevailed, and secession was no longer on the agenda.

[27] The War of 1812 may be properly seen as the second stage of the American Revolution, the stage in which America confirmed the independence won in the Revolutionary War. The Third stage was the American Civil War, a war which concluded the American Revolution.

in the widely unpopular embargo. It seemed certain that he would have to send America into war with Britain within the next year or two. He would be without the assistance of the sixty-six-year-old Jefferson, who was worn out and desperate to return to private life. Montpelier needed Madison, and he wanted to be there, but it was not going to happen any time soon. And if all that wasn't enough, he had to endure an inaugural ball that featured a very hot, jam-packed room full of very loud people who weren't interested in quiet, intellectual conversation. How he envied Jefferson and ached for Montpelier.

Dolley, however, was in her element. At Jefferson's request, she had assumed the duties of White House hostess for the various receptions and such that the bachelor President found himself having to put on. By the time her husband's presidency began, Dolley already had a keen appreciation of the role she would play in assisting him. One tactic for which she became famous was organizing the seating for White House dinners, using a number of small tables instead of one large one. She would then assign the seating so that persons holding views in opposition to each other sat at the same table. The atmosphere was of course socially congenial, the parties were too close to ignore each other, and the hope was that they could open channels of communication and find some common grounds of understanding. Dolley's ice cream socials were also a Washington fixture, which again mixed men and women of all stripes and factions together in a congenial atmosphere. Dolley was the quintessential Washington Hostess, a charming lady doing serious business.

On the morning of August 24, 1814, at Bladensburg, Maryland, British forces defeated a hastily assembled and poorly organized mob of militia and prepared to march into Washington. The British had only a thirty-five mile march from their troop ships, but their pace had been leisurely in the extreme, taking a week to cover the distance. Their slow progress only served to give the local defense forces more time to put on an impressive display of disorganization and general ineptitude. The United States had actually begun to field some excellent armies by this point in the war, with capable young generals, such as Winfield Scott and Andrew Jackson, but those people were a long way away from Washington in August of 1814. The War of 1812 was about to become close and personal for Mr. Madison and the Federal City.

Madison had borrowed a pair of dueling pistols from George Campbell, his Secretary of the Treasury, and he had ridden off earlier in the day to see what he could do. The small-statured, intellectual, soft-spoken Father of the Constitution thus became the only President of the United States to actually carry weapons and serve in a combat zone while in office. At some point during that day, Madison is supposed to have discovered that he was between the British and American lines. It may have briefly encouraged him to have found an American line anywhere.[28]

Just a few months earlier, Madison had suffered yet another of his many spells of sickness. It was probably the worst in his experience, and for three weeks, his survival had been in some doubt. Fortunately, Madison was now fully recovered, and he could at least inspire and encourage with his Presidential presence in the face of the British assault. Presence, unfortunately, has its limits.

Dolley was left back in the White House, trying to save what she could. The British had long ago promised that they would burn Washington, and now they were coming to do it. Government papers and property rumbled out of town by the wagon load. A popular story involving Dolley is that she commandeered a wagon and filled it with Madison's papers, the White House silver, and some household items. The most widely-recounted act from that occasion is her ordering that the Gilbert Stuart full length portrait of George Washington be cut from its frame, rolled up, and put in the wagon. She left a meal on the dinner table for her husband, and she rolled off with her small cargo of White House treasures.[29]

In the interval between Dolley's departure and the arrival of the British, Madison arrived, looked around briefly, and left. Even if he had time to eat the meal set out for him, he probably had no appetite. The British ate it before torching the White House, along with a number of the other government buildings. In less than forty-eight hours, the British troops were through burning and looting and were gone, heading back to their ships.

It had to be the low point of Madison's administration. Much as the sun follows a thunderstorm, however, the government was quickly reestablished in Washington, and the British, overextended worldwide and meeting increasing American resistance, agreed to negotiate a peace. Andrew Jackson's crushing defeat of the British at New Orleans was a fitting conclusion to "Mr. Madison's War." It was fought after the peace treaty had been signed in Europe, but word concerning it had not reached America.

---

[28] Ketcham, *James Madison*, p. 577; Rakove, *James Madison*, p. 166. Madison also was exposed to cannon and rocket fire. Some Civil War buffs accord the first and only presidential combat exposure to Abraham Lincoln. Wrong.

[29] Paul Jennings, Madison's body servant begs to differ, reciting that the first alarm sounded so imminent that Dolley had to leave almost at once, taking almost nothing. He recalled that during the unexpected hiatus before the British actually arrived, the White House staff who had stayed behind saved many items, including the portrait.

## J. A Well-Earned Retirement

The remainder of Madison's Presidency went relatively smoothly. America was strong and prospering, the international community was appropriately respectful, and the election of Madison's friend, James Monroe, as his successor seemed certain. Dolley had a great time restoring the White House, and best of all, they spent two months of 1815 and most of the summer of 1816 at Montpelier. Between 1809 and 1812, Madison had undertaken another major renovation/addition project at Montpelier. Extensive landscaping had taken place, including the construction of a columned garden temple over a brick ice house; wings were added to each end of the house, and, as seemed to occur with each renovation, the arrangement of the interior rooms was changed yet again. Now they were finally about to enjoy all that had been done.

There was an extended round of balls and parties which followed Monroe's inauguration in 1817, but by early spring the Madisons were at Montpelier. At age sixty-six, Madison, like Jefferson eight years earlier, had come home to stay. Farming in Orange County among family and friends — it was the most thoroughly satisfying time of his life. He had fully earned the right to rest and retirement, and he was making the most of it.

Madison's retirement, however, was not all unalloyed pleasure. His stepson, John Payne Todd, had evolved into an alcoholic and a gambler, and not a very good gambler at that.[30] He came to Montpelier with his mother and stepfather when they left Washington, but trips away, followed by urgent messages back to them for money, soon started again. Once or twice Todd was already in jail by the time the response to a message was received. In just his retirement years alone, Madison evidently paid out over $40,000 to cover Todd's business debts and gambling losses, and he was not the only family member providing support. Todd had come into Madison's life as a preteen stepchild at a time when national and international affairs had first priority on his famous stepfather's attention. Such supervision and control as Madison may have had time to attempt made no visible impression, and unfortunately, for all of her ability to assess people

---

[30] Payne Todd was not the only cross Dolley had to bear. Her sister's husband went bankrupt, losing funds that the Madisons had placed with him and requiring their additional financial assistance. Her brother, John C. Payne became an alcoholic and frittered away such wealth as he had. John eventually took up residence near Montpelier and helped some with the editing of the Madison papers.

and deal with them, Dolley seemed incapable of doing anything with her son beyond bewailing his excesses and loving him unconditionally.

Shortly after Madison returned home, America was hit by a major agricultural depression. In addition, much of the land east of the Mississippi was worn out. A series of droughts drove many planters to the brink of ruin. A migration of Virginians, mostly to the south and west, had taken upwards to a million of them out of the state by the time of the Civil War. Madison moaned and groaned about the difficulty of trying to turn a profit, but he did not indicate any desire to revive his father's ironworks.

The Missouri Compromise of 1820 signaled that America remained bitterly divided over slavery. Woven into the problem was an ideological division between the commercial/industrial northern states and the agrarian South. Later, a tariff issue which had its roots in that division, led to the Nullification Crisis of the 1830s. As the arguments escalated, Madison found both sides quoting him for their positions. Much disturbed by those developments, Madison pointed out to any who would listen that he stood for the union of states, not for their division. Madison's heart must have fallen to his shoe tops when President Andrew Jackson announced his willingness to raise troops and send them across Virginia to subdue South Carolina.[31] Fortunately, those issues were patched up long enough to keep Madison from having to witness a test of his Constitution at bayonet point. To almost everyone, however, that test seemed inevitable.

In 1829, Nelly Conway Madison, by then widely known as "Mother Madison," died. She was 97 years old but had continued to read without glasses until nearly the end. She had lived comfortably for years in her (south) wing of the Montpelier house with her own personal servants and eating from her own kitchen in the basement under the wing. Because Mother Madison kept her own schedule and did not normally appear at her son's gatherings, guests often came by her sitting room to pay their respects before entering into social events farther up the hall. Like her son, Mother Madison had suffered bouts of indifferent health, but she had been able to avoid the life-claiming epidemics which periodically swept through the county.

On the other hand, all was not gloom and worry during Madison's final, and extended, retirement to Montpelier. Madison's greatest satisfaction came from running the farming operation. From a person who ini-

---

[31] Virginia's reaction to that possibility was to advise President Jackson that it would secede before allowing such a troop movement.

tially spent more time away from Montpelier than within its bounds and for whom agriculture was probably more of an intellectual pursuit than a hands-on business, Madison had evolved into an enthusiastic and knowledgeable farmer. Jefferson, with characteristic generosity, once labeled his friend "the best farmer in the world." The Albemarle Agricultural Society made him its President, and one of his addresses dealing with ways of reviving exhausted soils is regularly quoted to evidence his farming expertise.

Guests from everywhere came to visit, some to stay a while. The Madisons charmed and entertained them all. In time, however, Madison's body, but not his legendary mind, began to fail. Ultimately, his legs became too weak to support him. A bed was set up in the downstairs room adjacent to the dining room. With the door open, he could converse with guests as in old times. With the door closed, he could rest and husband his declining strength.

By the time of Madison's eighty-fifth birthday in 1836, it seemed certain that he would not live to see another. By late spring, they were counting the days. In June, Madison was consulted by his physician: Jefferson, Adams, and Monroe had all died on July 4. Would Mr. Madison wish to receive medication which might prolong his life to July 4?

No.

On June 28, 1836, James Madison, Jr., the Father of the Constitution and the last of the Founding Fathers, died. As his body servant Paul Jennings recalled, Madison was one moment alive and responding to his niece Nelly Willis. The next moment he was dead, "as quietly as the snuffing out of a candle."

How long Dolley had been living a life of quiet desperation before her husband's death is not known, but it now became clear that she was. There was nowhere near enough money to support her and Montpelier as in times past. Farming had not been a profitable venture for quite some time, and debts had been incurred. Compounding the troubles were Payne Todd's usual wasteful and destructive habits, which were now intensified by his efforts to build his own plantation, "Toddsberth," near the farm mill on Madison Run.[32]

An ongoing project in Madison's retirement years had been the assembling and editing of his official papers for publication after his death,

---

[32] The Toddsberth site is on high ground currently occupied by a farm building on the south side of Route 639 (Madison Run Road), about 100 yards east of its intersection with Route 15.

including the detailed notes he took at the time of the Constitutional Convention. He had no intention of publishing his private correspondence and personal notes. It was a project that he never fully completed, and his death was followed by the destruction and scattering of many of the originals of his papers. Dolley did save the 1787 Constitutional Convention notes plus some other material, all of which she sold to the U. S. Government for $30,000 in 1837. By 1848, she had assembled an additional collection, for which the Government paid $25,000. The second sale was conditional upon her using $5,000 to pay immediate debts and agreeing to the balance being put in a spendthrift trust that son Payne Todd could not get at. The ensuing years have seen the ongoing assembling and publishing of those significant Madison papers which still exist.[33]

Dolley began to spend more and more time in Washington, leaving the "management" of Montpelier to Payne Todd. Payne started to loot and liquidate Montpelier property. His marble quarrying venture at Toddsberth failed, and the creditors began closing in.[34]

Probably a combination of factors triggered Dolley's decision to sell Montpelier, but one definitely had to be the letter she received from Sarah, one of the slaves living there. Sarah advised Dolley that things were so bad that the Sheriff was due to come and start selling individual slaves at auction, thereby breaking up families. If that was not the final straw, it was close to it. In 1844 Dolley sold Montpelier.

Dolley lived out her days in Washington in genteel, but grinding, poverty. Her death in 1849 produced the largest funeral held in the Federal City to that time. In his eulogy, President Zachary Taylor referred to Dolley as having been America's "First Lady," the title now automatically accorded to Presidents' wives. Payne Todd died in 1852, and the story is that his funeral was attended by a single mourner. Probably a creditor.

---

[33] The University of Chicago and the University of Virginia initially collaborated on the project, with Virginia assuming full responsibility in 1970. The Introduction to Volume I, describing the dispersal of the papers and the various efforts to publish them, reads like an adventure story. See *The Papers of James Madison* in the bibliography.

[34] An unfortunate by-product of Todd's creditors' sale was the decision by family members to destroy almost two rooms full of original Madison papers that Todd had taken from Montpelier (probably to sell), rather than let them be auctioned off. Copies of some of those papers have since been located.

## K. The duPonts to the Rescue

Montpelier went through a time of being bought and sold, enduring six owners between 1844 and 1900. Finally in 1900, an agent for William and Annie Rogers duPont bought it for his clients. For the property and its new owners, it was a Madison/duPont reunion.

In 1778, Pierre Samuel duPont, an economic advisor to French King Louis XVI, assisted in the drafting of the treaty of friendship and commerce between his country and the new revolutionary government in America. Well born, duPont was initially educated to be an engineer. He then proceeded to learn and practice medicine. All that was before he discovered that economics was his passion. Through all of his career changes, duPont was recognized as an accomplished poet and playwright.

Government duties brought duPont into contact with Jefferson and Madison, and he corresponded with them over time. When the French Revolution began, duPont soon discovered that he was going to be an outsider, whose assistance with any new government would not be welcomed. He was actually jailed for a time when Louis XVI attempted to flee the throne. Finally, in 1799, with the revolution destroying his country, duPont sailed for America. The ship captain became lost twice, and the trip took 93 days.

Matters of business required duPont to return to France by 1802, and while there, that old economic advisor did what he could to help bring about the Louisiana Purchase. It may not have been much, but it reflected an attitude towards America that duPont put into words in a letter to Madison the year he returned:

"When the United States were established, I already held some responsible positions, and not without success I endeavoured to be as of much service as I could. I gave them my sons as soon as they reached manhood. To them and to the republics that are being formed on your continent, I am now consecrating the labors of my last years."[35]

In that same year, 1815, and at Pierre duPont's request, Madison assisted Pierre's grandson, Samuel Francis duPont, in securing a midshipman's warrant in the United States Navy. Rising to the rank of Admiral in the United States Navy during the American Civil War, Samuel duPont served with distinction, beginning with his capture of Port Royal, South Carolina, in November 1861 and continuing as commander of the

---

[35] Letter of July 25, 1815. Quoted in the forward of *The Correspondence of Jefferson and du Pont de Nemours*, Johns Hopkins Press, 1931, p. cvii.

South Atlantic Blockading Squadron. He requested and received reassignment in 1863 as his health began to fail him. He died in 1865, still on active duty. His grandfather would have been proud of him.

William duPont, the new owner of Montpelier in 1900 was Pierre's great-grandson. He had bought himself into right much of a mess. Considering how many hands Montpelier had fallen through since 1844, the fact that only two Madison-era structures survive to the present is rather understandable.[36] Things were probably in poor shape when Dolley sold, and most structures then suffered an additional sixty years of neglect.[37]

William, and his children after him, went to work. There are currently over 130 structures on the property, and the Montpelier mansion is roughly twice the size of the one of the Madison era. For those who feel that the duPonts should have preserved Montpelier as it was and not add on, keep in mind that the mansion had been reconstructed and remodeled so many times it was hard to tell how much of what they saw was historic and how much was not. Moreover, credit the duPonts with preserving what was left of Montpelier during a time when the rest of America wasn't interested in it. In much the same way that Uriah Levy saved Monticello for America, the duPonts saved Montpelier.

William duPont died in 1927, leaving Montpelier to his grandchildren, with lifetime possession granted to his own children. Of William's children, only the son, William, Jr., had offspring. The daughter, Marion, after two marriages had none.[38] But Marion loved Montpelier intensely. A renowned horsewoman, Marion duPont Scott elevated Montpelier to the top ranks of international horse racing when her Battleship won the English Grand National, the first American bred horse to do so. When her brother died, Marion was left as the sole custodian of Montpelier, at least until her death. She pondered at length on Montpelier's legacy and its future.

---

[36] The core of the mansion house and the garden temple in the front lawn.

[37] During the time of the Carson ownership (1857-1881), the assessed value of Montpelier's buildings declined from $8,000 to $3,500. Miller, "Historic Structures Report: Montpelier, Orange County, Virginia; Phase II," 1990, p. 123.

[38] Marion's second husband was George Randolph Scott (1898-1987), who had been born in Orange County, raised in North Carolina, and returned to graduate from Woodberry Forest School. Randolph went on to become a highly acclaimed movie actor in the 1930s, '40s, and '50s. Hollywood required his presence, Marion would not leave Montpelier, and their marriage did not survive.

The source of Marion's financial independence was a sizeable trust fund which would be disposed of as she directed in her will. Upon her death in 1983, it was learned that her will offered that trust fund to brother William's children, providing they deeded their just-inherited Montpelier over to the National Trust for Historic Preservation. There followed something which can best be described as a family ruckus, involving battalions of lawyers. When the dust settled, Montpelier was owned by the National Trust.

In 1987 Montpelier was opened to the public, and in 2000 the National Trust authorized the creation of the Montpelier Foundation which attends to the management of the property and to the fund-raising efforts necessary to support its continuing development. Another separate organization, the Montpelier Steeplechase and Equestrian Foundation, continues the practice of staging the Montpelier Hunt Races on the first Saturday in November, a steeplechase event begun by Marion duPont Scott and run annually since 1934. As of this writing, the evolution of Montpelier into a publicly accessible property where Americans can learn about the fourth President of the United States and the Father of our Constitution continues. While Madison would probably be uncomfortable with all this fuss over him and Montpelier, Dolley and Marion would surely be delighted.

Employing leading-edge skills and computer software, the Montpelier Foundation has acquired the ability to trace the changes made to the mansion since the last Madison remodeling. That knowledge thus permits the re-creation of the Madison-era mansion, and the decision has now been made to do exactly that. A $20 million grant from the Mellon Foundation, the largest ever made to a presidential home, has been promised, and work begins as this book goes to print. Returning visitors will probably be most impressed by the sight of one story side wings instead of the current two, and the removal of the stucco coating to reveal brick exterior walls. The interior will also be changed to bring back the Madison-era rooms.

*Above:* The Federal II Corps advancing west along the Orange Turnpike (today's Route 20) towards Robinson's Tavern (today's Locust Grove) during the afternoon of November 27, 1863. The tavern is on the right at the top of the rise, the ca. 1814 residence portion of which still stands a short distance from the site shown. Heavy skirmishing with Confederate forces just west of the ridge has begun and the Mine Run Campaign is starting to become serious. Alfred Waud's sketch for *Harpers'* gives the Turnpike a generous width. Reproduced with permission.

*Below:* Confederate trenches in Saunders' Field, Orange County. The Orange Turnpike (Route 20) runs through the field just out of view to the left. On May 5, 1864, Ewell's Corps had time to dig this trench line plus a reserve line before Federal forces attacked across the field to begin the Battle of the Wilderness. National Park Service property photographed by Bernice Walker. Reproduced with permission.

# CHAPTER V

# *The Civil War: Too Close for Comfort*

## A. A War by Any Other Name is Still a War

As a local historian/guide, this writer has probably heard all of the descriptive names for the war which convulsed America from 1861 to 1865. Some qualify as cocktail party humor, others as serious political statements. It is clear that the Confederate government wanted to exist separate and apart from the Federal government, not overthrow and replace it. From that standpoint, the struggle easily earns the title of "War for Southern Independence." Beyond that, the naming issue gets fuzzy.

The Federal government, for all of its pronouncements about dealing with a domestic internal rebellion against it by a dissident minority — a "civil war" — blockaded Southern ports to all shipping, agreed to a prisoner parole and exchange protocol with the Confederate government, and engaged in a systematic and widespread destruction of the infrastructure and the economy of the South. Those acts in combination were routinely seen in nineteenth century contests between belligerent nations, but almost never in civil wars.

That said, America's 1861-65 war is being called a "Civil War" in this work. Three reasons: First and foremost, the North won, so they get to name it. Second, it is a short, universally-recognized title for the conflict. Lastly, the story of the impact of that war on Orange County and its residents is more important than any debate over what to call it.

The American Civil War affected every citizen of Orange County regardless of age, race, or gender, and irrespective of whether one was in any way connected with the military. It was a time of duty and honor, blind stupidity, grand romance, panic, dangerous high adventure, terror, awesome courage, pain, suffering, and crushing loss, with Orange County finding itself involuntarily sharing in all of it.

We can say with some certainty that the Civil War era for Orange County began with the local musters following John Brown's October 16, 1859, raid on Harpers Ferry and that the last significant local fighting took place with the repulse of Sheridan's Christmas Raid aimed at Gordonsville in late December 1864. The war period is thus not much more than an eyeblink in the historic timeline of one of the older counties in the oldest colony of British America. The world for Orange County, however, was traumatically and permanently changed in that eyeblink.[1] Wars tend to collapse time, and changes that had seemed certain to take place in the county during the next generation, or maybe two, occurred between 1859 and 1865. There is a price for such rapid "progress," and there are times today when we can tell that it is still being paid.

Following Robert E. Lee's April 9, 1865, surrender at Appomattox and the subsequent surrender or disbandment of Confederate forces elsewhere, it took months for the surviving Orange County veterans to straggle back from Southern battlefields and Northern prisons. The cessation of combat and the return of survivors, however, does not end the story of the American Civil War. A significant segment of America's population had been defeated in a destructive and depopulating war, and their persons and property subjected to the occupation and control of the conquerors. Accompanying that was the collapse of their social, political, and economic system, a system that had dominated America for almost two centuries. Like the astronomer's Big Bang, the echoes of that experience have not died out. Many of those echoes bring back unpleasant memories, but if there is one general good to come out of remembering, it is that we are constantly reminded that neither the concept nor the reality of a "United States of America" should ever be taken for granted.

## B. The Pot Boils Over

As the Disunited States lurched into the mid-1800s, it became clear that the social, political, and economic systems of the slave labor states differed so much from those of the wage labor states that it was going to be extremely difficult for the two to co-exist under the same government. More to the point, there were influential leaders in both systems who did

---

[1] "We Lived Years in as Many Days," is the expressive title of chapter 4 in James Marden's *The Children's Civil War*. Children constituted almost a third of America's Civil War era population and became a generation marked by it.

not <u>want</u> them to co-exist under the same government. For Virginia, a threshold problem was determining which kind of state it was.

In the western counties, much of the Valley, and even in areas of Northern Virginia, the state was prepared to call itself "free." It was a minority of Virginia's whites (less than 10%) who owned slaves, and those ownerships were small compared to the Lower South. Of the Virginia families who did own slaves, only 20% owned more than 25 individuals of both genders and of all ages. Of Orange County's slave-owning families, which were themselves a minority in the county, only 8% owned as many as 25 slaves, even though the county was considered to be in the labor-intensive "Tobacco Belt."[2] All whites, however, were acclimated to and dependent upon a social, economic, and political system which had as a foundation the use of a cash-free, racially determined, permanently bonded labor force, i.e., slaves.

Harriet Beecher Stowe's *Uncle Tom's Cabin,* published in 1852, dramatically presented an abolitionist's view of the moral depravity of slavery and was wildly popular in the North. Its distribution in the South was suppressed, and Stowe was dismissed as a hysterical Yankee preacher's wife who simply did not understand the Southern system, admittedly points not totally without merit. There was, however, another book, written by a member of a North Carolina slave-owning family, which attacked the economic foundations of the slave labor system. In 1857 Hinton Rowan Helper published *The Impending Crisis of the South: How to Meet It.* Helper cited census data detailing how the Southern economy was being eclipsed by that of the North. Number after number, table after table, Helper documented the South's growing inferiority in virtually every economic category. Helper asserted that the cause was the South's dependence upon the inefficient system of slave labor. For a time Helper was one of the most widely known authors in America; however, his highly confrontational personal and prose style finally alienated him from Northern supporters, and that, plus a crushing Southern repression of his book, caused both it and him to slip from memory.

Among other things, the South's slave-labor-based agrarian economy made the region both a major exporter of raw materials and America's largest importer of manufactured goods. With the Federal government relying on import tariffs for much of its income, the South saw itself as being required to support a government which it increasingly distrusted. Many argue for tariffs as the sole cause of the war. Imports and the tax on them,

---

[2] Benson, *Edge of the South,* pp. 61, 63.

however, were symptoms of the South's problems, not the malady. The concentration of so much Southern capital in a non-entrepreneurial planter class and the low incentive for an efficient use of labor produced the South that Helper described.[3,4]

In 1832 the Virginia House of Delegates had only narrowly defeated a bill to abolish slavery in the state.[5] Robert E. Lee was understood to be among those who felt that it would not be much longer before there would be a vote to adopt such a measure. A brief review of the deliberations and comment before and after that vote, however, provides no real comfort for such optimism.[6] That vote also came just after the bloody Nat Turner uprising, which had polarized many whites against freeing slaves, ever.

In the "Tobacco Belt" (counties just east of the Blue Ridge), in the Southside, and in the Tidewater, one saw a Virginia heavily dependent upon the old English plantation system of agriculture, which in turn had historically depended upon the use of cash-free, bonded labor. Antebellum Virginia was controlled by the planter aristocracy from those regions, a group who saw themselves as representing the America of the Founding Fathers, who saw the similarly-controlled slave states to the south as "sister states," and who viewed the North with ever-increasing suspicion. While in no way universally acceptable, secession was the choice of the people who ran Virginia. Some residents evidenced their disagreement by leaving the state or by joining Federal military units, and in 1863 the entire western portion of the state elected to secede from the secessionists, forming a territory which to this day seems to be seeking its identity and heritage.

---

[3] An aged James Madison dissected and dismissed the tariff argument. Ketcham, *Madison*, p. 628 and accompanying notes. For a fictionally presented, but factually based, dialogue giving the mid-nineteenth century Southern position on slavery and economic issues, read Morton, *Marching Through Culpeper*, p. 193, *et seq.*

[4] Article 1, Section 8, of the Confederate Constitution limited tariffs and duties, and the expectation was that Southern ports would be duty-free. The South was thus hoping to attract virtually all of North America's import trade while the Federal Government's income dried up and Northern ports sat idle, a prospect which caused the city of New York to initially consider seceding. The Federal government's attitude towards internal improvements and a national bank are also cited as non-slavery causes for the war.

[5] The vote to adopt the emancipation bill, taken January 25, 1832, was 58 "Ayes" and 65 "Nays."

[6] For a report that captures some of the fervor of the time in addition to supplying good detail, see: Whitfield, *Slavery Agitation in Virginia.*

Orange County had its share of residents who did not desire a separation from the Union for which their ancestors had sacrificed so much to create. Whatever their numbers, they could not match the secessionists' ability to "talk big, talk loud, and look as if they were breathing thunderbolts and had breakfasted on fried lightning."[7] One of Orange's delegates to the Virginia secession convention, Dr. Jeremiah Morton of Morton Hall, was one such fire-eater, and he countenanced no objection to his states' rights arguments. He was a major factor in both Orange and Culpeper Counties sending pro-secession delegations to Virginia's 1861 secession convention.

It turned out that there was enough pro-Union sentiment represented at the convention to initially cause that assembly to vote against secession. That sentiment, though, could not hold against the wave of secession fever which swept the state after the bombardment of Fort Sumter and Lincoln's subsequent call for Virginia troops to subdue the South.[8]

The vote to secede added to the rush of young Virginians to enlist in the host of military units across the state. A similar rush to arms was taking place in the North. It is widely and correctly understood that lofty principles and patriotic goals motivated most volunteers, whether Union or Confederate, with conscription serving as the ultimate motivator for the rest. It wasn't all that hard, however, for thoughtful and informed folks to see that the fundamental problem was and had long been slavery.[9]

Leaders, both North and South, proclaimed that should secession bring on hostilities, they would not involve the slavery issue. Actually, it would have been nigh on to impossible in 1861 to have found enough people on either side to create armies to fight over slavery. The North was glad to be rid of it, and there seemed to be no quick way of rooting the "peculiar institution" out of the South, short of dismantling its social, political, and

---

[7] From Took, Horne; *Whose Overcoat Have You Got On?* A partisan pre-war pamphlet published in New York, referring to a contentious trial in which that question was especially incendiary.

[8] Overcome, but not silenced. The vote on April 17, 1861, was 88 for secession, 55 against. A pro-Union delegate from Orange County was Lewis Burrell Williams of Yatton. A later public referendum confirmed the decision of the convention.

[9] Worth reading on this subject is McPherson's *For Cause and Comrade, Why Men Fought in the Civil War.* For summaries on how the slavery issue had been dividing America for decades, read chapter II ("Mexico Will Poison Us") in McPherson's *Battle Cry of Freedom* and/or chapter 3 ("The Silence") in Ellis' *Founding Brothers,* and/or chapter nine ("Other Persons") in Miller's *The Business of May Next.*

economic systems. That was an unacceptable alternative in 1861, though the North felt little remorse in doing just exactly that a few years later. The South took the position that the slavery issue was one to be resolved after the new Southern Nation had been created and that the slave labor system for all its faults was better than the impoverished squalor of the immigrant-exploiting, crime-fostering, wage peonage system imposed on the northern working class. There was much blustering, posturing, and misinformation on both sides, and there is great wisdom in the one word answer that Pulitzer Prize-winning historian Dr. Douglas Southall Freeman used to give when asked his assessment of the cause of the Civil War: "Politicians."

By the time Lincoln's Emancipation Proclamation of January 1, 1863, made slavery an issue to be decided on the battlefield, the Southern commitment to war was seen as irreversible. There had been too much destruction and there had been too many husbands, fathers, sons, and brothers killed or maimed by then to start negotiating with the invaders. Reinforcing that commitment may have been the fact that Lincoln's proclamation appeared during the Army of Northern Virginia's "Year of Miracles." That year had begun with the Seven Day's Battles that saved Richmond in mid-1862 and ended at Gettysburg almost exactly twelve months later. During that year it appeared to many that Southern independence might actually be won.

## C. The Traditional Home Front Evolves

Once the initial war excitement died down, it seemed clear to the locals that Orange County was not in any immediate danger. Local militia units had promptly gone north to Harpers Ferry to seize Federal supplies and equipment, to organize and train, and to make a closer acquaintance with a discipline-driven former Virginia Military Institute professor named Thomas J. Jackson.[10] Back in Orange, the Hero of Fort Sumter, General P. G. T. Beauregard, passed through on his way north to defend Virginia's borders. On July 21, 1861, the Federals were routed at Manassas/Bull Run,[11] and as the year waned, the Confederate army made plans to winter in north-

---

[10] Some Orange County militia men had been guards at Harpers Ferry for the John Brown trial and execution and had encountered Jackson and his V.M.I. cadets at that time.

[11] Early in the war the Federals tended to name battles by nearby streams. Later, like the Confederates, they usually named battles after nearby communities.

ern Virginia. Local routines were disturbed by the constant passage of men, supplies, and equipment, and the periodic arrival of sick, wounded and dead, but the Real War was "up north." It would come south soon enough.

Shortages of consumer goods surfaced as early as the summer of 1861, and for some items, the situation quickly became acute. Local diarist Fanny Page Hume noted on October 4, "Hattie made an attempt to get a calico dress but could not succeed. What will we all do, all the stores are nearly all empty. Nothing is to be had except at enormous prices."[12] Things only got worse with time, and turning seams, reworking sleeves, and patching worn and rent clothing became the custom. In August 1865 Hannah Garlick Rawlings, then working as a governess at Piedmont Farm in Rapidan, recalled those times to her Pennsylvania sister: "In fact there never was a time-serving politician who underwent as many metamorphases as a garment in the hands of a Southern girl. . . ."[13]

Fanny Hume also found herself having to act as the Confederacy's quartermaster for a brother in service: "A note came from Frank asking for boots, pants, overcoat, quilt and gloves. Mr. Dailey [sic] sent me word that he could not make the boots, neither could Jack nor Wat Jones. Poor fellow! What am I to do."[14]

In 1862, and repeating a decision made at the onset of the American Revolution, the County Fathers laid in a supply of salt for the citizens. Salt was not naturally available locally, and without it a great deal of food, particularly meat, could not be preserved.[15] The county thereafter periodically appointed salt agents to procure and distribute salt to its citizens for the remainder of the war. Fanny's problems also returned in 1862: "Had a letter from Frank dated 'Bunker Hill,' 12 miles from Washington; says he wants shoes and winter clothes."[16] This time Fanny didn't even bother to comment on the enormous and probably impossible task of meeting her

---

[12] Cortada, *Hume Diary* (1861), p. 70.

[13] See "Reconstruction in Orange County, Virginia," 75 *VaMagHisBio* 459.

[14] Cortada, *Hume Diary* (1861), Entry of October 28, p. 75. Alexander Daley was probably still running his shoe factory, but the Confederate government did not allow general public sales of such essential items. Wat Jones was one of the county's free blacks.

[15] The county's representative was instructed to purchase 6,000 bushels of salt "or so much as they will furnish." Order of May 26, 1862. Orange County Minute Book for 1856-67. (Neither the book nor its pages are numbered.)

[16] Grymes, *Hume Diary* (1862), Entry of October 2, p. 155.

brother's needs. By then everybody understood that the only people who had access to such items in any quantity were the enemy.

As the war ground on, the county leaders, with Richmond's authorization and support, undertook to help the county's many "men-less" families.[17] Widows and orphans quickly became a special concern, as death took both the soldier and the soldier's pay from the household. Initially, special commissioners were appointed to call on affected families and to provide them with support payments. Near the end of the war, and possibly taking a realistic view of the worth of Confederate currency, the county leaders not only authorized money payments, but also the distribution of foodstuffs, empowering the commissioners to impress (seize) the needed items if necessary.

## D. Where Have All the Young Men Gone?

The Civil War was not even a year old when "young men" joined the long list of shortages experienced by Orange's citizens. They were in uniform and away. A brief downgrading of the state militia system in the early 1850s had been followed by an 1857 militia law that called for regular musters and training. The local muster fields had once again resounded with martial music and shouted commands as units went through their drills, sounds that mingled with the conversation and applause of the civilian spectators who attended and brought the all-important refreshments. With the start of hostilities, those fields were swept clean.

As soon as the secession ordinance was adopted, Virginia militia units quickly went into state service. There were three Orange County infantry companies, all of whom went into state service on April 17, 1861, the day of the secession vote. All were subsequently incorporated into the 13th Virginia Infantry Regiment. The "Montpelier Guard," which had been active for several years, became Company A. The "Gordonsville Grays," for whom no organization date is presently known, became Company C.[18] The "Barboursville Guard," organized in 1859, became Company F. Com-

---

[17] Example: On October 31, 1863, the Virginia Legislature passed "An Act for the Relief of Indigent Soldiers and Sailors of the State of Virginia Who Have Been or May be Disabled in the Military Service, and the Widows and Minor Children of Soldiers and Sailors Who Have Died or May Hereafter Die in Said Service, and of the Indigent Families of Those Now in the Service."

[18] A 2002 issue of a catalog offering historic artifacts for sale displayed a flag, the design of which contained among other things the wording, "Gordonsville Grays. June 14, 1860." The flag sold during the winter of 2002-2003 for $97,750.00.

pany B was the "Culpeper Minute Men," a storied unit in which Orange residents had served during the early days of the Revolution. Company D was the "Louisa Blues." The 13th also exhibited some of the diversifying effect of the war in that it included one company from Maryland and two from Hampshire County in what would become West Virginia. (Most soldiers on both sides were destined to travel farther and see more of America than either their fathers or their grandfathers.)

The 13th Virginia was part of the force sent into the Valley in the spring of 1862 to fight under that stern disciplinarian they had met at Harpers Ferry, "Stonewall" Jackson. The 13th thus became part of his famed "foot cavalry," which garnered international fame during Jackson's spring 1862 Valley Campaign. At the conclusion of that campaign the 13th went with Jackson to Richmond to join Robert E. Lee and his Army of Northern Virginia. It then participated in every major engagement involving Lee's army until the siege began at Petersburg in the summer of 1864. At that time the 13th was taken back into the Valley where it participated in an offensive which took it to the outer defenses of Washington. Ultimately the Valley forces were crushed, and the remnants of the 13th returned to Petersburg for the winter of 1864-65. The 13th was one of the units surrendered by Lee at Appomattox on April 9, 1865.

The first commander of the 13th was Ambrose Powell Hill of Culpeper, who went on to command the third corps of the Army of Northern Virginia. Following Jackson's death, the 13th was assigned to the second corps under Richard S. Ewell. Numbering 550 men at Harpers Ferry in 1861, the rolls of the 13th list the names of some 1,500 individuals who served in it at one time or another. Following its defeats in the Valley during 1864, the regiment was down to about 90 men. At Appomattox, 63 remained to surrender.[19]

THE ORANGE MEN CONSTITUTING THE "HAZELWOOD VOLUNTEERS" WENT INTO active service only six or eight weeks after the secession vote, but it was already too late to be a part of the 13th Virginia. Almost all of the Hazelwood Volunteers from Orange went into Company C of the 7th Virginia Infantry Regiment. The regiment was primarily from Culpeper, but its first commander was James Lawson Kemper, a Madison native who served a term as Governor of Virginia after the war, then retired to Orange County.

---

[19] Technically, a regiment was supposed to be composed of ten 96-man companies. In practice, a 500-man regiment was considered "full."

The 7th Virginia regiment ultimately became a part of the first brigade of Pickett's division of Longstreet's corps of the Army of Northern Virginia. Kemper, promoted to Brigadier General, led the brigade. As a part of Pickett's division, the 7th was one of the units which marched up Gettysburg's Cemetery Ridge to its destruction on July 3, 1863. During the summer of 1864, the reconstituted but much diminished 7th served in North Carolina for a time, returning to the Army of Northern Virginia just prior to the start of the Petersburg siege. During the retreat to Appomattox, the 7th was among those units cut off and surrounded at Sailor's/Sayler's Creek on April 6, 1865, and the war ended for all but a handful of its surviving members that afternoon.

A CAVALRY COMPANY, THE "ORANGE RANGERS," WAS MUSTERED INTO service at Rhoadesville on May 4, 1861. Shortly thereafter, the company rode to a rendezvous point in Culpeper County, where it became Company I of the 6th Virginia Cavalry Regiment, the "Little Fork Rangers." The 6th saw service all across the state during the war. When Lee was cornered at Appomattox, the 6th broke out and roamed the countryside for more than a week before finally surrendering.

The Reverend Richard T. Davis of St. Thomas' Episcopal Church in Orange was granted a leave of absence by the vestry to ride with the 6th as its chaplain. On his rather frequent visits home, Rev. Davis was accustomed to returning to the pulpit. One such time was noted by Fanny Hume: "Less, Hattie and I walked up to church. Mr. Davis gave us a fine sermon from the text `And He shall come to judge the world.' It was very solemn. The first time I have been to church since it was used as a hospital-it is still very dirty, though it has been repeatedly cleaned. . . ."[20] Those "dirty," presumably bloodstained, floorboards existed as a somber reminder of the war for Reverend Davis and his parishioners long after the fighting had ended. When work was done on the current church floor during 2000, it was discovered that an old floor was under it, almost certainly the one from the Civil War era.

The captain of Company I was Gustavus Judson Browning, who returned after the war to live at Oakley, adjacent to the Fat Nancy trestle and its locally famous train wreck. "Jud" Browning became a featured character in the post-war writings of the widely-known local humorist Dr. George Bagby. Never known to be anything but quietly serious, Browning tolerated Bagby's torrent of tomfoolery without a murmur.

---

[20] Grymes, *Hume Diary*, p. 93, Entry for May 11, 1862.

AN ARTILLERY UNIT, KNOWN VARIOUSLY AS "PEYTON'S BATTERY," "FRY'S Battery," and the "Orange Artillery," was organized March 20, 1861. Its first captain was Thomas Jefferson Peyton, who with his brother, Charles Snyder Peyton, had run Peyton's Mill, a complex of water powered enterprises on the Rapidan two miles downstream from Madison Mills/Barnett's Ford. Peyton's Ford at that location was on what was then a heavily traveled road from Orange to Culpeper which paralleled the Barnett's Ford Road for a ways before joining it. A flood destroyed the mill facilities in April of 1861, but the ford and road remained heavily used throughout the war. Neither exist as such today. Several mill stones were pulled from the Rapidan near the ford in the mid-1900s, and Ellen Peyton Donnelly of Rapidan, a descendant of Charles Snyder Peyton, has one of them.

Thirty days after being issued its guns, the Orange Artillery was in the field in the Peninsula Campaign — much too soon for the men to have learned their complex new trade.[21] While in the Peninsula, Captain Peyton was disabled by illness, and Charles W. Fry assumed command. In July 1863 the Orange Artillery was the first Confederate battery to go into action at Gettysburg. On May 12, 1864, in the initial Federal attack at Spotsylvania's Bloody Angle, half the battery was captured.

ON JULY 1, 1861, A GROUP OF 66 MEN ASSEMBLED NEAR VERDIERSVILLE TO enlist with Captain George Pannill for three months' service. The enlistment term reflected a widely-held belief that the war would be over in one summer and that a person needed to join up right away to have any chance of being a hero. Captain Pannill marched his new recruits to Culpeper, where they became Company K of the 46th Virginia infantry regiment. The company adopted the name "Orange County Minute Men." At the conclusion of their enlistment term, most of the Minute Men joined other local units, while a few stayed on in a re-formed Company K.

Another unit with a significant Orange County connection was Taylor's battery, whose roster during the spring of 1862 listed 33 Orange men among its total complement of 182. The unit was sometimes called "Eubank's Battery," in recognition of its first commander;[22] at other times "the Bath

---

[21] An 1864 field artillery manual in this writer's possession is over 300 pages long. An artilleryman, for example, was supposed to be able to recognize and respond to 39 different bugle calls.

[22] A real Civil War trivia item: Battery commander J. L. Eubank, who retired from field duty for health reasons, became the postmaster of the Army of Northern Virginia.

Artillery," in recognition of the large number of its members coming from the Bath/Berkeley Springs area of what would become West Virginia.

Many more Orange County men volunteered or were conscripted for Confederate service than just those making up the organizations described above, but they were widely scattered among the host of Confederate units which came into being during the Civil War. Orange County historian W. W. Scott, for example, was one of four Orange County natives in the "Black Horse Troop," a Warrenton-based cavalry contingent which became Company H of the 4th Virginia Cavalry. The 4th fought at Gordonsville in December 1864, as well as on many other fronts. Another county native, eighteen-year-old Jaquelin Beverly Stanard, died on April 15, 1864, at New Market, fighting alongside his VMI student cadet classssmates.

In his county history, W. W. Scott began the difficult task of assembling information on Orange's soldiers and came up with some fifteen pages of unit rosters and notes. In her work *Soldiers, Stories, Sites, and Fights,* Patricia Hurst significantly reorganized and supplemented that earlier effort, and in so doing has assembled probably the most complete roster of Orange veterans that can be created. Also, the Regimental History Series project of the H. E. Howard Company of Lynchburg VA has brought into print the histories of most of the Virginia regiments, troops, and batteries in which Orange County men served.

So many of Orange County's young men went off to serve in distant fields that the locals began to feel unprotected. On April 22, 1861, a Home Guard Association was organized out of the "old men and young boys" remaining in the county. The volunteers agreed to meet and drill once a fortnight or oftener, wearing civilian clothes and carrying personally owned weapons. As the South's manpower pool started drying up, expanded conscription laws made most of the youngsters "old enough" and most of the oldsters "young enough," and off they went. Near the end of the war, Orange County again assembled a home guard unit, identified as Company F of the 1st Virginia Battalion Reserves. It wasn't long, however, before they too were ordered off to the trenches at Petersburg.

## E. The Rapidan Line:
## The Home Front Becomes the Front Line

Even with all the hustle and bustle, county residents in 1861 could comfort themselves with the knowledge that neither their persons nor their property were in any real danger. Orange was a rear area, and its citizens were settling into their roles of attentive, anxious, and (mostly) loyal supporters of the boys at the front. Richmond, however, was starting to see things differently.

Following some additional Manassas-type successes elsewhere during the fall of 1861, the Confederacy proceeded to suffer reversals on almost every front except the one in Virginia. Many of those reversals involved the Federals' use of water transport and naval fire power.[23] With the Federals already holding a Chesapeake base in Fort Monroe, with the capture of Richmond being a primary Federal goal — and with too few troops to defend the Confederacy's northeast border to the banks of the Potomac and along the shores of the Chesapeake simultaneously — Virginia looked especially vulnerable.

It was imperative that the Confederate Army of the Potomac (that was its name at the time) be put in a position from which it could move quickly to repulse advances from either the Potomac or the Chesapeake. But where was such a position? Orange County, as it turns out. And why Orange? It was the result of the combination of a number of the natural and man-made features in the county.

First and foremost is that ridge of the Southwest Mountains which traces the northern border of Orange County and serves as the south bank of the Rapidan. It is a natural military breastwork, which the Confederates over time enhanced with multiple lines of trenches, rifle pits, and gun emplacements. By the end of the winter of 1863-64, there was a twenty mile long battle trench along that south bank of the Rapidan, running from Liberty Mills (Somerset) to Morton's Ford (a mile or so east of Palmyra Church in eastern Orange County). That trench, along with its supporting earthworks, camps, and connecting roads, was the heart of what became known as the "Rapidan Line."

---

[23] Fort Clark NC on the Hatteras inlet was taken without resistance on August 27, 1861. Fort Hatteras was captured the next day, leading to the subsequent captures of Roanoke Island and New Bern. Port Royal SC was captured November 7, 1861, and was quickly converted into a home port for the Federal Southern Blockading Squadron. Its fall also led to the capture of the adjacent Hilton Head/Sea Island area. Fort Henry on the Tennessee River and Fort Donelson on the Cumberland River were captured during February 1862, opening those waterways to Federal navigation. Federal transports unloaded troops near Nashville TN on February 24, 1862, and the city was taken without opposition the next day. Also, the Federal blockade of Confederate shipping, initially a nuisance, began to dramatically curtail Confederate imports and exports during the winter of 1861-62. See those successes and others chronicled in Long, *The Civil War Day by Day*.

Protecting the eastern end of the Rapidan Line was the Wilderness, that seventy-square-mile Virginia jungle, which during the over 100 years of its existence had gotten only marginally more passable. Protecting the western end were the bad roads and inhospitable terrain of the Blue Ridge foothills. Efforts to turn the line by either flank would be slowed, giving its defenders ample warning and time to react.

Clark Mountain served the Rapidan Line as its primary observation post and signal station. While having an elevation of only 1,082 feet, the mountain happens to be at the northeasternmost end of the Southwest Mountains. There is no higher mountain visible to the north, east, or south. In those directions, the land falls away from Clark Mountain in a broad plain. Cavalry vedettes and infantry pickets were required to supplement observations from that mountain, but nothing could replace its day-in/day-out usefulness.

Certain man-made features in Orange County also enhanced the military importance of the Rapidan Line. The arrival of railroads in the 1840s and 1850s had led to the development of Gordonsville into a major rail center. The Virginia Central, Richmond's rail lifeline to the Valley, went through Gordonsville. The Orange & Alexandria, running north from Gordonsville through Orange, Rapidan, Culpeper, and Manassas, was a line supporting Confederate advances north (and Federal advances south). Numerous battles were fought in the corridor that railroad served. As the junction point for those two rail lines, Gordonsville was the site of track and equipment maintenance and repair shops, storage yards, warehouses, and rail management offices. Associated with that were a host of local railroad-related enterprises. The railroads were essential to maintaining any meaningful Confederate presence in this region, and in addition to its defense-of-Richmond role, the Rapidan Line was intended to protect them.

Significant highway development had also taken place in Orange County, with the Rockingham and Blue Ridge Turnpikes connecting Gordonsville to the Valley, and with the Orange Turnpike and Orange Plank Road connecting Orange to Fredericksburg. Also, a strategic travel way existed in the form of a graded railroad bed that stretched from Orange to Fredericksburg. The onset of the war had stopped construction before cross ties and track could be laid. During the war the Confederates used portions of that roadbed to move troops with considerable success.

In short, an army behind the Rapidan Line was in a strong defensive position from which it could monitor nearly all of the northern and eastern land routes to Richmond and from which it could move quickly to oppose enemy advances along them. Over time, the importance of the Rapidan Line to the Confederacy grew to the point where General Lee noted in an

April 15, 1864, letter to Confederate President Jefferson Davis: "If I am obliged to retire from this line, either by a flank movement of the enemy or the want of supplies, great injury will befall us."[24] Within three weeks of that letter, Lee and his army had to abandon the Rapidan Line, and Virginia and the Confederacy started to experience the full weight of Lee's prophecy coming to pass.

Near the end of the first winter of war, the Confederacy signaled its decision to pull back to the Rapidan. In late February the just-built Samuel P. Moore Military Hospital in Manassas was dismantled, and it and its patients were moved to Gordonsville. Next came the "retrograde movement" of Confederate General Joe Johnston and his army to the Rapidan. Johnston tarried briefly at Culpeper, but his ultimate destination lay elsewhere.[25] The recently-built Camp Henry at Culpeper was abandoned and dismantled. For practical purposes, the northern border of the Confederacy in our area had become the Rapidan. The folks north of the river were not told that in so many words. They learned about it the hard way.[26]

Local diarist Fanny Page Hume saw great peril in this turn of events. She wrote on March 8, 1862: "Jackson is said to have evacuated Winchester, and part of the Manassas army has fallen back to 'Rappahannock Bridge'[Remington]. Cannon and all kinds of supplies have been sent back to Gordonsville. It is thought all places will be burnt, if they fall back. God help us all if the enemy should get this far."[27]

But Miss Fanny's alarms were premature. In the spring of 1862, "Stonewall" Jackson conducted his brilliant Valley Campaign and turned himself into an international legend in the process. At about the same time, Federal General George McClellan began an attempt to take Richmond from the east. Both actions drew the combatants away from the Rapidan until midsummer. The Federals during this time did occupy Fredericksburg and conduct raids and "scouts" into this area, but Culpeper and Spotsylvania coun-

---

[24] Dowdey/Manarin, Eds., *Wartime Papers,* p. 700.

[25] A portion of Gen. Johnston's March 12, 1862, message to Richmond: "A reserve depot was established at Culpeper Court-House, the stores in which I have ordered to be removed to Gordonsville. I will remain here to cover that operation unless otherwise ordered." O.R., Ser. I, Vol. 5, p. 527.

[26] Some Northern Virginians had spent the winter of 1861-62 in Federally occupied territory, and their experience was chilling. Read Noel Harrison's award-winning article "Atop an Anvil," referenced in the bibliography. For more current reasons, locals have again begun referring to Northern Virginia as "occupied Virginia."

[27] Grymes, *Hume Diary* (1862), pp. 58-59.

ties bore the brunt of that activity. Orange County remained comparatively quiet.

From mid-July to mid-August 1862, things became serious in the Orange area, but then Jackson defeated Federal General John Pope at Cedar Mountain. Following that victory, Jackson pulled back across the Rapidan, camped in the meadow adjacent to Woodley, just south of Orange, and awaited orders from General Lee. Lee brought the rest of his now-named "Army of Northern Virginia" to Orange County and then took it to Manassas once again. He followed up on his victory there with an invasion of the North.

Returning from Maryland in late September 1862, Lee soon learned that Federal forces were concentrating on the Rappahannock River just across from Fredericksburg. Moving to Fredericksburg, Lee developed a defensive position very similar to the Rapidan Line. Marye's Heights took the place of the Southwest Mountain ridge. Telegraph Hill substituted for Clark Mountain. The Richmond, Fredericksburg, & Potomac railroad substituted for the Orange & Alexandria. Possibly not quite as formidable as the Rapidan Line, but good enough. On December 13, 1862, Federal attacks against the Rappahannock Line were repulsed with heavy losses.

In the spring of 1863, the Federals tried to turn Lee out of his Rappahannock defenses in what became known as the Chancellorsville Campaign. The resulting Federal defeat was followed by Lee's second invasion of the North. Calm reigned along the Rapidan, but that was about to change.

On July 3, 1863, Confederate Generals George Pickett, James Pettigrew, and Isaac Trimble sent their troops up Cemetery Ridge at Gettysburg, and the result was a "Fredericksburg in reverse." Supplies were about gone, the army's ranks depleted and exhausted — it was time to go home.

On August 1, General Lee telegraphed Confederate President Jefferson Davis from Culpeper: "I SHALL NOT FIGHT A BATTLE NORTH OF THE RAPIDAN, BUT WILL ENDEAVOR TO CONCENTRATE EVERYTHING BEHIND IT. IT WOULD BE WELL TO SEND ALL REINFORCEMENTS IN RICHMOND TO ORANGE COURT HOUSE."[28] Get ready, Orange County, here they come!

On August 4, General Lee offered a bit more detail to General Samuel Cooper, Adjutant and Inspector General of the Confederate Army: "I could find no field in Culpeper offering advantages for battle, and any taken could be so easily avoided should the enemy wish to reach the south bank

---

[28] Dowdey/Manarin, Eds., *Wartime Papers,* p. 566.

of the Rapidan, that I thought it advisable to retire at once to that bank."[29] Lead elements of the Army of Northern Virginia were behind the Rapidan Line by August 1.[30] Within a few days, all of its divisions were assembled along the Rapidan to re-equip, resupply, and retrain. The strength of that position was obvious, and with the usual exceptions for raids, scouts, skirmishes, ambushes, etc., the Federal army kept its distance.

With little happening along the Rapidan, Lee agreed to Longstreet's corps being detached to duty in Tennessee. That was mid-September, and Lee was not feeling well. By early October, the General was in better health, and he decided to take his remaining two corps and see if he could run the Federals out of Virginia, while at the same time capturing some desperately needed supplies. It is called the Bristoe Station Campaign, which began October 9, 1863, and lasted almost exactly a month. During that campaign, the advance of Lee and his army was turned back at Bristoe Station (just south of Manassas) with significant losses in Hill's corps. Then on November 7, they failed to contain a river crossing at Kelly's Ford and suffered an outright defeat at Rappahannock Station. Lee's already thin ranks were now even further depleted, and his army had been roughly handled in the process. The protection of the Rapidan Line was sorely needed.

The Bristoe Station Campaign marked the last time in the Civil War that Culpeper County would be rejoined with the Confederacy. The Federal occupation of Culpeper, which had been off and on since mid-1862, became continuous for the winter of 1863-64, and the people of Culpeper found themselves in a world vastly different from the one in Orange.[31] The differences between Orange and Culpeper, clearly noticeable up to the mid-twentieth century, have fueled innumerable local discussions. Those differences may be explained in part by what the people in those counties experienced as a direct result of which side of the Rapidan Line they were on during the Civil War.

Upon his return to Orange County after the Bristoe Station Campaign, Lee established his headquarters beside the Orange Turnpike and a little over a mile east of the town of Orange. He had A. P. Hill's third corps

---

[29] *Ibid.,* p. 568.

[30] Pfanz, *A Soldier's Life,* p. 330.

[31] A readable and well-documented report on the experience of Culpeper County in the Civil War is found in Sutherland's *Seasons of War.* Morton's *Marching Through Culpeper,* a historically-based novel, offers a personalized perspective on that same era through the eyes, words, and thoughts of her characters.

holding the Rapidan Line from Liberty Mills to a little north of Rapidan Station. General Ewell's second corps extended the line downstream from there. Hill established his headquarters at Mayhurst, and Ewell at Morton Hall. Mayhurst still stands in the town of Orange, but Morton Hall's ruins are fast disappearing. Lee's headquarters was about where the two corps joined, making him equally accessible to both. The army's Quartermaster and Provost Marshall maintained offices in the town, but Lee proposed to join his men for another winter in the field.

Not surprisingly, General Lee's headquarters was a field tent. It was his practice of long standing, and it would continue well after he left Orange.[32] The previous winter, Lee had written his wife Mary: "The weather has been wretched. More unpleasant than any other part of the winter. The earth has been almost fluid & my tent even muddy."[33] Mud or not, he didn't move. In a letter to Mary the following winter, he offered an explanation/ excuse for his tenting practice: "The people are very kind in giving me invitations to take a room in their house, but they do not know what they ask. I cannot of course go alone or be alone, as a crowd is always around me."[34]

There was something different about the winter in Orange County, however. General Lee had not been a well man for the entire war. He suffered from what he called "rheumatism" and which most doctors studying the sketchy medical record today think was probably angina. There was periodic chest pain, usually triggered by cold weather, and which in its severe stages was accompanied by arm numbness. At Fredericksburg in the spring of 1863, Lee had also experienced what may have been a full-blown heart attack. As the winter of 1863-64 approached, he wrote Mary:[35] "I do not know what I shall do when the winter really comes, I have suffered so from the cold already. I hope I shall get used to it. But I have felt very differently since my attack of last spring, from which I have never recovered."

General Lee's transition into winter was also not without some outside disturbances. The Federal army undertook what is known as the Mine Run Campaign, coming into eastern Orange County on November 26, 1863,

---

[32] After surrendering at Appomattox, Lee started for Richmond. En route he spent one final night in his tent, pitched in the yard of his brother's house.

[33] Dowdey/Manarin, Eds., *Wartime Papers,* p. 419.

[34] *Ibid.,* p. 652.

[35] *Ibid.,* p. 616.

and after some maneuvering in weather that anyone would call "wretched," left the county on December 2. Lee had moved his headquarters tent to the yard of the Rhodes' house at New Verdiersville (the intersection of Routes 20 and 621) during that campaign, but with the Federals gone, it was time to settle into winter quarters for real.[36]

Lee's officers and men took as good a care of their chief as they could. By the time winter really got going, his tent featured a wood floor and a brick fireplace with a chimney. He reported to his wife that actually he was pretty comfortable.[37] Also, there is reason to believe that in spells of very severe weather, the General was prevailed upon to spend a night or two in a nearby home, his reluctance to do so notwithstanding.

When spring came, the armies began preparations to move. At midnight, May 3, 1864, the entire Federal army began marching out of Culpeper County into the Wilderness, just east of the Rapidan Line. Spotswood's old Germanna Ford was, as usual, one of the major crossing points. Some time the next day, General Lee's tent was struck and taken away, leaving the floor, fireplace, and chimney.[38] Lee spent one more night in Orange County, again in the Rhodes' yard at New Verdiersville, and then it was down the Plank Road — and into an eleven-month death struggle with Grant, Meade, and the Army of the Potomac. The man[39] whose concept of and commitment to duty made the war a personal and professional tragedy from the day it started, and whose almost legendary life and character would come to symbolize the virtues of an entire society, was gone, never to reside in Orange County again.

---

[36] The military significance of the two Verdiersvilles came from the fact that the road connecting them afforded the last good chance to switch between the Plank Road and the Turnpike before entering the Wilderness.

[37] *Ibid,* p. 652.

[38] As a boy, the late Wallace Walters used to play around the remains of the camp. Later, as the features of the camp began to disappear, Walters and his friends erected a small monument on the site. It is located on private property, approximately a mile off of Route 20.

[39] Separating the real Lee from the Lee created by the myth-makers is a difficult task. One aid is Flood's *Lee: the Last Years.* Mr. Flood details the post-war life of Lee, when the uniform had been put away, the army gone, and Lee had to stand or fall on his own. The man was not without faults, but he was still magnificent.

## F. Into the Wilderness One Last Time

While Lee and the third corps of his army left Orange County via the plank road (Route 621) on May 5, 1864, his second corps remained in the county, traveling east on the Orange Turnpike. Early on the morning of May 5, that second corps, commanded by Richard S. Ewell, arrived at Saunders' Field, not much over two miles from Wilderness Run and the Spotsylvania County line. Saunders' Field is now a part of the Fredericksburg and Spotsylvania National Military Park. Where today's Route 20 runs through it, the highway is on the roadbed of the old Swift Run Gap Turnpike, locally called the "Orange Turnpike," the western end of which underlies today's Main Street in Orange. The Park has now cleared Saunders' Field on the south side of the road to its wartime dimensions.[40]

Under orders to wait and allow A. P. Hill's third corps to come up on the plank road (about 2.5 miles to the south) to a position approximately parallel to theirs, the second corps units used the time to dig in along the western edge of the field. Lee's plan generally was to tie the Union army down in the Wilderness with his second and third corps, and when General Longstreet and his first corps arrived, see what opportunities presented themselves. Longstreet, recently back from a winter campaign in Tennessee, had been camped south of Gordonsville. His corps was roughly a day's march farther away from the Wilderness than the other two. Even after Longstreet arrived, Lee's army would still be outnumbered almost two to one, but Lee intended to use the Wilderness vegetation and terrain to eliminate the increasingly effective Union cavalry and artillery from the coming battle and to disrupt Federal attempts at massed infantry assaults.

Near midday May 5, 1864, Union troops launched an attack across the dry overgrowth of Saunders' Field, initiating the Battle of the Wilderness. After some early success, the Federals were repulsed, but only back to their own defensive lines. Subsequent attacks by both sides only succeeded in strewing Saunders' Field and the adjacent Wilderness with dead and wounded, whereupon the portion of the field south of the turnpike caught fire. The shrieks and screams of wounded trapped in the flames and the sound of their cartridge boxes exploding shook even hardened soldiers.

---

[40] The Park Service has also laid out a Saunders' Field battlefield walk originating at the information shelter on the north side of Route 20. Is not a difficult walk and it rewards Civil War buffs and outdoor lovers alike. A Civilian Conservation Corps (CCC) camp building, left over from the Depression, will be seen on that trail.

Later in the afternoon, two soldiers from opposing sides who had been trapped together in a ditch running through the field, grew sufficiently displeased with each other's company to step out into the turnpike and engage in a fist fight. Combat generally ceased while this spectacle held the attention of Yank and Reb alike. Following that personal war, the general war started up again.

General Ewell was able to conduct a successful defense of his position on the turnpike during the fighting on both May 5 and 6. A. P. Hill on the Plank Road (at that point in Spotsylvania County) did not fare nearly as well. By nightfall on May 5, his third corps was "fought out," and Longstreet was going to have to relieve it. On the morning of May 6, before Longstreet arrived, the Federals attacked and began to rout Hill's men. When Longstreet appeared, he was able to check the Federal attack and launch one of his own.

Longstreet's attack met with considerable initial success, but then the general was severely wounded by friendly fire. The pause while new leadership assumed command and the attack reorganized was enough to allow the Federals to regroup and hold their ground. When Longstreet's condition was stable enough to permit moving him, he was taken back to Meadowfarm in Orange County, where he stayed briefly before taking a train out of Orange to a more secure place of recuperation.[41]

On a comparatively quiet May 7, the leadership of the opposing armies came to the same conclusion: the enemy held too strong a position to attack successfully. By nightfall, both armies were heading to Spotsylvania Court House. The Rapidan Line stood abandoned, and the Army of Northern Virginia was gone, marching on roads that would ultimately lead to Appomattox.

## G. No Battle was Unimportant if You Were in it

Orange County's portion of the Battle of the Wilderness is easily the most significant engagement that took place in the county. It was, however, by no means the only one. Federal efforts to force the Confederates out of the Rapidan and Rappahannock defenses turned the corridor be-

---

[41] Erasmus Taylor of Meadowfarm and Spring Garden had become Longstreet's Adjutant while the corps was in Tennessee. Taylor stayed on to the end of the war, and his brief but interesting memoirs are on file at the Orange County Historical Society.

Ellwood. A 1799 insurance policy showed it completed except for porches. Now a property of the National Park Service, the residence has been the backdrop for its fair share of eastern Orange County's colonial, Revolutionary, and Civil War history. Over the years it has hosted among others Light Horse Harry Lee, the Marquis de Lafayette, Confederate wounded, Federal generals Burnside and Warren, and U. S. President Warren Harding. The Orange/Spotsylvania line runs within yards of the house. Photographed by Bernice Walker. Reproduced with permission.

tween Orange and Fredericksburg into the most heavily fought-over ground in America. The few action summaries which follow will still have to leave out the hundreds of smaller engagements that were constantly taking place between and around the major battles.[42]

APPROXIMATELY TWO MILES NORTHEAST OF LOCUST GROVE, EAST OF ROUTE 611, is a property called Payne's Farm. On November 27, 1863, during the Mine Run Campaign, a major battle was fought there between a Confederate division of 5,300 men and two Federal corps amassing some 33,000

---

[42] For instance, there isn't space for the stories of how Stonewall Jackson's amputated arm wound up being buried at Ellwood; of the July 17, 1862, occupation of the town of Orange; or of the numerous skirmishes throughout the county. For a lively and vastly more extensive presentation on Orange County actions, see: Hurst, *Soldiers, Stories, Sites, and Fights.*

men. This was again in a portion of the Wilderness, and the Federals were unable to get a good assessment of the force opposing them. Also, the Federals had already been lost twice in the web of roads, paths and trails through the thickets, and they seemed to be in no hurry to leave the Payne's Farm clearing and revisit that mess.

The Battle of Payne's Farm was yet another disruption in the already much-disrupted plans of Union General George Meade and his Army of the Potomac to mount a year-end offensive against the Confederates. The hope had been to at least force the enemy out of the Rapidan Line and to relieve the enormous pressure from Washington on Meade and his army to DO SOMETHING to follow up on their successes in the recently-concluded Bristoe Station Campaign.

Meade's Mine Run Campaign, which lasted from November 26 to December 2, 1863, turned into as much of a losing struggle against the Virginia winter and Orange County mud as it did against the Confederate army. Meade finally gave up and ordered his cold, wet, and exhausted troops back to Culpeper County for the winter. The Confederates had fared little better, and the men were glad to return to their camps on the Rapidan.

IN THE SPRING OF 1864, MEADE AND HIS ARMY RETURNED, THIS TIME accompanied by General U. S. Grant, the newly-appointed overall commander of all Federal forces. With the Mississippi cleared, Grant saw the defeat of the Army of Northern Virginia as the final step to a complete Federal victory, and he had attached his headquarters to the Army of the Potomac. Grant had some strong opinions about how to wage war, and beginning with the Battle of the Wilderness, Meade's army essentially fought Grant's war in Virginia.

With the Battle of the Wilderness, Grant initiated his Overland Campaign against Lee and the Army of Northern Virginia, a campaign which continued in varying formats until Lee surrendered eleven months later. Saunders' Field showcased Grant's willingness to hurl vast numbers of men at Lee's army and trade losses, employing what President Lincoln termed the "awful arithmetic." Grant knew other ways to fight, but in Lee he had an opponent who not only made few mistakes but who also was legendary in his ability to recover from the ones he did make. Grant's appointment as overall Federal commander did contain a benefit for Orange County, because he supported General Meade's request to shift the Army of the Potomac's primary mode of transportation from railroads to coastal shipping. That change spared Orange County many traumatic months of existence as some version of a Federal transportation/ supply center.

WITH FEDERAL GENERAL MCCLELLAN'S 1862 PENINSULA CAMPAIGN bogging down, Lincoln and his advisors had assembled an "Army of Virginia" out of various available units and placed it, as well as McClellan's army, under the command of General John Pope. The plan was for Pope to move south through central Virginia, destroying the Gordonsville and Charlottesville rail centers, and then assisting McClellan if possible. Pope moved slowly, and Lee and the Confederates had time to bottle up McClellan on the James River, freeing Jackson to come north and, in Lee's words, "suppress Pope."

On August 2, 1862, there was a cavalry battle in Main Street Orange, and while it was not a large affair, it was located where it got the full attention of the locals. On the morning of that day, Federal cavalry stormed into Orange from the east, along the turnpike. They had briefly occupied the town without opposition on July 17. Now, however, Stonewall Jackson was at Gordonsville, and A. P. Hill's division was on the way to reinforce him. Jackson was almost ready to take on Pope. The opposing infantry and artillery units were still miles apart, but their cavalry had been skirmishing here and there for the last week or so. On August 2, they made the residents of Orange an involuntary audience to another of their meetings.

The initial fighting on August 2 took place in Main Street, and its narrow width allowed the numerically inferior Confederates to hold their own and buy time until help arrived. The Federal advance stalled right at today's Main Street/Madison Road intersection. About then William F. "Grumble" Jones and elements of the 7th Virginia Cavalry entered the fray.

Jones hit the Federals on the front and flank and initially chased them out of town. Once in the open, however, the Federals reorganized, and the fact that they vastly outnumbered the Confederates was obvious. Also, having learned a bit about the roads in and around the settlement, they were ready to use those numbers. The Confederates were hustled through and out the other side of Orange in fairly short order. At that point the Federals broke off their pursuit and busied themselves with poking around the town and thoroughly upsetting the residents. Before dark the enemy was gone. Diarist Fanny Page Hume reported in part for that day: "A sharp fight took place in the Village; a Yankee Colonel or Major was killed just before Mr. Robinson's door & many were wounded on both sides."[43]

---

[43] Grymes, *Hume Diary* (1862), p. 129. The T. A. Robinson house was in the northeast corner of the Main Street/Madison Road intersection.

ON DECEMBER 23, 1864, THE BATTLE OF BELL'S MOUNTAIN PASS WAS fought. It marked the repulse of the final attempt by Federal forces to capture Gordonsville. The pass is located at the point where the Blue Ridge Turnpike (Route 231) crosses today's Cameron Mountain. (Bell's Mountain became "Cameron Mountain" after its purchase in the 1870s by Col. Alexander Cameron.) The battle was the climax of "Sheridan's Christmas Raid," undertaken by Alfred T. A. Torbert, the Chief of Cavalry under General Philip Sheridan, overall commander of the Federal forces in the Valley.

Sheridan's interest in Gordonsville had been prompted by intelligence received to the effect that the town was largely undefended. Washington also urged the capture of Gordonsville and the destruction of its rail facilities. Subduing Confederate resistance in the Valley during the fall of 1864 took first priority, however, and the intelligence was old news by the time it was acted on. On December 19 Sheridan finally dispatched Torbert and some 5,000 troopers to Gordonsville. He telegraphed Washington to the effect that the men were on the way but not to expect great things.

Enduring snow, sleet, and freezing rain, plus all of the other inconveniences and discomforts of a Virginia winter, Torbert's men forced a crossing of the Rapidan at Liberty Mills (Somerset) after dark on December 22. The defenders of the Liberty Mills crossing had delayed the Federals by burning what was the last covered bridge in the region and by occupying and expanding the Rapidan Line earthworks on the Orange County side of the river. During the hours consumed by Federal cavalry columns to reach and cross fords above and below Liberty Mills, units of the main Confederate army at Petersburg began moving to counter the threat.

The next morning, Torbert's men resumed their push to Gordonsville, driving a mixture of Confederate regular cavalry and home guard troops up the Turnpike ahead of them. At Bell's Mountain, the Confederates dug in, and initial Federal probes were repulsed. Frontal assaults on prepared defensive positions during the Civil War were almost always a disaster for the attackers, and Torbert prudently ordered another flanking maneuver. Before the movement could be completed, a brigade of South Carolinians arrived from Richmond by train, creating a force that Torbert deemed inadvisable to take on. He withdrew to the Valley, having lost seven men and 258 horses.

County historian W.W. Scott, a member of the Black Horse Troop of the 4th Virginia Cavalry, participated in the repulse and noted with some satisfaction that the Confederates had tricked Torbert into pulling back. Scott wrote that the defenders took an available locomotive, backed it up the tracks quietly and then, whistle screaming, roared into Gordonsville to a greeting of martial band music and the cheers of locals, all in on the ruse. The Confederates apparently repeated the ploy several times to give the appearance of a huge force arriving from Richmond. Torbert for his part reported seeing the South Carolinians filing into the defenses, but then that sight could have also been staged. In any event, the Federals, particularly their mounts, had a generally miserable time of it, and Gordonsville escaped occupation once again.

ON THE MORNING OF FEBRUARY 6, 1864, UNION TROOPS CROSSED THE Rapidan at Morton's Ford, right at the far eastern end of the Rapidan Line. The assaulting force was quickly bottled up, thanks in part to the fact that the Confederates guarding the ford had just been relieved, and both the old and new guard details manned the defenses. Confederate second corps commander Richard Ewell also hurried over from his headquarters at nearby Morton Hall and ordered up additional reinforcements. After a day of taking losses, the Federals pulled back across the river during the night.

At some point after sunset on the 6th, either a Federal detachment skirmished its way upstream to Raccoon Ford or Federal cavalry crossed directly at the ford. In any event, much of the Orange County side of that settlement was put to the torch. This act dealt a significant blow to a river crossing and a commercial center that had thrived from the earliest days of the county. On the Culpeper side today a road to the ford site and a small settlement remain. On the Orange County side, Route 611 and a house or two are in the vicinity of the ford. That's all that remains.

Some time on February 6 or 7, Federal cavalry under the command of General Wesley Merritt arrived at Barnett's Ford beside Madison Mills. The troopers were being called upon to threaten a river crossing and keep the Confederates there from reinforcing the Morton's Ford defenders. A telegram from Merritt reporting on his activities described the roads in the area as "terrible" and expressed concern that his command could possibly run afoul of Confederate infantry on its return. One of the several young Union leaders referred to as "boy generals," Merritt found that Barnett's Ford in February 1864 offered no opportunities to showcase his talents.

It turned out that the Battle of Morton's Ford was supposed to have been a feint, designed to occupy the Confederates on the Rapidan while General Butler, far to the southeast at Fort Monroe, made a dash to Richmond. A politically appointed general of ordinary ability, Butler had lost his nerve and called off the raid. The Union losses at Morton's Ford had gone for nothing. Federal General John Sedgwick, in charge of the Army of the Potomac during General Meade's illness-extended leave, complained

Built in 1860, the Gordonsville Exchange Hotel oversaw one of the busiest rail centers outside of Richmond. The building was pressed into Confederate service during the Civil War and became the headquarters of a huge receiving hospital complex. Now the centerpiece property of Historic Gordonsville, Inc., the former hotel houses an excellent museum. Photo by Bernice Walker. Reproduced with permission.

extensively about the futility of the attack, both before and after it took place. It subsequently took the combined efforts of Generals Meade and Grant to save the competent and well-liked Sedgwick from the wrath of an embarrassed Washington.

Another sharp fight took place at Morton's Ford on October 11, 1863. Two days earlier, Lee and his army had begun their attempt to march around the Federal right via Madison Court House in the opening moves of the Bristoe Station Campaign. The initial Federal response was to make a reconnaissance "in force" of both Morton's and Raccoon fords, leading to small but briefly intense battles at both places. The force left behind by the Confederates was sufficient to hold the fords, but the Federals still learned enough to make them hurry off to catch up with their army. Fords all along the Rapidan Line were natural focal points for numerous small actions. For example, on July 29, 1862, Federal cavalry forced a crossing at Barnett's Ford, then formed a skirmish line in the front lawn of William Clark's home, Willow Grove. They exchanged fire with Confederates on the low ridge across from them for several hours before withdrawing. Characteriz-

ing such actions as small or routine provided little comfort to the participants. No battle was unimportant if the metal was singing and buzzing
around your ears.

One gauge of the level of military activity in our region is the number
of casualties being produced. The only surviving patient register of the
Gordonsville Receiving Hospital shows that there were 23,642 admissions
between June 1, 1863, and May 5, 1864.[44] That latter date was the first day
of Grant's Overland Campaign, and the record-keepers may have been
overwhelmed by the flood of Wilderness and Spotsylvania casualties. As
the war moved farther south, however, admissions were described as drop-
ping to "a trickle." The only other known surviving official record of the
hospital from that time is Prescription Book #2, containing entries from
May 1864 through March 1865. Some 700 patients are identified in
that record.[45]

Following the Battle of the Wilderness, the main Federal and Confederate forces left the Orange County area, and for the remainder of the war
the county was technically behind the Union lines. Grant and Meade were
out to crush Lee and capture Richmond, however, not occupy territory, so
a certain amount of what passed for calm returned to the county. The greatest
post-Wilderness excitements were caused by the periodic appearances of
Federal raiding parties, the brief return of the Confederate horse artillery
during the winter of 1864-65, and "Sheridan's Christmas Raid" aimed at
Gordonsville. For the most part, Orange residents were able to take a deep
breath and ponder their decidedly uncertain future.

## H. Spies, Spies, SPIES!

Civil War spy stories often seem to dwell on personalities such as Belle
Boyd and Allan Pinkerton, as though becoming a public figure was the
best way to do undercover work. In fact, there were several very capable
northern spies and informers who worked in the Orange County area at
one time or another. Because they were good at what they did, we knew
little to nothing about them until the archives of the Bureau of Military

---

[44] The register is at the Museum of the Confederacy in Richmond.

[45] The prescription book is in the rare book collection of the Alderman Library at
the University of Virginia. Historic Gordonsville volunteers are working on creating
a list of the patients' names shown in that record.

Information (BMI) were discovered in 1959, leading to the publishing of a book detailing their accomplishments.[46]

The BMI was not formed until the late winter of 1863 when Federal General Joseph Hooker took over the Army of the Potomac, but its archives also held information on earlier Federal intelligence gathering efforts. The information in hand also directed investigation into other archives and private paper collections, thus helping to fill in the record. Some of that record involves Orange County.

BY MID-JULY 1862, IT WAS CLEAR THAT THE FOUR-MONTH CRAWL OF General McClellan and the Army of the Potomac up the peninsula towards Richmond had been wasted effort. Also by then General Pope and his "Army of Virginia" were doing their own crawl south along the Orange & Alexandria Railroad corridor. The thing that wasn't clear to the Federals was what the Confederates were doing in response to all this. Pope in particular directed that his field commanders be extra diligent in gathering information, including the sending of spies out among the enemy. Franz Sigel, a St. Louis school administrator-turned general, produced a spy for Pope who probably saved the army — temporarily.

The spy was Thomas O. Harter, a sergeant in the 1st Indiana Cavalry, whose civilian occupation had been as a railroad locomotive engineer. After volunteering, Harter was given money, civilian clothes, and directions to assess enemy activity in the area between Staunton and Gordonsville. His spy training was apparently to be "on the job," and initially things did not go well.

Harter was arrested near Staunton and thrown into a Winchester jail for two weeks. By the time he arrived in Richmond for further questioning, his story about being a refugee looking for work on the railroad had gotten much better. He succeeded in talking himself out of his handcuffs and into a job running trains for the Confederacy. It probably helped that there was a huge need for Harter's kind of expertise right at that very moment, a need which fit in neatly with his spying assignment.

---

[46] The single most important source of information for this section comes from Edwin Fishel's *The Secret War for the Union*. In his introduction, Mr. Fishel reports that "researchers" who have gone through the BMI archives since his discovery of them have so ransacked the repository as to make him believe that it might now be impossible to find all the information which was available to him when he wrote his book.

By the time Harter had reached Richmond, Jackson had already defeated a portion of Pope's army at Cedar Mountain in Culpeper County. Jackson had then pulled back into Orange County while the full strength of Pope's army concentrated at Culpeper. Pope next moved into the southeastern end of Culpeper County to await additional reinforcements coming by water from the peninsula. The idea was to shorten their overland march from a river landing point. What it also did, however, was insert his army into the "vee" between the Rapidan and Rappahannock rivers and leave it vulnerable to attack.

What Harter learned was that Lee did intend to attack and crush Pope before the peninsula troops could arrive, and for that purpose, the bulk of the Confederate troops remaining near Richmond were being moved to Orange County as quickly as possible. From the train load of troops Harter took to Gordonsville, he learned that Pope was to be attacked as soon as sufficient Confederate troops were on hand. The soldiers there were already poised behind Clark Mountain, waiting for the order to push across the Rapidan and bottle up Pope's army.

Harter decided he had learned enough, and he fell in with a Confederate unit marching from Gordonsville to Clark Mountain. Once there, and as soon as it was dark, Harter swam the Rapidan and quickly made contact with Federal pickets. Before morning, his report had reached General Pope, and orders for a withdrawal of the army were issued. Additional intelligence on the Confederate buildup came in during the day, not the least of which were the dispatches captured along with J.E.B. Stuart's hat at New Verdiersville, but Pope was already on the move by then.

LOCAL CIVILIAN INFORMERS WERE A VALUABLE SOURCE OF INTELLIGENCE TO the Bureau of Military Information. The dedicated ones could be given some instruction, which converted them into resident spies whose occupations concealed their activities. There were a number of disgruntled unionists lying low among the local residents, and one or two did go to work for the BMI.

One of the best was a farmer named Isaac Silver. Originally from New Jersey, Silver owned a small farm in Spotsylvania County on the Plank Road southwest of Zoan Church. He also had some sort of business interests in Orange County, possibly rented land, which provided the excuse for extensive traveling through our area. His reports of Confederate unit strengths and positions were among the more accurate received by Colonel Sharpe, Director of the BMI.

Silver had already proven his worth during the winter of 1862-63, when the Army of Northern Virginia wintered along the Rappahannock. By the spring of 1863, Colonel Sharpe knew the location and strength of every regiment in Lee's army, thanks in great measure to Silver's untiring efforts. When the Army of Northern Virginia returned to the Rapidan Line in Orange County in August 1863, Silver was ready. His reports, written in plain, albeit unlettered English, and delivered by one of his farm workers, again provided Sharpe with valuable information. Silver's spying was occasionally suspected and he was arrested at least once, but nothing came of it. His reporting continued until the end of the war.

A SPY WHO HAD AN ENORMOUS IMPACT ON ORANGE COUNTY WHILE PROBably never setting foot in it during the war was Samuel P. Ruth. Ruth was the Superintendent of the Richmond, Fredericksburg and Potomac Railroad. His offices were in Richmond, but his job made him aware of much of what was going on in our area. The spy ring Ruth operated in Richmond, along with another ring in that city operated by Elizabeth ("Crazy Bet") Van Lew, provided some of the most important strategic intelligence the Federal government received during the war.

Ruth also had a specific impact on Lee and his army when they were wintering here in 1863-64. His job put him in a position to delay and disrupt the flow of supplies to Orange County, and he made the most of it. An overworked single track railroad operating patched-up equipment over a badly deteriorated road bed had its own built-in delays and disruptions, but Ruth apparently took advantage of opportunities to make matters worse. After the war, he was officially commended for his efforts to starve Lee out of the Rapidan Line.

General Lee suspected something was not right, and he wrote more than one of his invariably respectful notes to Richmond during that winter, complaining that his men were starving and freezing while he understood that other Southern armies were faring much better.[47] Early in 1864, Lee publicly apologized to his army for the deplorable supply situation.[48] What-

---

[47] A sample: "I have been mortified to find that when any scarcity existed this was the only army in which it is found necessary to reduce the rations. . . . I understand that at the present time the army of General Johnston is receiving full rations of meat, bread, rice, molasses, and some whiskey, while in this army only a quarter of a pound of salt and three-quarters of a pound of fresh meat are being issued. . . . I am always glad to hear of troops receiving abundance of provisions at any point, but think all ought to fare alike, if possible." From a letter to the Commissary General dated 5 January 1864. Dowdey/Manarin, *Wartime Papers,* p. 648.

[48] General Order No. 7, Dated 22 January 1864.

ever Richmond was doing, if anything, wasn't helping. As bad as it evidently was, the gritty, dedicated soldiers stuck it out, with many referring to their winter in Orange County as their "Valley Forge."

## I. Wars Within the War

There were times when the Civil War became very personal for some of its participants. The fist fight in Saunders' Field during the first day of the Battle of the Wilderness was one such personal war. There were countless others, with several memorable ones occurring in Orange County. Two in fact happened on the same property, the Higgerson Farm, now part of the Fredericksburg and Spotsylvania National Military park. The farm is located on Hill-Ewell Drive a little over a mile south of Saunders' Field. The widow Permelia Higgerson and her children were living there when the Battle of the Wilderness began in May 1864.

The first indication that Permelia had of her being in the middle of a battle came when troops of Federal General James Wadsworth's division appeared on her farm. They were part of the Federal attacking force which was initiating the Wilderness fighting. Permelia didn't have any use for a war. Life was hard enough as it was. Her protests that General Lee was nowhere around and that they should go away were met with grins and chuckles, as her fences were pulled down and her garden trodden underfoot. She then announced loudly (and rather profanely) that they would be coming back before long, running like rabbits. Laughter.

A short time later, with their lines broken and Confederates hard on their heels, the Federal troops scrambled back cross the Higgerson clearing. The survivors were a while getting over the sound of Permelia's cackling laughter mingling with the noise of combat.

Her personal war won, Permelia's compassion for fellow suffering human beings returned. When the fighting had moved away, she took in several wounded Federals to nurse them, her earlier tirades notwithstanding. One had smallpox, and son Benjamin Higgerson caught the disease and died. She buried him on a nearby hill and marked his grave with upturned stones. After the war, Permelia remarried and moved west. Hopefully, she found the better life she deserved.

The Higgerson Farm was also the scene of the concluding acts of a drama that has come to be called "van Valkenburg's Revenge." It had begun almost eighteen months earlier during the December 13, 1862, Battle of Fredericksburg.

On that December 13, James D. van Valkenburg was a company level officer in the 61st Georgia infantry regiment. His regiment was fighting at the far southern end of the Fredericksburg battlefield, and it had gotten itself into a jam. The 61st and several other regiments had pursued retreating Federals out onto a broad plain in front of the main Confederate line and had become the target of concentrated Federal artillery fire. The enemy infantry had also received support, and further advance was out of the question. For the most forward of the Confederate troops, a retreat in the midst of the cross-fire was equally unthinkable.

Van Valkenburg and some of his men wound up pinned down in a stream bed. They found themselves joining a group of Federal soldiers who had earlier sought the same shelter. After some argument, cooler heads prevailed, and it was agreed that whichever army wound up controlling that stream bed would determine who was whose prisoner. The soldiers then settled down to wait, conversing with their enemy counterparts, sharing canteens, writing notes home — anything to pass the time. After the fighting died down, Federal pickets advanced beyond the stream bed, and van Valkenburg and the other Confederates surrendered. Their companions, and now captors, were members of the 7th Pennsylvania Volunteer Infantry Regiment. The prisoner parole and exchange convention was in effect in 1862, and van Valkenburg was eventually exchanged for one or more Federal prisoners held by the Confederates.

On the first day of the Battle of the Wilderness (May 5, 1864) van Valkenburg was a Major in the 61st Georgia and participating in the rout of Federal General James Wadsworth's division across the Higgerson Farm. The Wilderness vegetation and terrain broke up the pursuit by the 61st, and van Valkenburg was finally left with just a couple dozen men. Everybody else was out in the bushes somewhere. About then van Valkenburg learned that a Federal unit had appeared in the Higgerson clearing behind them, but that it was just standing there, doing nothing. Later it was learned that the unit had been sent to join Wadsworth's attack, but having found no one where they were supposed to be and with fighting going on in the thickets behind them, they had stopped to try to sort things out. At that moment, van Valkenburg appeared.

Taking a few of his tiny force with him and leaving the rest in the edge of the woods, van Valkenburg went out to the Federal unit. He asked for the commanding officer, and a Federal colonel was pointed out. Van Valkenburg approached the colonel and delivered a surrender ultimatum. The ultimatum was summarily rejected, and a heated discussion began.

The point at which van Valkenburg realized that he was dealing with his old captors, the 7th Pennsylvania, is not certain. He probably spotted their regimental flag sometime during the proceedings. Evidently none of his former captors recognized him, and he elected to not add anything else to an already tense situation.

With negotiations going nowhere, van Valkenburg turned to the woods and shouted to his brigade commander that this Federal unit was refusing to surrender. Of course neither the brigade commander nor his brigade were anywhere nearby, but the woods began to ring with shouted commands and the sounds associated with a large unit being readied for attack. That was enough for the colonel, and he surrendered his command.

After the 7th Pennsylvania had stacked arms and moved away from the stacks, the rest of van Valkenburg's little rag-tag command came sauntering out into the clearing. They had been the source of all the impressive military sounds in the woods. The mortification of the Federals was extreme. Men loudly cursed their officers. One of the color bearers who had surrendered his flag collapsed to the ground, weeping. Van Valkenburg had won his private war. There was an unfortunate and cruel twist to the story. The prisoner parole and exchange convention was not in effect in the spring of 1864, and the 7th Pennsylvania wound up in Southern prison camps.

Somerset Plantation is almost at the opposite end of Orange County from the Higgerson Farm[49]. In the private war which took place at Somerset, a 16-year old girl took on 5,000 Federal cavalrymen — and won.

In the 1840s Ebenezer Goss of Albemarle County had bought Somerset, a tract of rich farm land lying along the Blue Ridge Turnpike (Route 231). When the war started, Goss did not volunteer, and he bought a substitute when the first Conscription Act was passed. Farming, not fighting, made sense to him. By 1864, however, the Confederacy was scraping the bottom of the manpower barrel and the next hike in the conscription age caught Ebenezer. His wife had just delivered a baby, and she had not had an easy time of it. She was going to be confined to bed for some time, but Ebenezer had to go.

The management of Somerset thus devolved on the eldest child, 16-year-old Anne Carter "Nannie" Goss. Late in 1864 Nannie got her test of fire. Word came that the Yankees were coming up the Turnpike and would be at Somerset before long. The timing of this means that it had to be General Torbert on his "Christmas Raid" to Gordonsville. Nannie got the

---

[49] There is another Somerset in the county, called "Somerset of Flat Run." That property is near Germanna. See: Miller, *Antebellum Orange*.

men to take all the large animals except for her riding pony up into the hills behind the farm. She gathered the women and children in the main house, putting the pony in the basement. Then they waited. The next morning's light revealed a small town of Federal tents in the front pasture, and before long there was banging on the front door.

Shouts through the door that there was nothing inside worth stealing just led to more banging, so Nannie called for the pony to be brought up out of the basement. Slipping out the back, Nannie mounted her pony and galloped around the house and down to the tents. She rode to the tent with all the flags in front of it, and a guard there demanded to know her business. Her business was with the commanding officer, who soon appeared. Nannie explained what was going on at the house, and the officer called for his horse. The two rode back to the house. The door was opened, and the officer was invited to inspect the premises.

Satisfied with her representations, the officer placed a guard at the Somerset house, and it was not looted. Sixteen-year-old Nannie had won as much of her war as she wanted to. She had saved the family property. In 1874, Anne Carter "Nannie" Goss married Robert S. Walker of Woodberry Forest, and they are this writer's paternal grandparents.

Written accounts from multiple sources substantiate much of the detail of the Higgerson and van Valkenburg stories.[50] The Goss story, on the other hand, still exists as one of the thousands of local, traditional legends. Some are totally imaginary. In the Goss story, we know that something along those lines happened, but the details are not yet (and maybe can never be) firmly established.

## J. Something Lost, Something Gained

The Civil War was fought in an era when a person was considered undressed, indeed exposed, without a hat on when outdoors. The sight of a bare-headed J.E.B. Stuart riding around in Orange County on August 18, 1862, then, was something that didn't pass unnoticed. The actual details of how he came to be hatless were a source of even greater mirth at Stuart's expense. This is how it all came about.

Following Jackson's victory over Federal General John Pope's "Army of Virginia" at Cedar Mountain on August 9, General Lee decided to seize

---

[50] *Blue & Gray* magazine, April 1995, pp. 59-60; Rhea, *Battle of the Wilderness*, pp. 157-167.

the opportunity to destroy that army before it could be reinforced by troops returning from McClellan's failed Peninsula Campaign. Pope's three division commanders were Irving McDowell, whom the Confederates had drubbed soundly at Manassas in 1861; Nathaniel Banks, whom Jackson had thrashed both in the Valley and again at Cedar Mountain; and Franz Sigel, a "political general" who wasn't expected to provide much in the way of a challenge.

Pope had also moved his army into the southeastern corner of Culpeper County, down into the Great Fork between the Rapidan and Rappahannock Rivers. He was positioning himself in anticipation of McClellan's troops disembarking from ships on the Potomac or Rappahannock and marching to reinforce him. Pope knew that he was vulnerable to an attack, but he figured that he would be reinforced and gone before Lee could react. Like a number of generals who faced Lee during the War, Pope seriously underestimated the speed with which Lee could move his army. He also was about to learn that McClellan, smoldering at being replaced by Pope as overall commander, was moving slower in retreat than he did on the advance.

Lee began moving his army to Gordonsville as quickly as feet, hooves, and worn-out rail equipment could manage. Once there, the troops were ordered to assemble on the south flank of Clark Mountain and its accompanying Southwest Mountain ridge. An attack launched from that position would have the army across the Rapidan and trapping Pope in the Great Fork in a matter of hours. The attack was initially planned for August 18; however, some units were not in position, and Lee ordered a postponement to August 20.[51] In the interim, J.E.B. Stuart and the Confederate cavalry were to make a reconnaissance in force, possibly resulting in another daring ride around an enemy army, just as he had done a couple of months earlier to McClellan.

In the early morning hours of August 18, Stuart was dozing on the front porch of the Catlett Rhodes' house, awaiting the arrival of division commander Fitzhugh Lee and the additional cavalry he would bring with him. The Catlett Rhoades' house was located at New Verdiersville, in the southwest corner of the intersection of today's Routes 20 and 621. Route 621 at that time was the Orange Plank Road. The Rhoades were Southern

---

[51] During this pause, Jackson had three deserters executed near Mt. Pisgah Church, the first, but by no means the last, such executions in his Corps. See "So Far From God and so Near to Stonewall Jackson,"111 *Va. Mag. His/Bio.*1, p. 33 (2003).

sympathizers and well known to the Confederate military. General Lee pitched his headquarters tent there during the Mine Run Campaign and spent his last night in Orange County camped, as he said, "in Mrs. Rhoades' yard."

Hearing riders approaching, Stuart reportedly said, "There's Fitz now." At that moment, gunfire erupted. Federal cavalry, making its own reconnaissance, had ridden right into the middle of Stuart's nap. In the pandemonium which followed, excerpts from the postwar observations of Ford H. Rogers, at the time a lieutenant in the 1st Michigan Cavalry, are pertinent.[52] After briefly pursuing a Confederate officer who had jumped on a horse and ridden away bareback, Rogers returned to the house:

"I threw my reins over a post and went on the porch, which I found covered with blankets, long shawls, hats, haversacks, revolvers, pipes, tobacco, etc., showing that a party of officers had camped there for the night, but I still had no idea of how distinguished a party it was whose slumbers I had so rudely disturbed.

"I immediately began gathering up such articles as struck my fancy. I took a gentleman's long shawl marked 'Chiswell Dabney,' a pair of revolvers, a broad-brimmed, light brown, soft hat with a long feather in it, which I immediately donned."

Rogers also picked up a patent leather dispatch case, which he gave to another Federal officer. That officer looked inside and discovered copies of various orders and dispatches to Stuart, revealing Lee's designs on Pope. Union spy Thomas Harter had already slipped across the Rapidan and given the initial alarm, but the cavalrymen didn't know that.[53] They decided that it was time to hurry back and report to General Pope. Returning to Roger's narrative:

"On our way back to rejoin the column we fell in with Adjutant Wm. M. Heazlett of the First Michigan Cavalry and a few men who had Major Norman R. Fitzhugh, Stuart's adjutant-general as a prisoner. Upon seeing me with the broad-brimmed hat on, Major Fitzhugh blanched and said in a quick troubled voice, 'Where is the man who wore that hat?' Upon being

---

[52] Excerpted from: " 'Jeb' Stuart's Hat, A Paper Read Before the Commandery of the State of Michigan Military Order of the Loyal Legion of the United States," by Ford H. Rogers. An authenticated copy of that paper is in the collection of the Orange County Historical Society. The date of the reading is not noted on the paper.

[53] See Fischel, *The Secret War for the Union*, pp. 191-192.

informed that he had escaped, he said with an air of great relief, 'Thank God for that, that's Jeb Stuart's hat.'

"The long shawl I now have at my house in this city. The hat I took to California with me, packed in a trunk, and being smashed very flat, I took it to a hat store in San Francisco to be put in order, where I allowed it to remain a long time, and when I called for it, it could not be found, having been cleared out with a lot of old second-hand hats."

Stuart later wrote his wife and spoke of his embarrassment and discomfort as a result of the hat losing incident. Described as a brilliant cavalry officer with an almost childlike need for attention and praise, Stuart was upset by this event more than he would let on. On a raid into Pope's rear at Catlett Station a few days later he got even when he captured Pope's full dress uniform. Stuart sent a message to Pope, offering to swap the uniform for the hat, but by then Pope was in no mood to deal. Lee had him on the run, and his defeat at Second Manassas was only days away.

IN THE SPRING OF 2001, ORANGE COUNTY WAS CONTACTED BY GEORGE Lawson, a Mason living in Yorba Linda, California. He had something that belonged in Orange County, Virginia, and did we want it?

Probably. What is it?

Lawson explained that about seven years earlier he had gone to Anaheim to see a Mrs. Eleanor Parker and to present her with a 50-year Eastern Star pin. Mrs. Parker showed Lawson a Mason's apron in a plastic package and told him that if he didn't want it, she was going to throw it out. The apron, about 17 inches by 13 inches, was in reasonably good shape and had writing on its back. That writing detailed the history of its ownership and its travels.

The apron had originally been the property of William H. Clore, and the note on its back states that it was taken from "Orange Court House" during an 1864 "fraying party." The apron was given to Federal Colonel H. H. Vinton, who later gave it to his son, North Dakota Indian Affairs Agent H. B. Vinton. H. B. Vinton eventually gave the apron to his daughter Vanita Vinton Jones, who still later gave it to her good friend, Mrs. Parker. Mrs. Parker and the apron subsequently moved to California and to a meeting with George Lawson.

Some things about the apron seem relatively easy to explain. Others are vastly more difficult. "Fraying party" almost has to be a foraging party, but when that took place and by whom it was done is a mystery. There is also no record of a William H. Clore being a member of the Orange Lodge during that period. There were lodges at Gordonsville and Barboursville, and "Orange Court House" was a Civil War location term that sometimes included those communities as well as the rest of the county. For that matter, Clore may have been a member of the several Madison or Culpeper Lodges, but living near the Orange County line, and the apron could have come from his house. Lodge records for the Civil War era are not necessarily complete, and an exact location for Mr. Clore remains elusive.

In the spring of 1864, Harvey H. Vinton was the Captain of "M" company, 6th Michigan Cavalry—one of Custer's "Wolverines." On August 16, 1864, James Kidd, who for a time commanded the 6th and later the brigade containing it, reported that "Major" Vinton commanded a picket line at Front Royal. Late in the war, Vinton finally made Lieutenant Colonel. The "colonel" notation on the apron then might not actually describe Vinton's status at the time he got it.

But how did Vinton get it? A scan of the record of the 6th Michigan for 1864 does not indicate that the regiment was in the Orange County area after the May Wilderness fighting, and even then the 6th was fighting in Spotsylvania County. After the main armies moved off to the James River during that summer and fall, some Federal cavalry showed up in Orange County from time to time, but there is no indication that any of it was from Custer's command.[54] All we know for sure is that Vinton somehow got this apron and elected to hang on to it. And that too is a mystery. What did he want with a Mason's apron?

Freemasonry was a very powerful movement during the mid-nineteenth century, and there are stories of opposing Civil War soldiers whose common loyalty to the Order was stronger than their status as wartime enemies. Unless he actually knew Freemasonry, however, Vinton couldn't be sure that a display of the apron would, say, win favorable treatment at the hands of captors. If he actually was a Mason (not determined), he may have been keeping it for a possible return to Clore at some future date. Without some reference to Freemasonry, though, the apron qualifies as a very strange Civil War souvenir.

All the unknowns and mysteries aside, it is clear that the apron came from the Orange area, and we are pleased to have it back. It is currently held in safekeeping at Independent Orange Lodge No. 138, and after historians have done what they can to clear up its mysteries, it will go on public display somewhere in the town. Our sincere thanks to the Vintons,

---

[54] For example, on September 19, 1864, the 16th NY Cavalry destroyed the railroad bridge at Rapidan Station. *Official Records,* Vol XLII, Part I, p. 875. Then on October 6, an unidentified cavalry detachment partially destroyed the bridge again. *Official Records*, Vol XLII, Part II, p. 886.

Mrs. Parker, and George Lawson for a combined 139 years of safekeeping and a safe return.

And it does help some to make up for the loss of the hat.

## K. There Have Indeed Been Other Wars

With the possible exception of the French and Indian War, Orange County has had at least some involvement in all of America's major wars. The Revolution and Civil War actually brought armies onto its soil, but for most of the others the local connection with the struggle was more tenuous. The county's experiences during America's two World Wars, however, contributed significantly to the county's later history.

For America, World War I was a short fight after a long, anxious wait. Our military involvement spanned less than a year, but it initiated changes in our society that foreshadowed World War II. WWI saw the extensive involvement of women as military support personnel. Among Orange County's WWI fatalities was Ann Bull Reverly of Rebel Hall, an army nurse who died in Europe during that massive and deadly influenza epidemic of 1918. Black units were organized and sent to Europe, and their world view was forever changed. Among the returning veterans were county citizens who had been gassed, maimed, or "shell shocked," and who were living reminders of what had been endured. Children played on a WWI cannon that stood in the court house yard. Patriotic speechmakers lauded our involvement in the "war to end all wars," a phrase which fell into disuse in the 1930s as it became clear that the industrialized world was almost surely headed back into another war.

WWII saw an even more extensive involvement of the county in the struggle. More of its citizens, male and female, black and white, went into uniform and then served at stations all over the globe. Some county citizens became members of the 29th Infantry Division and on D-Day were among the first wave of troops to meet the German firestorm of resistance on Omaha Beach. The experiences of the veterans who survived and returned helped to create a county citizenry significantly different from the one which they had left. Securing work off the farm (and in many cases out of the county) and an increasing appreciation and dependence upon machines to do labor were among their hallmarks.[55]

---

[55] For profiles of some of those people, see: Rowe, *The Greatest Generation of Orange*, and Audibert, *Local Folks*.

On the WWII home front, there were War Bond fund drives to help finance America's massive war expenditures. Local and national celebrities lent their time to those efforts, and the local post offices sold the "victory bonds" year-round. The "victory garden" promotion by the government had little impact on a still-largely rural Orange County, but it was amusing to read of city folk trying to learn how to grow food.

There was a large aluminum collection drive early in the war. An early scrap metal drive gobbled up the old WWI cannon on the court house yard. Food cans were cleaned, flattened and turned in for recycling during the entire war. Whole families went out into the fields to gather milkweed seed pods,, the feathery seeds being needed for navy life jackets. Ladies groups knitted thigh-length, heavy wool socks for North Sea sailors to wear inside their boots. Business executives came out of retirement to run newly-created government departments, working for a dollar a year. People reflected on the accounts of enemy submarines sinking American ships within sight of Virginia Beach. Then there was "rationing." Leather goods, sugar, meat, butter, whiskey, etc., most especially gasoline. Every household had a collection of ration books and tokens which permitted the limited purchase of rationed goods whenever they happened to be available.

Route 15 was a major north-south artery, and the roar of truck convoys added to the sounds of the steady stream of trains passing through the county – one every ten minutes during peak levels. Workers at the silk mill were making parachutes and glider tow ropes. Snead & Co. was making bridge pontoons. Clark Manufacturing was producing fuse bodies. Several local factories flew the blue Army/Navy "E" flag, denoting outstanding commitment to the war effort. There were local civil defense drills and blackouts, and volunteer airplane spotters worried about distant dots overhead. Patriotic posters reminded everyone that "loose lips lose lives" and that "Uncle Sam Needs You." The Selective Service, or "draft board" had assigned all conscription age males a number, and periodically someone was notified that his number had "come up" to report for military service. All in all, it was a tense, heady, emotional roller coaster ride, at the end of which rural Orange County found itself totally immersed in the twentieth century with no way of going back.

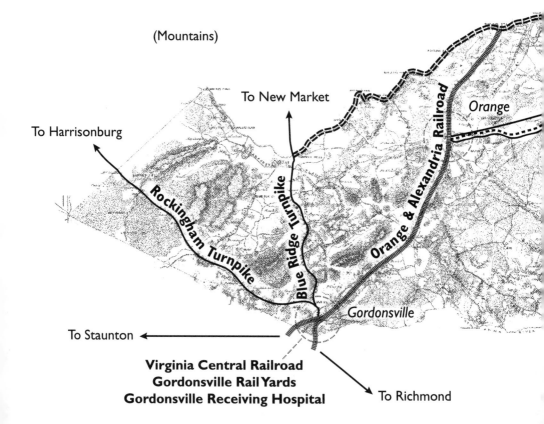

CHIEF ENGINEER'S OFFICE D.N.V.

MAJ.GEN. J.F.GILMER CHIEF ENGINEER.

## Map of
# O R A N G E .

From surveys and reconnaissances by Walter Izard 1ͭ Lͭ Engͬ P.A.C.S.
Made under direction of A.H. CAMPBELL CAPͭ ᴇɴɢͬ in charge Topͦ Depart.
1864
SCALE 20.000

(Mountains)

To New Market

To Harrisonburg

*Rockingham Turnpike*

*Blue Ridge Turnpike*

*Orange & Alexandria Railroad*

*Orange*

To Staunton

*Gordonsville*

**Virginia Central Railroad
Gordonsville Rail Yards
Gordonsville Receiving Hospital**

To Richmond

Jeremy Francis Gilmer Collection

63     ORANGE COUNTY, 1864

The Rapidan Line. A twenty-mile long complex of earthworks was built into the Southwest Mountain ridge forming the north border of the county. It both protected and was served by the vital transportation network immediately to its rear. When the line was occupied, the soldiers lived in camps just behind it. Fourteen such camps have been found on

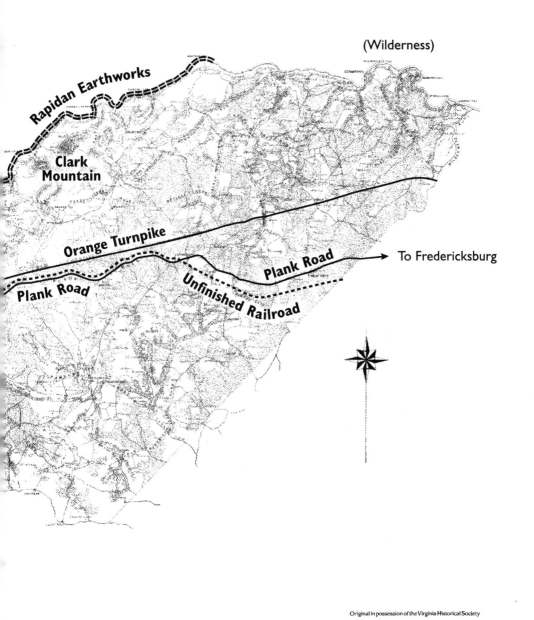

Montpelier alone. The Rapidan Line reached its peak development when Lee and his army spent the fall and winter of 1863-64 in the county. The 1864 county map was prepared by the Confederate Engineering Department and is reproduced courtesy of the Virginia Historical Society. The highlighted features superimposed on the map by Design 3 Studios.

Blue Run Baptist Church. The core of this structure dates to 1769. A combined race church prior to the Civil War, the black members of the congregation bought the sanctuary from the white members after the war. It continues to support an active and growing congregation. Photo by Bernice Walker.

# CHAPTER VI

# Reconstruction & Race, and Times of Slow & Uneven Adjustments[1]

## A. Virginia Becomes a Slave to the Slaves

The arrival of a Dutch slaver at Jamestown's docks in 1619 and the ensuing sale there of its human cargo is routinely cited as the moment when slavery was introduced into the Virginia colony.[2] If one refers only to enslaved Africans, that date is probably as good as any, though a few may have arrived in the colony earlier by way of England.[3] To restrict the consideration of slavery in British America to only that of Africans, however, is to avoid an understanding of the use of bonded labor in the Virginia colony, which over time evolved into a labor system using only racially determined, permanently bonded labor, i.e., enslaved Africans. It doesn't make the practice any more morally defensible, but it helps in gaining an understanding of why and how anything like that could have ever happened.

Initially, slavery in Virginia had many faces. The first settlers in 1607 quickly discovered that the Indians with whom they were dealing owned slaves, typically the booty of war and trade. The settlers soon captured or traded for Indian slaves

---

[1] One of the advance readers noted that the title might be read as indicating a completed adjustment. For some people, that is true. For others, it has yet to begin.

[2] Ironically, 1619 was also the year the Virginia Company established the House of Burgesses, thought by many to be the first freely-elected representative assembly in the western hemisphere. The Iroquois might beg to differ.

[3] Slavery was not abolished in England until 1833.

of their own.[4] Also, temporary slaves, called "indentured servants," were among the earliest arrivals from England. Dr. Charles Bryan, Director of the Virginia Historical Society, estimates that approximately 80% of all the settlers who came to the Virginia colony during the first century of its existence were indentured servants.

Most indentured servants were "contract slaves," that is individuals who had agreed to serve a master as his/her slave for a specified period of time in return for the master doing something for them. Most often the master was paying the servant's passage from England to the colony, for which seven years' service was the usual indenture ("debt" in today's words) owed by the servant.

Other indentured servants were people sentenced by the English courts to transportation to the colonies for sale into service. For the most part, they were debtors and petty criminals. At the relatively late date of 1763, the *Beverly* was reported as having sailed up the Rappahannock with a cargo of convict servants, the sale of whom was to be held first at Leedstown, Westmoreland County, on Monday, November 14, and with the rest to be sold at Port Royal, Caroline County, a week later.[5]

Orphans and other wards of the local government were also routinely indentured, and indenture was one of the punishments which could be imposed for certain local crimes. When indentured servant Mary Madden bore her illegitimate mulatto child, for example, not only could she have been fined and sentenced to be whipped at the public whipping post, she also could have had her indenture extended. We know that her child, Sarah Madden, was indentured by law to age thirty-one and became the servant of James Madison, Sr. That was the indenture which he later gave to his son Francis and which Francis still later tried to convey to someone in Pennsylvania.

Wherever an indenture might wind up going, the person serving it of course had to follow. If a master died, his servants' indentures were inherited by the heirs. It was also generally understood that indentures were a sub-class of persons, that they could be housed as poorly and beaten as

---

[4] For a time, the Indian School at Williamsburg was buying slaves from the Indians and making them members of the student body.

[5] Reported in Fall, *Hidden Village*, p. 198. On that same page, Jonathan Boucher notes that: "Not a ship arrived in Virginia either with redemptioners or convicts, in which schoolmasters are not regularly advertised for sale, [as well] as weavers, tailors, or any other trade; with little difference, that I can hear of, excepting perhaps the former do not usually fetch so good a price as the latter."

regularly as the master desired, and that if one died, questions were not necessarily asked. It wasn't routinely called "slavery," but for most indentured servants and their masters it certainly operated and felt like it.[6]

Many indenture agreements recited requirements for the master to teach the servant a trade, and at the conclusion of the indenture, to send him/her off with something, such as new clothes, tools of a trade, a sum of money, etc. The conclusion of an indenture could, therefore, mean not only the loss of a trained servant, but also the incurring of costs. Some masters either tried to ignore those obligations or seek ways around having to perform them. That could include overlooking the obligation to set the servant free.[7] Forever circulating through the colonies were stories of masters who used and abused their short-term indentured servants, while taking better care of the slaves who would be staying with them. Probably most of them were just stories, but not all.[8]

Initially, even Africans were not necessarily consigned to the permanent bondage system that dominates present-day thinking on slavery. Some were sold as indentured servants. Africans were also allowed to own property, including slaves of their own.[9]

As Virginia's farms and plantations grew in size and number, the demand for workers increased. At the same time, however, the flow of European indentured servants to the colony began to decline. Court ordered transportation and commitment to indenture by English courts was ultimately outlawed. Also, persons needing the price of a passage were not necessarily agreeing to long-term or slave-type indentures any more.

More and more African slaves were used to meet Virginia's need for laborers. At the same time those slaves slowly but surely became both an

---

[6] One Madison County Heatwole recalls that his indentured ancestor was beaten so badly that he fled to the Valley, where he remained, permanently scarred and constantly afraid of being captured and returned.

[7] One former indentured servant filed suit in Orange's court against her former master for the sum she had been promised upon her release. A group of Spotswood's Germans had to sue him and get a court determination that their indentures had been served before Spotswood would agree to let them go.

[8] On the docks at New Orleans, it was common for masters to hire Irish immigrants to do jobs deemed too dangerous to risk their investment in a slave.

[9] For a snapshot of that period, see: "Seventeenth Century Virginia's Forgotten Yeomen: The Free Blacks," by Breen and Innes in the Summer 1982 number of *Virginia Cavalcade*. ("…I know myne own ground and I will work when I please and play when I please.")

isolated and a vulnerable laboring class. Acts were passed, particularly during the later years of the seventeenth century, which began to legally separate slaves from the rest of society.[10] With the consolidation of the state's various slave laws in 1705, "chattel slavery," the slave labor system as it is popularly characterized today, started to become a reality. Unlike indentures, slaves were from thenceforth to be considered "real estate," not persons, in the eyes of the law. As real property, slaves were now included as security for the planters' loans, thus binding Virginia's agrarian economy even more tightly to the "peculiar institution."

With the population of Africans in the colony starting to grow to what was seen as threatening numbers, such freedoms as the slaves had enjoyed were sharply curtailed. The right of slaves to assemble was effectively eliminated. Plantation owners organized patrols, the "patterollers," to monitor slave activity. Free blacks "without papers" were rounded up and forced into slavery. Others were sentenced to slavery for imagined offenses.[11] Underlying all of this was the whites' abiding fear that some day the blacks would rise and massacre them all.

Freedmen who stayed in communities where they were known, who "knew their place," and "minded their manners," were often left alone, even though Virginia enacted laws at various times requiring all free blacks to register and to leave the state within a certain time after being freed.[12] Some freed slaves did take the risk of going to where they were not known and moved to Virginia's urban centers where more profitable work could be found.[13]

African slaves constituted a major portion of this area's earliest settlers, but they were almost certainly not among the first. While much of the

---

[10] Example: A 1670 law forbidding free Negroes or Indians from owning christian [European] servants, but allowing them to buy "any of their own nation." II *Hening Statutes* 280-281.

[11] Persons illegally enslaved did have access to the courts, but the results were not encouraging. Existing court records from the 1790-1800 period show only 19 Indians and 7 Negroes recovering their freedom. 106 *Va.Mag. of His/Bio.* 431 (August 1998).

[12] Two of the several registration acts were passed in 1783 and 1797. One Orange County registration list identifies 129 free Negroes in which the latest date any had been freed was 1850. One of the several banishment laws was passed in 1806, but the legislature then adopted act after act especially excusing specific individuals from the effect of the law.

[13] By 1810, 57% of Petersburg's population was black, and approximately one-third of them were free. 106 *Va. Mag. Of His/Bio.* 431 (August 1998).

work in establishing Fort Germanna in 1714 was of the type routinely assigned to slaves, the Germans were themselves indentured servants and did not approve of slavery at the time. That said, it was surely not long before groups of slaves were coming into the uplands to do the "seating and planting" required to convert their masters' patents into legal titles to the land.

IT COULD BE YEARS, IF EVER, BEFORE A MASTER MIGHT ARRIVE TO SETTLE ON the land which his slaves and servants had been clearing and farming. For example, Ambrose Madison received the patent to the land that we now know as the Montpelier tract in 1723. He did not arrive with his family to settle there until 1732. Ambrose's arrival at Mount Pleasant (later to be called "Montpelier") triggered another facet of slavery which haunted the white population.

In a matter of months, Ambrose Madison was dead, and Pompey, a slave, charged with his murder. Ultimately Pompey was found guilty and executed. He had been a slave from another plantation, probably rented or on loan to Madison. As required by law, the court set a value on Pompey, and since the government was taking a master's private property by executing him, that sum was paid to the master. Two Madison slaves, convicted as accomplices, were ordered punished and returned to the brand-new widow. As far as we can tell, Frances Taylor Madison simply put them back to work, a situation which has spawned a subset of never-to-be substantiated speculations about how unlikeable her husband may have been.[14]

Easily the most notorious execution of a slave in Orange County for the murder of a master was the burning of Eve at the stake. It was charged that on August 19, 1745, Eve committed treason by administering poison to her master, Peter Montague, who "did then languish" until December 27 of that year. The trial was held on January 23, 1746. Eve pleaded not guilty and put herself at the mercy of the Court. The Crown produced witnesses, one of whom came from some considerable distance, and Eve was found guilty. Back in the 1500s, the English Parliament had made the murder of masters by slaves an act of treason punishable by death, and Eve's execution was so ordered.[15]

A day or so after the trial, Eve was hauled to the execution site on a hurdle (called a "slide" today), tied to the stake, and wood stacked around

---

[14] For an expanded dissertation on this incident, see Miller, *The Short Life and Strange Death of Ambrose Madison.*

[15] 4 OCDB 454. Eve was valued at £50.

her. The Sheriff, Thomas Chew, threw a rope over a notch in the top of the stake and looped one end around Eve's neck. When things got too bad, he pulled on the rope, long and hard. Eve's execution site is near Orange County's first court house, specifically on the hill at the intersection of Routes 522 and 611. Fittingly, a church now stands near that site. The late R. Monroe Waugh, former county Supervisor and long-time owner of that property, often said that if the land were ever developed, he wanted one of the streets to be named "Eve's Wail." Lest we forget.[16]

Guilty verdicts and executions were not automatic. On May 26, 1748, Letty was tried for two murders by poison. It was alleged that on August 1, 1746, she poisoned a white overseer named Richard Sims and that on September 30 of the same year she poisoned a Negro named Simon.[17] Sims finally and mercifully died the following January. Simon languished until May, both deaths typical for the compounds in use in the African poisoning culture of the day. The Orange County court found Letty innocent and released her to her mistress. On another occasion, a 17-year-old youth who had raped a white girl was found guilty but was, because of his youth, recommended for either executive clemency or transportation out of the colony.

Slaves would sometimes be granted the "benefit of clergy" for a first offense. That ancient theory of punishment mitigation grew out of a need to preserve persons who could read and write for the good of a mostly illiterate society. The theory's name reflects the time when ministers did most of the teaching. That plea, however, tended to work only once. In 1767, Tom, the property of John Baylor, was found guilty of having gone into the house of Erasmus Taylor and taken items worth about 25 cents. Tom's biggest problem was that he had already received the benefit of clergy for an earlier offense. He was executed.[18]

As Orange County's larger plantations developed, portions of the acreage were assigned to separate work crews, usually each with their own

---

[16] There were relatively few executions by burning at the stake in Virginia. In 1714 in New York City, 29 slaves were sentenced to be executed by burning/ hanging for involvement in a spree of arsons and lootings. Pritchard, *Lost History*, p. 77.

[17] Overseers were an obvious target of slaves' wrath. The January 11, 1786, entry in the *Diary* of Orange County's Francis Taylor notes: "A Negro of Capt. C. Conway's yesterday wounded his overseer with an ax . . ."

[18] In his *History of Orange County Virginia*, W. W. Scott chronicles additional incidents in a chapter entitled "Crimes and Punishments," pp. 133-137.

overseer or foreman. Those people would live in their own settlement, or "quarter," near the land they were responsible for. One of the most well-known quarters in Orange County was Sawney's quarter on Montpelier. Sawney, the slave overseer of that quarter, was known to produce high quality tobacco, and buyers looked for his special mark on hogsheads coming from Montpelier. There was also a "Peg's quarter" at Montpelier, but as of this writing, nothing more is known about Peg or his/her quarter.

The naturally rich soils in the western areas of Orange County and access to an extensive transportation system kept the county in the "Tobacco Belt" long after farmers in other areas had switched to hay, grain and livestock. Tobacco tended to be the crop of large farm operations, and the constant tending requirements for that crop meant that those operations had comparatively larger slave populations. Even in Orange County, however, there was a peaking out. In 1850, the farms of Orange and Greene counties combined averaged 209 acres of open land. Ten years later, on the eve of the Civil War, that figure had dropped to 186 acres. In 1820, the median number of slaves held by a single slave-owning household in Orange and Greene counties was 21.5 individuals. By 1860, that figure had dropped to 18.7.

Along with their decrease in acres, more of those farms were producing something other than tobacco, thereby lowering their labor requirements. The general agricultural depression of that period also had to be a factor in those lower numbers. When working with slave population statistics, keep in mind that data from the several huge plantations, such as Montpelier and Barboursville, can tend to skew the numbers. Also, remember that only a fraction of most Orange County plantations' slave populations were routinely members of its work force. Not available were the very young and the very old. Also, women not working in the main house were usually sent into the field only in emergencies or during peak planting and harvesting times. For example, while the county's 1860 median holding (the middle number in a graduated array of numbers) was 18.7 slaves, the average Orange County farm utilizing slave labor that year had six workers in the field.[19]

A specific example of the declining slave holdings in Orange County involves Ellwood, the Lacy plantation in the far eastern end of the county. Slave census data tells us that Ellwood's slave population averaged 90 persons for the 1810 and 1820 censuses and averaged 36 persons for the 1850

---

[19] Data cited in "The 'Social Economy' of an Upper South Community," by John T. Schlotterbeck, published in *Class, Conflict, and Consensus, Antebellum Southern Community Studies*, Burton & McMath, Eds., Greenwood Press CT 1982.

and 1860 censuses. Ellwood never grew tobacco, so its owners probably hired laborers or pooled their work force with neighbors at peak times in those later years, but some of that decline had to reflect permanent reductions in labor needs.[20] As their need for slaves lessened, Orange County owners no doubt contributed to their state being the South's largest exporter of slaves prior to the Civil War. With the exception of the depression-era census counts for 1840 and 1850, however, the total number of African-Americans in Orange County increased steadily until the 1880s. Surprisingly, the 2000 census report shows that the county's current African-American population has now declined to the 1782 level.[21]

THE FIRST BLACK UNION TROOPS TO ARRIVE IN ORANGE COUNTY DURING THE Civil War were members of Ferrero's division of Ambrose Burnside's Ninth Corps. When they crossed the pontoon bridge at Germanna on May 6, 1864, they were also the first USCT (United States Colored Troops) soldiers to appear on a Virginia battlefield. They did not see their first combat until May 15, in connection with the Spotsylvania Court House fighting, but their arrival in Orange County had been an historic event in itself.

As the fortunes of war go, some USCT soldiers were captured, and at least one was brought to the enclosed yard around the Orange Court House, where captives were held until they could be shipped off to prison camps. On the morning of May 8, 1864, a USCT prisoner was hanged from a tree in the court yard.[22] It is not known if other black prisoners were present and that this particular individual had done something to arouse the guards' ire, or whether this was the sole USCT prisoner there.

To many Southerners the arrival of USCT troops did indeed mean that the massive slave uprising which had long been feared was actually underway. Additionally terrifying was their understanding that it was the Federal government which was arming, training, and sending former slaves to massacre Southern whites. The response of some Southerners to this perceived nightmare-come-true knew no bounds.

The advent of the Civil War put many of Orange County's Africans in a quandary. Virtually all desperately wanted freedom, but many were un-

---

[20] Slave census data is available on microfilm at the Orange County Historical Society Research Center.

[21] The 2000 U.S. census figures show an African-American population for Orange County of 3,679 persons, comprising 14.2% of a total county population of 25,881.

[22] As reported by white prisoner Charles Hopkins, 1st. NJ Infantry, VI corps.

## POPULATION BY RACE
## ORANGE AND GREENE COUNTIES (VA), 1782 TO 1900*

| Year | Total | White | | Black | | Black % of Total |
|---|---|---|---|---|---|---|
| | | No. | %Change | No. | %Change | |
| 1782 | 7,763 | 4,223 | | 3,540 | | 45.6 |
| | | | 28.7 | | 26.7 | |
| 1790 | 9,921 | 5,436 | | 4,485 | | 45.2 |
| | | | 13.3 | | 17.9 | |
| 1800 | 11,449 | 6,160 | | 5,289 | | 46.2 |
| | | | -7.3 | | 25.0 | |
| 1810 | 12,323 | 5,711 | | 6,612 | | 53.6 |
| | | | -6.6 | | 15.9 | |
| 1820 | 12,997 | 5,336 | | 7,661 | | 58.9 |
| | | | 21.0 | | 6.9 | |
| 1830 | 14,637 | 6,456 | | 8,181 | | 55.9 |
| | | | -6.7 | | -10.3 | |
| 1840 | 13,357 | 6,022 | | 7,335 | | 54.9 |
| | | | 10.1 | | 6.8 | |
| 1850 | 14,467 | 6,629 | | 7,838 | | 54.2 |
| | | | 14.2 | | 6.0 | |
| 1860 | 15,873 | 7,568 | | 8,305 | | 52.3 |
| | | | 16.2 | | 2.2 | |
| 1870 | 17,276 | 8,792 | | 8,484 | | 46.5 |
| | | | 16.2 | | 2.2 | |
| 1880 | 18,882 | 10,215 | | 8,667 | | 45.9 |
| | | | 4.6 | | -10.6 | |
| 1890 | 18,436 | 10,687 | | 7,749 | | 42.0 |
| | | | 10.7 | | -10.3 | |
| 1900 | 18,785 | 11,833 | | 6,952 | | 37.0 |

*Greene's totals are added to permit comparison with the numbers for the years prior to its formation out of Orange in 1838.

Source: *Plantation and Farm: Social and Economic Change in Orange and Greene Counties,1716 to 1860*, a PhD dissertation submitted to Johns Hopkins University in 1960 by John T. Schlotterbeck. The numbers for 1782, 1820, and 1870 were adjusted for underenumeration. The full text of Dr. Schlotterbeck's dissertation is available at the Research Center of the Orange County Historical Society.

sure of what their freedom would mean in the middle of a war. Most also felt some attachment to their masters and mistresses. Some did run away and seek the protection of the Union army. Others remained with their "families." No matter what, in 1865, all were free and expected to learn how to get along on their own. Extremely unsettling times lay ahead.

## B. A Virginia Gentleman[23]

Paul Jennings was born at Montpelier in 1799. His mother was a slave; therefore, he was one also. His father was understood to be Benjamin Jennings, an English merchant and the source of Paul's surname.

Jennings may have spent a few childhood years doing "boy's work," such as thinning corn, pulling weeds, and carrying drinking water to the field crews. Before his teens, however, he had already become the body servant of James Madison. This may have occurred at about the same time that Madison was elected President, because Jennings' earliest personal memories seem to be of his Washington years. They speak of his moving into an unfinished White House and of enduring the mud and dust of an unpaved Pennsylvania Avenue. Jennings described the new Federal City as "dreary," a sentiment he shared with most of its early residents.

As one would expect, Jennings' most interesting memories of Washington deal with its capture and burning by the British in late August 1814. While such local militia as could be found to defend Washington from the British were judged to be of not much account, there was a small force of mixed sailors and marines, regular troops, that the British would also have to fight their way through. Jennings reported that a number of the sailors were black and that the entire force fought valiantly and suffered heavy losses before being overcome.

Jennings was in Washington when the defense forces were overrun at Bladensburg, Maryland. Madison and much of his cabinet had gone to Bladensburg and nothing had been heard from them for an ominously long time. The first post-battle news to reach reached the White House apparently convinced everyone that the victorious enemy would be at their doorsteps in a matter of minutes. According to Jennings, Dolley Madison and several of the other house servants hastily gathered a few items and left, and the remaining White House staff found themselves having to run off local looters who began roaming through the building.

---

[23] The primary source of information for this subchapter is Jennings, "A Colored Man's Reminiscences of James Madison."

When it became evident that the British were going to take their time getting into the city, Jennings recollected that he and some of the remaining White House servants started collecting other valuables and getting them onto wagons for transport to safety. It was at this time, Jennings recalled, that the doorkeeper and the gardener cut George Washington's portrait out of its frame and put it into a wagon. Dolley has long been given the credit for having saved the Washington portrait, but Jennings obviously begs to differ. As he recollected, Mrs. Madison needed to leave too quickly to deal with such things as portraits. In the unexpected space of relative calm which then followed, there arose the opportunity to save additional items before everyone left.

Jennings had also set the White House dinner table for a 3:00 p.m. meal, a customary eating time in that day. When the British finally did arrive, their officers ate the meal and then set fire to the White House and other buildings in the city. Fearing that large bodies of militia and colonial troops were being mobilized to cut them off from their ships, the invaders soon vacated Washington and headed back down the Potomac. They left behind an absolute mess, and there was talk of moving the seat of government to another location. Madison, however, was determined to rebuild and restore the damaged structures and keep the Federal government in Washington. He had played a major role in the original choice of that location between the northern and southern states, and he understood the need to stay there.

The remaining months of Madison's term as President were unexciting by comparison, and Dolley and the servants followed him into an active retirement of farming at Montpelier. As the years went by, Madison grew less able to care for himself, and grew more dependent upon Jennings and others. Jennings recalled that for the last sixteen years of Madison's life, he shaved his master, every other day. He attributed Madison's shaving schedule and his conservative dress (one suit at a time, everything black) to Madison's desire to demonstrate frugality to less affluent members of his extended family. There may have been something to that, but it also fit well with his master's tastes and personality.

It was Paul Jennings who was with Madison on the morning of June 28, 1836, and who reported the last moments of that great life. Madison was being fed breakfast, and his "favorite niece," Nelly Madison Willis of Woodley, was present. Jennings recalled that a slight change of expression crossed Madison's face. When Nelly asked if anything was wrong, he responded, "Nothing more than a change of mind, my dear." With that, Madison died, passing from life to death, Jennings observed, as quickly and quietly as the snuffing out of a candle.

Hard financial times followed Madison's death, and Dolley moved to Washington, taking Jennings with her. Ultimately, Dolley sold Jennings to Senator Daniel Webster, providing her with some badly-needed cash. Jennings and Webster, for their part, agreed to an arrangement whereby Jennings would work off his purchase price and would then be a free man. Jennings expressed no hard feelings about the transaction, and he actually may have had a hand in arranging it.

At times, Webster would send Jennings around to see his former mistress, usually with a market basket of "provisions." During those visits, Jennings was also checking to make sure that Dolley was all right and that she had what she needed. Jennings noted that on occasion he personally gave Dolley some small sums from his own pocket to help her along. Her situation doubtless pained him, for as he recollected Mrs. Madison was a "remarkably fine woman...beloved by every body in Washington, white and colored."

Jennings also expressed high regard for his former master, describing Madison as "one of the best men that ever lived" and noting that Madison never struck a slave nor allowed an overseer to do so. Even so, Jennings was keenly aware of the plight of his people. A few years prior to the Civil War, Jennings determined to do something. He eventually assisted with the financing and the planning of a slave escape attempt involving the ship *Pearl*. The attempt failed, but Jennings had at least tried.

Smart and worldly-wise, accustomed to dressing well, displaying good manners, and evidently comfortable dealing with Washington's society, Jennings soon found employment with the government. At the time his reminiscences were being taken down, Jennings was in his mid-sixties. The writer described Jennings as an intelligent colored man whose character for sobriety, truth, and fidelity was unquestioned. In sum, he looked and acted like what he was: a gentleman, a Virginia Gentleman.

## C. William Byrd vs. Freedom

The usual working arrangements on a farm or plantation left its slaves with a certain amount of free time. "Quittin' time," as dramatized in the opening scenes of *Gone With the Wind*, commonly ended the work day in our area. Further south, most plantations used the "task" system, in which a task was assigned to one or more slaves, and when it was completed to the taskmaster's satisfaction, they were done for the day. As for weekends, even the notorious slave driver John Kelly of Culpeper County shut his mills and shops down for the week on Saturday afternoons.[24]

During peak planting and harvest times, working from "can see" to "can't see" was tolerated as being necessary. Other than that, a certain amount of free time was expected, and to unreasonably deny it was to expose a master to "labor unrest," which tended to produce anxiety and tension on both sides of the master/slave relationship, even if nothing else came of it.

There is almost nothing on the use of slaves in an industrial setting in Orange County; however, we do get one interesting glimpse into that area when William K. Smith mortgaged his Vaucluse mining property in 1843. The property securing the loan was listed as follows:

"The Gold Mine Tract, 120hp. steam engine & related appurtenances, grist mill, 6 Chilean mills, 2 Mexican mills, eighteen stamps [type of rock crusher], eighteen amalgamating mills, 3 dolly tubs, one washing machine, 18 horses & mules, 3 wagons, 10 carts with harness for all, 2 lots blacksmith tools, one large winch with blocks & chains, 8 windlass chains, buckets, six pumps two horsepower, & all the picks shovels & blasting tools, and wheelbarrows now in use at the Vaucluse gold mine, also two slaves Sam and Davy."

Long before 1843, Virginia law had made slaves real estate, thus allowing them to be included as security on mortgages. This admittedly deplorable practice caught the master, the slave, and the plantation together in an economic snare which drew ever tighter as the agricultural economy faltered in the early 1800s. Mr. Smith at the Vaucluse, however, was evidently sidestepping that trap. Sam and Davy were obviously not going to run all that equipment. Smith was going to hire almost every bit of the labor he needed. If a man got sick or was hurt, he didn't have to be Smith's problem. If the mine had to be closed for a time, the workers could be sent home without pay if Smith so chose. Sam and Davy were probably counted on to keep an eye on things when the mine was down, and, depending on their experience, they may have had special jobs, like firing the steam engine, when things were running. Except for those two men, Smith was avoiding being locked into his labor force, something the planter saw as inevitable.

ENTERPRISING SLAVES USED AT LEAST PART OF THEIR FREE TIME FOR PROFIT. Some raised pigs, chickens, and garden vegetables and sold them, often to

---

[24] See Rosengarten, *Tombee*, pp. 79-82; Sutherland, *Seasons of War*, p. 11 *et seq.*

their masters.[25] Others might do special sewing or take in laundry outside of their regular work. In addition, masters and mistresses sometimes gave "tips" to slaves who did special tasks for them. The sums received, though, were usually small.

A few slaves, however, gained access to serious money. In cases such as Dolley Madison's servant, Paul Jennings, a third party might advance the necessary funds for a slave to buy his/her freedom from the master, receiving in return what amounted to an indenture. The new master might be doing it out of the goodness of his heart, but more often he was looking to secure honest, intelligent, hard-working help.

While many masters "hired out" (leased) their surplus workers, some also allowed their skilled artisan slaves to "hire their own time." Hiring one's own time meant that when the slave's skills were not needed at home, the slave was given papers allowing him to travel away from the plantation and to contract his services to third parties. Usually, the master was going to receive a portion of the slave's earnings in return. The rest of the money was the slave's to use as he saw fit.

An Orange County example of a slave operating in a blend of hires comes to us from Francis Taylor's diary.[26] Taylor, a grandson of Col. James Taylor II, owned "Midland," a property which for much of the twentieth century was called "Yatton," but which is now being called by its earlier name. Taylor's diary covers the 1786-1799 time frame, and several of the entries made in the week between Christmas and New Year's of 1792 are pertinent:

December 26: "I agreed to give carpenter Moses for working on Over-seers house 1/3 p day [one shilling, three pence per day] in Holidays & he went to work." December 28: "Raised a house intended for Overseer to live in. Carpenter Moses at work upon it." December 31, two entries: "I came by M^r T Bells, who agreed to let Robin come here tomorrow to get boards to finish the house begun for the overseer, Moses is to go to morrow

---

[25] A sample entry from Francis Taylor's *Diary*: "10 chickens of Sary 3/9" [three shillings, nine pence]. Entry of July 18, 1799. When Tombee plantation's owner learned that a neighboring slave to whom he owed ten dollars for a hog was being sold, he made a point of getting the money to the slave before he left. Rosengarten, *Tombee*, p. 80.

[26] Taylor's diary is in the Archives and Records Division of the Library of Virginia. It was transcribed as a project of Gunston Hall Plantation, and a rough copy is available at the Orange County Historical Society Research Center. For an associated article, see: 30 *Virginia Magazine of History and Biography* 387 (1922).

to M$^r$ John Waughs who has hired him of his master," and "p$^d$ Carpenter Moses for 4 days work on overseers house a 1/3 - .5" [Five shillings]. Moses, as it turns out, is a slave who hired out his own time for a few days of his Christmas week vacation, and whose master then hired him out immediately thereafter. It should come as no surprise to learn that slaves would be working in a variety of roles reflecting everything from the sweat-service of a supervised laborer to something akin to free enterprise. The bottom line, however, was that, at the end of the day, they were all still slaves.

Slaves intending to hire their own time usually wanted to go to the larger cities where their skills could earn the highest dollar. There they would join a population of locally owned slaves, slaves who were being hired to city people by out-of-town masters, local freedmen, and white laborers. It helps to explain, for example, why over half of the pre-Civil War populations of Richmond and Petersburg were black. One writer characterized the slaves who were living in that environment as entering a "twilight" or "quasi freedom" zone in the slave labor system.[27] The effectiveness of their competitive skills was reflected in the howls of protest raised by white artisans and the occasional, ineffective efforts by them to have the hiring practice outlawed.[28]

IN ANY EVENT, A SLAVE USUALLY HAD TO BE BOTH ENTERPRISING AND FRUGAL to save up enough money to buy his/her freedom, but a number did just that. Some were able to go even further and buy the freedom of spouses and other family members. The following is a story involving a slave purchasing his freedom. Variations of this story abound, and this particular encounter may not have actually taken place. It does, however, characterize the respective attitudes of the parties involved.

The characters in this story are the wealthy, powerful, and arrogant William Byrd II of "Westover" being confronted by one of his slaves. Quite some time earlier the slave had asked Byrd to name the price of his freedom. Byrd quoted some figure, probably confident that the slave would

---

[27] Douglas R. Egerton, "An Upright Man, Gabriel's Virginia and the Path to Slave Rebellion," 43 *Virginia Cavalcade* 59 (Autumn 1993). In Egerton's assessment, Virginia slave laws by the late eighteenth century were "in a state of collapse." Locally, the Chatham uprising in Spotsylvania County in 1805 and the George Boxley uprising in Louisa County in 1816, did much to resurrect those laws.

[28] Even in rural Culpeper County, the whites eventually called for the control of competition for jobs by the local freedmen. Sutherland, *Seasons of War*, p. 17.

never be able to accumulate that sum of money. Now, here is the slave, polite but determined, tendering the agreed amount.

Byrd realizes that he is in real danger of losing a valuable worker. With the financial roadblock to freedom eliminated, Byrd assumes the uncomfortable task of trying to persuade his slave to reject freedom.

"All right, now. You know you would have to move off the plantation and find somewhere else to live. I don't have any obligation to house you if you're free."

"Yassuh."[29]

"And you know I won't be responsible for your house, like I am now. If the roof leaks, or a window breaks, you'll be fixing that on your own time and paying for it out of your own pocket."

"Yassuh."

"And if you get sick, I won't be around to see how you are doing, or sending you food from my kitchen, or paying your doctor bills, like I do now."

"Yassuh."

"And whatever work we have here is going to my slaves first. I can't promise you regular work, and I might not have anything for you."

"Yassuh."

"And when you get old or broken down, I won't have any obligation to take care of you."

"Yassuh."

"Well, what do you think about freedom now?"

"Massa Byrd, I'm sho' everything you said is so, an' I ain't goin' to argue you on it. But, to tell you the truth, I looks forward to the <u>looseness</u> of it."

Exit Mr. Byrd.[30]

## D. Sink or Swim Time

At the conclusion of the Civil War, most of the surviving Confederate veterans returned to their homes and farms or businesses and began re-

---

[29] There is a growing body of scholarship which points to the speech of the 17th-century poor whites in the south and west of England providing the basis for what is called "Black English" today.

[30] Byrd lived in the eighteenth century. By the mid-nineteenth century, laws controlling freedmen had become so restrictive that some freedmen were petitioning the courts to be enslaved to certain masters. See Davis, *Madison County*, p. 120.

building their lives in any way they could. If they came back to an area which had been largely untouched by the war, their situation might appear promising. For others, including some eastern Orange County residents, the return was to a devastated and depopulated landscape. Few buildings, no crops, no animals, no fences, no workers, and little to no money available to recreate any of it.

At the conclusion of the Mine Run Campaign in December 1863, General Lee filed an action report with the Confederate War Department. When withdrawing from Orange County, the Union army vented its frustrations on the countryside, and Lee observed:

"I cannot conclude without alluding to the wanton destruction of the property of citizens by the enemy. Houses were torn down or rendered uninhabitable, furniture and farming implements broken or destroyed, and many families, most of them in humble circumstances, stripped of all they possessed and left without shelter and without food. I have never witnessed on any previous occasion such entire disregard of the usages of civilized warfare and the dictates of humanity."[31]

Jubal Early, who commanded the Confederate units that fought at Payne's Farm and along the Turnpike during Mine Run, expressed his growing anger over Federal atrocities, an anger which was instrumental in changing him from an anti-secession delegate in 1861 to the clarion voice of the Lost Cause following the war: "I saw on the enemy's track, which I pursued, abundant evidences of the most wanton barbarity. A small tanyard near Locust Grove, used solely for the purpose of tanning hides on shares to furnish shoes to the women and children of the neighborhood, had been burned, the hides taken from the vats and cut to pieces, and the house of the owner also burned. Smoke-houses had been broken open and helpless women plundered of every mouthful of provisions; the most common country carts and farming implements destroyed, and a number of other outrages perpetrated, which could have been only perpetrated by a cowardly foe, stung with mortification at this ridiculous termination of so pretentious [an] expedition."[32]

---

[31] O.R , Series 1, Vol. XXXIX/1 (Ser#48), p. 830. The report is dated April 27, 1864. Less than two weeks later the armies were fighting the Battle of the Wilderness in eastern Orange County.

[32] O.R., Vol XXIX, Part 1, Series 1, p. 835. The tanyard was across Route 20 from Johnson's Funeral Home, west of Locust Grove. Some of the tanning tools were saved and are in a local private collection.

As a destitute Willis Madden of adjacent Culpeper County would be able to attest, it made no difference whether you were white or black when soldiers came plundering. The Orange County communities of Germanna and Raccoon Ford would completely disappear before the fighting ended. In all fairness, Confederate units also routinely took food and firewood from the civilian population, but more extensive destruction of private property by Confederates in the South was rare.

There is a grim joke which drifts through the American South to the effect that the reason why it came through the Great Depression of the 1930s as well as it did was because that era was sensed by the average Southerner as only a short and comparatively mild extension of post-Civil War Reconstruction. The message in that statement and others like it is that a substantial portion of the American people had experienced something worse than anything an economic downturn could produce. That particular heritage of defeat, subjugation, and ruin is something that the rest of America seems to have difficulty comprehending.[33] It takes days off from work, parades, and speeches to help people remember a victory. You can't forget a defeat.

Most Confederate veterans found themselves coming home to clusters of civilians, both black and white, who had decided to stick it out where they were. Many were friends, family, or neighbors. Some were former slaves who saw this part of the world as much their home as it was to any white or freedman. Whatever their relationships, the story of the efforts these people made to rebuild their parts of the South constitutes one of the great sagas in American history. Unfortunately, that saga tends to be overshadowed by another, more grim saga that began at the same time: the struggle to deny the Negro an equal status in American society.

## E. Reconstruction: Social Engineering in Old Virginia

Before the Civil War had ended in Virginia, Northern organizations were already into the work of educating former slaves and of supporting their economic ventures. The people active in that work implored the Federal Government to take the lead role in those efforts and in building something out of the wreckage of what used to be the "Southern Way of Life."

---

[33] In truth, the Depression in the South was as bad as anywhere else. Former U. S. President Jimmy Carter grew up in Plains, Georgia, during that time, and he recalled the grinding poverty in *An Hour Before Daylight* (Simon & Schuster, 2001).

Initially, however, the Federal position seemed to be one of wanting to ignore such problems and let the South rebuild itself.

Lee surrendered at Appomattox on April 9, 1865. A presidential proclamation removed Southern public officials from office in May 1865, and elections were held the following July. In most cases, the former office holders were simply reinstated. By January 1866, the Federal military presence in Virginia was only a shadow of what it had been a year earlier.

The Federal army left behind a deeply humiliated white population and a black population whose delight at being free was muted by uncertainties about the future. Many blacks became disillusioned by what they saw as a lukewarm commitment by the Federal government to helping them through those uncertainties. There were in both groups persons whose lives became dominated by a sense of betrayal and a deep, corrosive bitterness. The whites, having control of the local governments, expressed themselves soon and openly. The blacks for the most part experienced an extended repression and had to bide their time. Decades later, when the National Association for the Advancement of Colored People (NAACP) decided to become a more militant organization, some of those frustrations finally found an outlet.

Initially, then, there was no "reconstruction." There was anarchy at best and chaos at worst. In the general lawlessness which prevailed, blacks, being both accessible and vulnerable, were the targets of what we today call "hate crimes." Very few specific Orange County stories have surfaced, though there almost have to be more out there.[34] Even so, the general sense of writings about that era is that things didn't get as bad in Virginia as they did in the deep South. Locally, things were probably seen as bad enough.

THE AVAILABILITY OF LAND AND EMPLOYMENT, PLUS A DESIRE TO REMAIN IN the community, led many of Orange County's emancipated blacks to remain in the area at various locations throughout the county. Over the years, the settlements became known as "freedmen's villages," and the Orange County Historical Society has identified the sites of fifteen such villages[35]

---

[34] In February 1867, the Gordonsville office of the Freedmens' Bureau became involved in an incident in which a colored man named Thomas Jefferson was whipped. By May, the matter had been settled, with Jefferson receiving $1,000 in damages. (From an unpublished research report on the operations of that office, the report done in 2001 for Historic Gordonsville, Inc.)

[35] The March/April 1999 newsletter of the Society contains a map showing the locations of the villages and gives a brief description for each.

in the county. Tibbstown, Little Egypt, Careytown, and Little Petersburg survive as viable communities to this day. Others, such as Possum Hollow, Cattail, and Freetown, have ceased to exist. Freetown remains probably the most widely known of the county's freedmen's villages, thanks in large measure to one of its former residents, Edna Lewis, becoming internationally known for her culinary skills.

Not all freed slaves elected to settle in the villages. George Gilmore, for example, who had been a Montpelier slave, bought land just across today's Route 20 from Montpelier, and in 1872 built his home there. The Gilmore house and farm, now owned by Montpelier, is undergoing restoration.

George Gilmore's home. Tree ring analysis of the structure's core logs gives a construction date of 1872. Speculation is that Gilmore found a place to live in the nearby remains of the 1863-64 winter camp of McGowan's South Carolina brigade until he could build his house. Montpelier Foundation property photographed by Bernice Walker. Reproduced with permission.

The South had put down its weapons, but for many of its leaders, the war was still on. Many Sunday congregations continued to hear that God was on "our" side and that they would eventually, somehow prevail. Political speeches were often laced with the same rhetoric. The "Bonnie Blue Flag" was sung in the streets, and Federal representatives were taunted and spit upon. The report of Robert E. Lee's response, however, was more indicative of how the majority of the South was actually thinking.

On a Sunday in June 1865, ex-General Lee was attending worship services at St. Paul's Episcopal Church in Richmond. Many Confederate notables were members of that church, and its sanctuary had become known as "the Cathedral of the Confederacy." On that particular Sunday, communion was to be offered, and at the appropriate time the minister took the communion elements from the altar and turned to the congregation. A black man, a stranger, described as "tall, well-dressed, and having a military bearing," was the first person to stride to the altar rail. While St. Paul's had long had black communicants, they sat separately and came for communion last. The congregation froze in silence. Finally, there was the sound of movement, and Robert E. Lee came to the rail to receive communion in the company of the black stranger. Lee's motivations in the light of the times can be argued from now to forever, but students of the General agree that the act was consistent with the character of the man.[36]

Other folks were also looking to heal the south. Their efforts, however, might have been seen more as trying to bring the south to heel. Late in 1865 the "Committee of Fifteen" on Reconstruction was formed by Congress and began holding hearings in Washington. This is the committee that subpoenaed Lee and took his testimony. This was also the group whose members were the primary authors of the Fourteenth Amendment, making slavery in America unconstitutional — at last. Another product of that committee's efforts were the Second Reconstruction Acts of March 1867.

With the Second Reconstruction Acts, the Radical Republicans in Congress were in full control, and "Military Reconstruction" was imposed on a recalcitrant South. For procedural purposes, the Commonwealth of Virginia ceased to exist, and that particular portion of conquered Federal territory became known as "Military District #1." There was a governor and a legislature, but their decisions were subject to being countermanded by the Military Governor, the first of whom was Brevet Major General John M. Schofield.

When a constitutional convention in Richmond adopted the Underwood Constitution on April 4, 1867, Virginia began to slowly emerge from Reconstruction. The new state constitution was found acceptable by the Federal government, and Virginia headed towards free public elections. It was not until 1874, however, that a popularly elected native Virginian would occupy the Governor's mansion. That person, as we know, was James Lawson Kemper, a Madison County native who would come to "Walnut Hills" in Orange County after his term of office and live there for the rest of his life.

---

[36] Sincere thanks to Philip J. Schwarz, St. Paul's Church historian, who supplied the author with copies of the two primary information sources on the incident. Both are reports of the recollections of Col. T. L. Broun of Charleston WV, who stated that he had been an eyewitness. Those who assert that the story is a fabrication note that revered Lee biographer, Dr. Douglas Southall Freeman, makes no mention of it. Several other Lee biographers, however, do.

Kemper had barely settled in as Governor when he was faced with a race related issue. The City of Petersburg had recently held town council elections, and some of the city's more influential residents were upset. Historically, Petersburg had a sizeable black population, and the elections had produced a town council which reflected the racial composition of the electorate. Now Kemper was looking at Senate Bill No. 5, which if he signed it into law, would replace the new town council with a board of commissioners appointed by the city judge. Kemper vetoed the bill and returned it to the Senate with a four page letter, pointing out that the bill went against everything a reunited America stood for. He was burned in effigy both in Petersburg and in Richmond, but his veto was upheld by the Senate. Kemper, a son of the Old South but a realist, had made his stand for Virginia's future.

Ardent secessionist and Civil War general, James Lawson Kemper became a leader in the New South after the war. This picture was taken during his term as Governor of Virginia, 1874-78, and is reproduced with permission of Mr. & Mrs. I. W. Jeanes (owners of Walnut Hills, Kemper's home) and of Harold Woodward, Jr., Madison County historian.

Kemper also displayed a "New South" attitude towards the state's pre-Civil War debt, payment of which was being demanded by nervous creditors, many of whom were British. A few Virginians were for "repudiating" the debt, effectively stiffing the creditors. The Old Guard were "funders," supporting payment of every penny owed, with interest, honoring their sacred obligation. Funders were also hoping they could thereby avoid having to acknowledge that Virginia, once the most prosperous state in all America, was now virtually bankrupt. Kemper, a funder in principle, realized that if Virginia did not renegotiate its debt, it would be decades, if ever, before roads, bridges, schools, etc., could be built. He therefore ran for governor as a "readjuster," a position that attracted the support of the then-powerful Mahone faction and effectively guaranteed his election.

A less than casual observer of the Orange County scene during Reconstruction was Marcus Sterling Hopkins. An Ohio native, Hopkins' first visits to our area were as a sergeant in the 7th Ohio Infantry Regiment, but disabling wounds to his face and shoulder during the Battle of Cedar Mountain in adjacent Culpeper County relegated him to the Veteran Reserve Corps for the remainder of the war. As soon as the Federal government created the Bureau of Freedmen, Refugees, and Abandoned Lands, he sought and received appointment as one of its field officers, or "agents" as they were often called. The official short name for the Virginia division of the Bureau was "BRFAL-VA," however everyone soon began calling it the "Freedmen's Bureau," since such work as it did with refugees and abandoned lands was overshadowed by its involvement in freedmen's activities.

Hopkins first served as an officer in the Bureau's Prince William County office, but in February 1867 he was transferred to the District Four offices in Gordonsville and placed in charge of Orange and Louisa counties.[37] By then he had bought a small farm near Manassas and had moved his wife and family there. Hopkins, however, had been attracted by the land and the climate, definitely not by the people.[38]

Initially, Bureau agents conducted Freedmen's Courts and tried cases involving freedmen, who had no standing in Virginia courts until the Civil Rights Act of 1866 was passed. After that, agents still had to attend local courts and monitor all cases involving freedmen. If a decision appeared improper, the agent could conduct an investigation and report to his superiors for possible orders to overturn the local court's decision. Bureau agents were also charged with providing food and medical care for the freedmen, and a Freedmen's Hospital was operated for a time at Gordonsville. There is no specific reference to the use of the Exchange Hotel and the old receiving hospital facilities, but there are references to using property of the former Confederate government, which the hotel and hospital most certainly were. The Bureau ceased operating a hospital at Gordonsville the same year Hopkins arrived.[39]

Bureau agents also assisted the various private organizations involved in the education of the former slaves. At the time Hopkins was here, there

---

[37] The District Four offices of BRFAL-VA oversaw Bureau activities in fifteen counties, and Hopkins' limited jurisdiction is described by one researcher as that of an "Assistant-Sub-Assistant-Commissioner."

[38] "I am anxious to have our section settle up with good, intelligent, and industrious northern people." Also, "I would be glad if I were paying [Virginia property] taxes for the same advanced and enlightened purposes as I would be in the North." Mugoleston, *Diary of Marcus Hopkins*, pp. 53, 54.

[39] Historic Gordonsville, Inc., Freedmen's Bureau research report, 2001, p. 34.

was a school in Gordonsville staffed by several members of the Freedmen's Aid Union Commission, one of the several private organizations engaged in educating Virginia freedmen. Jane Hosmer of Concord, Massachusetts, and William P. Lucas were the only Gordonsville teachers named in Hopkin's diary. Various other sources report that Harriet F. Stone, Mary A. Fowler, and Marie Perkins, all of Massachusetts, also taught at Gordonsville at one time or another. John W. and A. S. Pratt, husband and wife, taught at Orange for a time. Lucas was a black man. It is not known if any of the women were black, but that would not have been unusual in a freedmen's school.

Bureau agents were also supposed to draw up and help enforce labor contracts for the freedmen. Hopkins does not specifically note doing so at Gordonsville, and probably by then, he, like most agents, had given up trying to deal in the employment relations of the former slaves with their former masters, as long as everything was relatively peaceful. Both sides routinely ignored such contracts until their enforcement could benefit the complaining party. Agents did what they could to resolve minor claims between whites and blacks and even attempted on occasion to resolve domestic disputes. Hopkins noted that both whites and blacks habitually carried concealed weapons, which definitely added to the excitement and urgency of his work.[40]

Hopkins had a decidedly low regard for the male versions of both the Southern white and Southern black. He did associate with Mr. Stratton in Gordonsville, but that was apparently because they were fellow Masons. He had very little to say about Southern women of either race. In his opinion, Northern men and women were clearly superior people. Because of what he saw as the depraved and degraded condition of the people he dealt with, Hopkins occasionally despaired of accomplishing anything of value. At the end of his term of service, however, he did point to some success which could be attributed to the work of the Bureau:

"As the Bureau is about to be partially discontinued, and this is the last report I shall be called upon to make as one of its officers, I deem it proper to note briefly some of the results of its establishment that appear within the limited extent of my jurisdiction, at this, the end of three years of my

---

[40] Hopkins' diary entry for July 31, 1867: "Miss Nellie Patterson shot at Lawrence Faulconer in the street for swearing falsely against her sister in court. She looked out for Snyder, but he did not come on the train. Snyder seduced her sister and abandoned her." Mugoleston, *Diary*, p. 88.

employment in its service. I desire to do this especially, as in looking at the present condition of the freedmen and their relations with the whites, so much of imperfection and evil is seen, so much to improve and reform is presented, so great the work yet to be done and so long the time yet to wait is felt to be, that one is apt to lose sight of the beginning, and thus fail to appreciate what has already been accomplished in the great and arduous undertaking of converting slaves into useful citizens, and slaveholders into the respecters of the rights of their fellow men."[41]

Hopkins would have deplored even more what he saw as the premature shutdown of the Bureau if he could have seen what the future would bring. As Virginia headed toward the twentieth century, another white aristocracy evolved, this one based more on commerce and manufacturing than agriculture, but it drew strong support from the farmers and from the poor whites, the latter a class Hopkins had thought more depraved than the Negro.

WITH THE ADOPTION OF THE 1902 STATE CONSTITUTION — WITHOUT A public referendum — much of the concept and many of the gains of Reconstruction were wiped out. Blacks and poor whites were effectively disenfranchised, and overt racial discrimination was the order of the day. The era of "Jim Crow," the era of state mandated and legally enforced racial discrimination and segregation, was underway. A number of local blacks growing up in Orange County during the Reconstruction and Jim Crow eras who did not have strong family ties or property ownerships holding them here, moved away. One of those was Nannie Helen Burroughs, who as a young girl in 1884 was taken by her mother to live in Washington DC. Nannie developed into a phenomenal educator, eventually founding the National Training School for Women and Girls in 1909. Religion and practical life lessons were taught alongside the arts and sciences, or as Ms. Burroughs put it, teaching "the Bible, the bath, and the broom." She remained headmistress of the school until her death in 1961. The school, which continues in operation today, was renamed the Nannie Helen Burroughs School, and in 1975 Washington's mayor proclaimed that from henceforth May 10 would be Nannie Helen Burroughs Day.

From 1925 to the 1960s, Virginia was ruled by the Byrd Machine, a state Democratic party organization for whom fiscal conservatism and white

---

[41] Mugoleston, *Diary*, p. 99. Bureau activities were scaled back and the regional headquarters moved to Culpeper in 1869.

supremacy were hallmarks. Its fiscal conservatism was usually expressed as "pay as you go." Its white supremacy, an accepted, uncontested reality by both races for years, came with an official race relationship policy of "separate, but equal." The typical response of blacks who lived through those times is: "I saw a lot of separate. Equal? Never." Initially, however, it would not have occurred to anyone, black or white, to openly challenge that position. It was simply a fact of life. The Second World War, the *Brown v. Board* decision in 1954, the collapse of Virginia's "massive resistance" to school integration in 1959, and the successful "sit in" protests all signaled the crumbling of the Byrd political empire. The resignation of the seriously ill Harry F. Byrd from his U. S. Senate seat in 1965 signaled its end.

Local school integration moved slowly and arrived late. Both characteristics are most clearly demonstrated by the fact that while *Brown v. Board* had been decided May 17, 1954, Orange County proceeded to build Prospect Heights School as a black-only segregated school and opened it as such on December 17, 1956. The Orange public school system was not fully integrated until 1968, a reflection of the local white leaders asking for, and being granted, time and patience from their black counterparts. Small wonder then that the white members of the Orange community don't recall any real problems with integration. The responses from members of the black community are more guarded, but virtually no one wanted riots and Federal troops in the county. That was a heritage that Orange County's citizens did not want to have to live with.[42]

## F. Victims and Heroes of the New South

There were notable individual stories coming out of the Reconstruction era, some tragic and some triumphant. One of each with Orange County connections bears mention.

BY 1860, JEREMIAH MORTON WAS DOING AS WELL AS HE COULD HAVE EVER dreamed. His education at Washington College and William & Mary had prepared him for a career in law, but he had readily succumbed to the "call" of farming. As a planter, Morton had accumulated large holdings in both Orange and Culpeper counties. To three, he assigned names that spoke to

---

[42] For a Spotsylvania comparison, in 1959 Fredericksburg's private Montfort School was the first to integrate, with the public school system fully integrating in 1968. See: Fitzgerald, *A Different Story*, p. 247, *et seq.*

both his wit and his prosperity: "Lessland," "Moreland;" and "Stillmore." The centerpiece of his holdings was "The Hall," the Orange County home place which had been in his family since 1756. Over the years, Morton family members had expanded The Hall operations to cover 3,500 acres. Jeremiah and his brothers, orphaned early, had grown up at The Hall with their great-uncle. Upon the uncle's death, Jeremiah and his brothers inherited The Hall, and he soon bought out his brothers' interests.

Morton was a man of many parts, one of which was as an uncommonly good architect and builder. As a "gentleman architect" in the Jeffersonian mold, Morton produced designs and constructed buildings that rivaled and in ways surpassed the work product of the professionals of his day. He extensively remodeled The Hall residence, combining a variety of popular architectural styles as he created what was essentially a new building. In performing that work, he did such things as installing cross-bracing between the joists and a fabric underlayment under the metal roof, features not seen in the work of other builders in the area. Morton's skill continues to be demonstrated in the residences of Lessland and Greenville, the latter in Culpeper County. The once grand but long-unoccupied Hall residence, that over time had become known as "Morton Hall," collapsed to the ground during the year 2000.

Morton had also tried his hand in politics, serving as a delegate to the 31st U. S. Congress (1849-51). His term was concurrent with that of brother Jackson, who had moved to Florida after selling his interest in The Hall to Jeremiah and who had been elected to the Senate from that state. An ardent secessionist, Jeremiah returned to Orange County and successfully fanned the flames of division. Thanks in large measure to his efforts, Orange and Culpeper counties sent delegations to the 1861 convention in Richmond with majorities committed to secession. With the outbreak of hostilities, Morton sold The Hall and put that money into Confederate bonds. He also secured a commission as a colonel in the Confederate cavalry and is reputed to have briefly served on Stonewall Jackson's staff.[43] There was absolutely no doubting the man's commitment.

At the end of the Civil War, Jeremiah was an old, bankrupt, and deeply disillusioned man, looking for a hole to crawl in and hide from the world until he could die. He found a roof to live under at Lessland with his daughter

---

[43] Richmond Battlefield Park historian Robert E. L. Krick is working on a book which when published will feature biographies of all staff officers who served in the Army of Northern Virginia. As of this writing, Mr. Krick had found no record of Jeremiah Morton's service in a staff position.

and her family. The only notable post-war work product from his once active and inventive mind is his brief lament, which may resonate with us for as long as anyone deals with Southern history:

"I was surrounded by every comfort the world could afford — a delightful home and happy family of whites and blacks, an income of $30,000 annually with a prospect of yearly increase — the scourge of war has swept all from me, and at the age of 68, I stand a blasted stump in the wilderness of life."

In 1878, at age 79, the Honorable Jeremiah Morton finally passed away at Lessland. Peace at last.

William "Billy" Mahone was not a local, but over time he created enough of a stir in Orange County for folks here to get to know him and keep up with him. Born in 1826, this rough and rowdy son of a Southhampton tavern keeper had been appointed a "state scholar" to the first class of the brand-new Virginia Military Institute. Scholarship student or no, young Billy lived well and dressed elegantly during his Institute years, thanks largely to his tavern-learned gambling skills. Fabulous at mathematics and poor at languages, he was educated to be an engineer.

Billy first surfaced in Orange County in the early 1850s as the survey team leader for the Culpeper to Orange segment of the Orange & Alexandria Railroad. Even before that project wound down, he took over as the Chief Engineer for the company that was building the Orange Plank Road. Those were high visibility jobs for this part of Virginia, and it quickly became clear that Mahone was up to the challenge. He liked being noticed. He also probably began to demonstrate to the locals that he had some real ability at managing people. Small, slightly built, with a thin, high voice, Mahone might not impress people immediately, but it wouldn't be long before they found themselves following his instructions.

Taking leave of his Orange County friends, Mahone went east in 1853 to design and construct a railroad right of way through the Great Dismal Swamp, the defining feat of his engineering career. That work was done for the Norfolk & Petersburg Railroad, and by 1859 he was its president. At the start of the Civil War, Mahone was appointed a colonel in command of an infantry regiment. By the end of the war, he was a Major General in command of a division.

As an officer in the Army of Northern Virginia, Mahone was in and out of Orange County a number of times. During his longest stay, the winter of 1863-64, Mahone used his Orange County connections to work out a deal with the members of Zion Church at Madison Run. Following Sunday services, Mahone's men would arrive to take the pews out of the church building and store them in a safe, dry place. Into the cleared chancel came soldier-shoemakers and their benches, and Zion Church became a weekday shoe factory. By the time the 1864 spring campaign began, Mahone's men were reputed to be the best shod troops in Lee's army.

Within 30 days of Lee's surrender at Appomattox, Mahone was back in the head office at the Norfolk & Petersburg, securing Federal hauling contracts. He also "secured" track repair crews and rolling stock from somewhere (probably the Union Army) and had the N&P back rolling, ahead of any other Virginia railroad. That bit of success did not go unnoticed. By 1866 Mahone was also the president of both the Southside and the Virginia & Tennessee railroads. He rebuilt those roads to the same gauge as the N&P, thus allowing uninterrupted rail traffic from Bristol to Norfolk.

William "Billy" Mahone. From civil engineer to Civil War general to railroad tycoon, the aggressive and capable Mahone rarely lacked for self-confidence. Mahone and his wife Otelia were elegant dressers and were sometimes called "the emperor and empress of Virginia." Picture reproduced courtesy of the Virginia Historical Society, Richmond.

Mahone then petitioned the Virginia legislature for authority to merge his three railroads. The opposition was fierce in the extreme, with one of the major opponents being John Strode Barbour, president of the Orange & Alexandria. Mahone prevailed, however, and created a rail system which, in cooperation with other rail systems in Kentucky and Tennessee, permitted him to offer rail service from the Mississippi to the Chesapeake, something that the Virginia "Old Guard" had fought to keep from happening.[44] Ultimately, Mahone's rail system became a major component in what is today's Norfolk Southern Railroad.

---

[44] The combined rail system was called the "A,M &O." Mahone's wife's name was Otelia, and wags claimed the new name meant "All Mine and Otelia's."

Mahone parlayed his business success into political power, and in 1874, he backed Orange County resident-to-be James Lawson Kemper for Governor. With that backing, Kemper won and became the first native born Virginian to be elected Governor following the Civil War. In 1880, Mahone himself was elected to the U. S. Senate, and two years later, one of his political lieutenants was elected Governor of Virginia. Mahone and the Democratic Party remained at odds, however, and as that party gained control of the state, Mahone's power waned. Already out of railroading, he eventually retired to private life and died in 1895.

Mahone's recovery from the Civil War was as dramatic and as inspiring as Jeremiah Morton's ongoing defeat was tragic. Can it be explained by noting that Morton's heritage was as one of the Old Guard planter aristocracy and Mahone's was as a dig-and-scratch poor white? Was it the nearly 30 year difference in their ages? Their vastly different educations? Hard to say, but there was a heavy sprinkling of Morton and Mahone types among that far greater majority of Southerners, black and white, who simply went out and worked every day to make their part of the world a better place in which to live.

## G. The Fried Chicken Ladies

One particular facet of Gordonsville's post Civil War rail-based economy involved an enterprising group of women in the town's black community. The core of that community was Brown Town, one of the county's freedmen's villages which a Brown family was instrumental in establishing. With so many passenger trains stopping in Gordonsville, the ladies saw a demand for some sort of food business that could offer passengers something to eat as long as it was instantly available right at the station.

Before long, the ladies were meeting trains with trays of items such as fried chicken, pies, and coffee. A tray would be held up to the passenger's window, the food selection made, and money in payment put on the tray. America was being exposed to fast food service in action at Gordonsville, involving folks whose grandchildren would later claim that fast food was an invention of their day. A few men and children also helped with the work, but the remembered symbol of the enterprise remains the "Fried Chicken Lady."

The food service worked beautifully, and rail passengers began to look forward to the Gordonsville stop, describing the community variously as "the fried chicken capital of the world," or "the chicken wing capital of the universe," or some other such high compliment. The business finally tapered off during the depression years, then was briefly revived in the early years of the WWII troop trains. Health Department regulations about food preparation and serving, the gradual move of railroads to cars with sealed windows, and some insist, the complaints of nearby hotel and restaurant owners to the town leaders, finally put the Gordonsville Fried Chicken Ladies out of business for good. But it is a time worth remembering. In the summer of 2002, a tourist information panel recalling the work of the Ladies was dedicated during a Gordonsville African-American street festival. It stands in the yard of the Exchange Hotel Museum, overlooking the railroad tracks where the Fried Chicken Ladies earned their place in Orange County's history.

## H. Orange County's Tuskegee Airman

In the 1930s, Andrew Maples, Sr., lived in a small frame house in the shadow of St. Thomas' Episcopal Church in Orange. Maples sold insurance in the local black community for the Home Beneficial Life Insurance Company and did various other jobs to help make ends meet. For example, when Mrs. Scott had a big occasion at Montpelier, she would ask Maples to help.

Maples' occupations and experiences, however, went beyond the norm. A New York native, he had served as a member of the $92^{nd}$ Division of the Allied Expeditionary Forces during World War I. He had been gassed, and doctors told him that his injured lungs couldn't handle the New York City air. But love was already providing an answer: He was going to marry Julia Blanche Michie and move to her home town of Orange, Virginia.

Julia Michie had also seen more of the world than Orange County and Virginia. She had lived and worked in Philadelphia for a time before moving to New York. Both Andrew Maples and his new bride understood what black people could do if they got a good education and operated in an environment that afforded more opportunities than the Jim Crow South of their day. In 1920, the Maples had their first child, and named him Andrew Maples, Jr.

Andrew Maples, Jr., spent his early years in Orange and attended the local, segregated, elementary school. He was evidently a bright youngster, and he was doubtless strongly encouraged by his parents to learn. As his education progressed towards the high school level, the decision was made for him to move to Washington DC, live with a relative, and attend Armstrong High School. At the time in Orange County, Lightfoot School in Unionville was reported to be offering a certificate program to black students which was supposed to be the equivalent of a high school education, but Armstrong offered the environment and education that Maples, Sr., felt would best fit his son for the future.[45]

Upon the completion of his high school education, Andrew was accepted at Hampton Institute in eastern Virginia. The Second World War was beginning as his Hampton years started, and somewhere, somehow, Andrew learned to fly airplanes. The Federal government had a Civilian Pilot Training Program in effect at a number of colleges and universities as early as 1939, but the program was not understood to be open to blacks. Probably Andrew had to arrange for his own instruction. In any event, with the war raging in Europe, Andrew withdrew from Hampton at the end of his sophomore year and entered the Flying School at Tuskegee Institute in Alabama.

The prestigious Tuskegee Institute, long known as the excellent black college whose programs had been initially developed and administered by Booker T. Washington, had applied to the federal government to become a flying school for black pilots. The school was approved conditionally, and in July 1941, thirteen pilot cadets began training. Nine months later, five of them graduated. The Army Air Corps was satisfied and authorized the school to continue. College students all over America were entering flying schools and being hit with cram courses in math, applied mechanics, meteorology, navigation, and aeronautics. The physical training and flying instruction was just as intense. The "wash-out" and resignation rate was high everywhere, but no higher than at Tuskegee. In the black pilots it graduated, Tuskegee was going to show America something.

Probably the average white person in the 1940s presumed that black people could do about as much flying as elephants, even though the Tuskegee Flying School was dedicated to turning out excellent pilots. One trainee recalled experiencing a mechanical problem and having to land in an Alabama road. There was a chain gang working on the road, all blacks, with white guards. When that trainee rose up out of the cockpit, his audience froze in stunned silence. They just knew he had to be from another planet.

The Army Air Corps wanted Tuskegee's pilots, with one possible exception: Andrew. Fighter plane cockpits were designed with no excess room, and the design contemplated an average sized body. Andrew was definitely not average sized; he was tall and lanky. Robert Eason, who also flew fighter planes in WWII and who has that same type of frame, says that he had to

---

[45] The George Washington Carver Regional High School (renamed the Piedmont Technical Institute in 1968) was not established until 1948.

figure out a way to fold himself into an airplane and then convince everyone that he was comfortable, which he wasn't. Andrew no doubt had to do the same.

On January 14, 1942, the Tuskegee Flying School honored its largest graduating class to date. Andrew Maples, Jr., was one of the 43 graduates, and along with his diploma, he received his pilot's wings and a Second Lieutenant's commission in the Army Air Corps. He thus became one of the "Tuskegee Airmen," the famed black fighter pilots of WWII. The Airmen began overseas operations in Africa and later moved to Italy. The 99th Fighter Squadron was joined over time by the 100th, the 301st, and 302nd squadrons, all Tuskegee Airmen. The four squadrons were incorporated into the 332nd Fighter Group, flying bomber escort missions deep into enemy territory. In 1945 some of the group actually tangled with German Me-262 jet fighter planes, but they kept intact a phenomenal

Lt. Andrew Maples, Jr., a picture apparently taken at his induction into the U.S. Army Air Corps following his graduation from the Tuskegee Institute flight school. Maples' education and determination were more than enough to meet the school's high standards. This much-copied photo was on the front page of the *Orange Review*.

record of never losing a bomber placed under their protection.

Andrew went to Michigan for advanced training. While there, he demonstrated a proficiency which earned him a promotion to First Lieutenant. He soon went overseas as a member of the 301st Fighter Squadron. By 1944 Andrew's command was flying the new P-47 Thunderbolts, planes combining a long range with more than adequate speed and firepower. On June 26, 1944, he was a member of the escort for a deep penetration bombing mission into Hungary. On the way home, Andrew ran into trouble.

At about 5:15 p.m., he radioed his base that the plane's engine had quit and that he was going to have to bail out. His last reported position was at 3,000 feet over the Adriatic Sea, some ten miles north of Termoli, Italy. Andrew radioed that he could just barely make out the Italian coast — and then he was gone. Two planes took off from Andrew's base and flew a search pattern over the reported bail-out area. Seeing nothing, they extended the pattern all the way to the coast of Yugoslavia, then came back to repeat it in the bail-out area. Nothing.

The Maples family was notified that Lieutenant Maples was missing, and the war went on. The family, with five sons in the military by that time, waited anxiously for news. None came for a long time, and when news finally came, it was bad. On June 27, 1945, the War Department notified the Maples family that a year had elapsed with no evidence that Andrew was alive. He was accordingly being declared killed in action on June 26, 1944. The family was devastated.

First Lieutenant Andrew Maples, Jr., was posthumously promoted to Captain, and Mr. and Mrs. Maples were awarded the Gold Star, symbolic of the loss of a child in the war. After the war, the local, segregated Veterans of Foreign Wars post asked the Maples family for permission to name their post in his honor. Permission granted. Still later, a monument honoring Virginia's airmen killed in WWII was dedicated at Richmond. Andrew's name is on it.

The name of Andrew Maples, Jr., has, unfortunately, been forgotten by a large number of Orange County's residents, both black and white. It should not be. He was, and is, a hero, a black American hero — from Orange County, Virginia.[46]

### I. "Bet My Money on a Bob-Tailed Nag . . . ."[47]

One of the most public displays of local black ingenuity and independence was the Orange Colored Horse Show, which became an annual event between the two world wars. Its success probably lay in the fact that it wasn't staged as an attempt to demonstrate ingenuity and independence, it was the black community responding as a whole to something a number of its members were really good at and loved doing.[48]

---

[46] The author is indebted to Doris J. Maples Walker and other members of her family for their help in bringing back the memory of her brother.

[47] "..., Somebody Bet on the Bay." For those who have no feel for the almost-addictive horse racing frenzy which once gripped America, listen to Stephen Foster's *Camptown Races* (the source of the subchapter title), then attend the Montpelier Races on a first Saturday in November.

During the first half of the twentieth century, there were quite a few owners of excellent horses in the area. Many of those people hired black jockeys, grooms, and stable hands, who thus had opportunities to work with quality horses, to develop high levels of professional skill, and to buy or be given horses of their own. Many of these black horsemen also got show experience by working in the white Orange Horse Show. That show had grown into a Triple-A rated event, licensed by the American Horse Show Association, and it attracted entrants and spectators from the mid-Atlantic region. The organizers of the Colored Horse Show surely learned a tremendous amount by being around it, but their show was uniquely theirs.

Prominent among such persons was Mr. Lewis Ellis, who owned a farm of some 200 acres on Route 612 opposite Meadowfarm. Ellis and his two sons, Marshall and Gus, built a show ring and a racing oval on a portion of the property, and races and shows there began drawing larger and larger crowds. Soon, local businessmen and horse lovers, particularly Andrew Maples, Sr., and Benjamin Bowler, teamed up with the Ellises. A corporation was formed, stock issued, and the Orange Colored Horse Show was a going concern.

It was called a horse "show," and showing took place. Maples and Bowler, for example, served as judges for some of the classes. Racing, however, appears to have been the main public attraction. There were flat track races, sulky races, jumping contests and mule races. A well-known local jockey was James Galloway, a/k/a "Peg Leg," who did not let the absence of a limb slow him down.

The primary emphasis was on having a good time. There was a sizeable grandstand and ample parking for the crowds which came from as far away as Kentucky, Pennsylvania, and New York. The show dates were chosen to coincide with the annual fall church homecomings and family reunions in the area and take advantage of those ready-made crowds of vacationers. During those "meeting" and "association" weeks, local blacks also routinely got extra time off work, and some of that time wound up being spent at the show grounds.

The quality of the competition was excellent. Not only did a number of blacks in the area personally own good horses, some also had permission to ride their employers' horses. Occasionally an out-of-state trainer would

---

[48] Construction was another area that offered early opportunities for capable black citizens to excel. For example, members of the Jackson family built an impressive bridge across Blue Run, as well as the complex of buildings currently housing Satchell's Funeral Home and Walker's Barber Shop in the town of Orange.

The 1938 Orange Colored Horse Show was advertised for a Wednesday and Thursday in late August. "Good order" means that the crowd will be well-behaved. That event drew William O. Klemm, staff photographer for the *Washington Post*. The archives section of the Post had a record of Mr. Klemm's employment, but none of his articles or photographs. The much-copied photograph is one of several which evidently accompanied a write-up on the show. Advertisement compliments of the Orange County African-American Historical Society. Photograph compliments of the Orange County Division of Tourism.

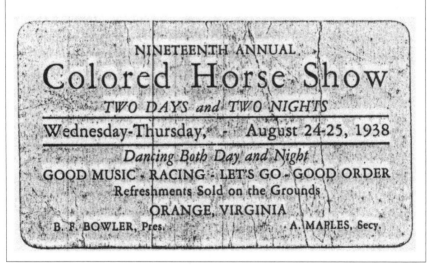

come with a horse. In addition to the usual winners' prizes of cups and ribbons, some races offered the added attraction of practical awards, such as small sums of cash, automobile tires, etc. Usually one of the mule races would be a contest in which the last to cross the finish line was declared the "winner." Riders strained to avoid earning that title.

Horses, however, were far from being the only attraction. There was good food, and lots of it. There was great music. Headliner bands that drew large audiences in big cities came to play at Orange. And there was dancing, oh mercy, was there dancing. Under the grandstand there was a large dance hall. An advertisement for the 1938 show announced "dancing both day and night." The lights blazed and the music blared into the wee hours of the morning.

Mr. Ellis passed away, but Marshall and Gus, accomplished horsemen in their own right, kept the show going with the continuing assistance of local black businessmen. One participant recalls the show continuing for five days and nights at the height of its popularity. A 1938 advertisement announced the Nineteenth Annual Colored Horse Show and called for a two-day event. The onset of the Second World War brought the show to an end. People became busier and traveled less, there was the possibility of civil defense blackouts cutting off evening and nighttime activities, and the mood of the country had turned deadly serious. It was time to do other things. After the war, the show was not resumed. Black baseball teams used the field some, but no horses. The white horse show survived into the war years, but it just wasn't the same. It too finally closed down.

Several other widely-known Orange County sporting activities lasted through most of the twentieth century. There were two "hunts," foxhound packs, with the associated Master, Whippers-in, Outriders, and "Field" of riders taking them out often enough for the hunts to be recognized by the New York-based Masters of Foxhounds Association. One was the Montpelier Hounds, which has an organization date of 1912. The other was a hunt first organized in 1902 as the Orange County Hunt, reorganized in 1905 as the Tomahawk Hunt, merged in 1933 into Carter's Hunt, and finally taken over in 1952 by Langbourne Williams and renamed the Rapidan Hunt.[49] In east-central Orange County, on Guy Lewis' Hawfield, one of the premier bird dog field trial events in America took place each year. All those activities ended with the deaths of their respective patrons. In recent years there has been a revival of the field trials, but the hunts, which demand an extended commitment of time, in addition to considerable money,  remain memories.

---

[49] V. R. Shackelford, Jr., who rode with the Montpelier Hunt for years, gave a talk to the Historical Society on foxhunting in this part of Virginia, and he kindly filed a copy of his notes at the Research Center. Those notes were extensively and gratefully consulted for this segment of the chapter.

*Above:* An 1848 lithograph of the Vaucluse Gold Mine Village located in the Wilderness of Orange County, just northeast of today's Route 3/20 intersection. The village could house 150 miners with their families and provided many on-site services, such as a resident doctor. The lithograph was probably created to show to prospective investors. Reproduced courtesy of the Virginia Historical Society, Richmond.

*Below:* Facilities of the West Virginia Timber Company in the Town of Orange. Madison Road now runs between the former Rapidan Railroad station in the foreground and the extensive sawmilling and wood drying operation in the background. The railroad brought logs from the Blue Ridge Mountains and unloaded them into a pond. A special conveyor at the sawmill dragged the logs into the mill. Today's silk mill building was built over that pond. Photograph courtesy of R. Duff Green.

West Virginia Timber Co.    Orange, Va.

# Chapter VII

## *The Commerce of a County*

### A. The Profession – Nay, the Calling – of Farming

The earliest arrivals to the Virginia colony soon confirmed the general expectation that Virginia held no treasure troves such as those discovered and looted by the Spanish to the south. The issue then became one of what one could do at a profit in this place besides struggle to survive. Initially, though, struggling to survive was a sufficient challenge to command the full attention and energy of everyone who came ashore from the supply ships. In point of fact, most of the early arrivals did not have long to consider their options because they were soon dead.

New arrivals first had to endure "seasoning," a baptism of ailments which usually featured malaria and which left them alternately roasting and shivering on their pallets for weeks. If seasoning was survived, then the hard work and the climate, most particularly the summers, sapped the strength and spirit out of folk and left them vulnerable to the periodic outbreaks of smallpox, cholera, typhoid, yellow fever, etc., that decimated even the seasoned. In addition to disease, such things as bad or insufficient food, childbirth, Indian attacks, accidents, and freak weather events all combined to send the weak, the unprepared, and the simply unlucky to early graves. To borrow a description from the eminently quotable Thomas Hobbes, life on Virginia's early tidewater frontier was "nasty, brutish, and short."[1]

Before Orange County was settled, however, the colonists had already begun to adapt and thrive in this new land. Also by then John Rolfe had cultivated the sweet Varinas to-

---

[1] During its seventeen year existence, the Virginia Company shipped some 6,000 persons to the colony. Of those, 4,800 (80%) died prematurely or unnaturally. For more, see "Unsettling Times at Jamestown" in the June 2002 issue of *National Geographic Magazine*, p. 74 *et seq.*

bacco on a James River plantation and demonstrated that it could be grown successfully in Virginia. That variety of tobacco was a highly prized item in Europe, and during the critical formative years of the colony, there was a rich and ready market for as much of it as Virginia could produce. While survival remained high on the settlers' lists of priorities, it was clear that what one could do in this wilderness to make a fortune was get land and grow tobacco.

The tobacco mindset was still firmly in place as the exploration of our region began, and a primary task for the Knights of the Golden Horseshoe on their 1716 jaunt was to assess the soils along their route for tobacco production. The settlers who followed did indeed grow tobacco, at least initially. It was the source of desperately needed cash, and what had to be done to produce a crop was generally known. Everyone from lenders in London to slaves in the rows "understood" tobacco. Later, as area soils became exhausted by tobacco's nutrient demands and as markets for other agricultural products evolved, more and more Orange County farmers switched to hay, corn, small grain, and livestock.

Whatever he produced, the farmer/planter was the King of the early Orange County economy. Farmers characterized themselves as practicing the consummate profession, and they spoke of being "called" to farming, mimicking the clergy who had long used the term. In their view, other professions: medicine, law, even the clergy, came second, and since the farmer/planter class was the wealthiest and most influential group in the county, it was hard to disagree with them. The Albemarle Agricultural Society, for example, elected James Madison to be its president, just as he was completing his term as President of the United States. He humbly accepted the post, and in 1818, addressed the group with a speech on crop and soil management that was printed and distributed widely, bringing even greater glory to agriculture and its practitioners.[2] Following Madison's presidency, the Society maintained its high profile by electing as his successor another Orange County resident: legislator, former governor, and U.S. ambassador to England, the Honorable James Barbour.

By the time Orange County was established, Virginia had begun to develop a manufacturing and commercial economy, but that had little impact out on the frontier. As late as 1850, over 68% of Orange County's free males were engaged in farming or farm-related occupations.[3] By compari-

---

[2] That address and its effect is detailed in: Hunt-Jones, *Dolley and the Great Little Madison*, p. 103.

[3] Schlotterbeck, *Plantation and Farm*, p. 238.

son, the 1990 U. S. Census shows that less than 1% of the county's work force was occupied in farming that year. Identifying and adding the persons occupied in servicing and supporting local agriculture in 1990 might triple the figure, but it remains clear that agriculture is far from being the dominant economic force in the county it once was.

People like to say that Orange County is a rural county, but that opinion now has to be based on the open spaces and wooded vistas that agriculture provides, plus the economic benefit to the county arising from the fact that its relatively large tracts of undeveloped land require almost no public services. "Rural residential" is probably the more accurate description of a county with every house identified on an E-911 map, a year-round leash law, and paid professionals in its rescue squads.

The county is already residential in terms of its tax base. The 1998 county real property value assessment figures available in the Commissioner of Revenue's office reveal that farms of 20 acres or more now make up less than 23.8% of the county's total real property tax base. The assessed value of residential real estate by comparison makes up 68.2% of that total.[4] Certain types of agricultural land qualify for a reduced assessment, called a "land-use" assessment. It is a badly-needed tax break for farmers, but one which further reduces the importance of agriculture to the county's economy.

From a business operations standpoint, local agriculture churns a lot of dollars (roughly $37 million during the last good crop year, according to the Agricultural Extension office), but with the exception of specialty operations, such as vineyards, profit margins are thin. As a farming friend of the writer observed recently, "Farming's not a whole lot of fun any more."

It was not until the 1920s that the status of the farmer/planter as the centerpiece of the county's economy was seriously challenged, and even then the farm vote remained a highly-desired political commodity. As late as the 1960s Virginia politicians courted the farm vote by reciting the mantra that farming was the backbone of Virginia's economy and that farmers were the moral core of its society. The politicians might not have believed it, but the farmers did. What's more, in their role as important and prin-

---

[4] Assessment classes #5 (Agricultural/undeveloped, 20-99 acres) and #6 (Agricultural/undeveloped, 100 acres and up) compared with assessment classes #1 (Single-family residential, urban), #2 (Single-family residential, suburban), and #3 (Multi-family residential). The only class not involved in the comparison is #4 (Commercial/industrial).

cipled people, farmers understood that they were above grubbing for dollars. Virtuous poverty was their badge of honor, and they proudly supplied the public with cheap food. Demands for import controls and higher support payments came later.

## B. Roads: Avenues of Commerce

As soon as the colonists began to move west of the fall line, there was a need for public roads. The broad, slow moving river highways of the Tidewater did not exist in the uplands. Backwoodsmen, explorers, and maybe a few frontier families might not mind using game trails or Indian paths, such as the Carolina Road, but that wasn't going to suit most people. A trail sufficiently cleared to permit travel on horseback was good, but a road along which wagons could be pulled and tobacco hogsheads rolled was the goal. With good roads, the colony's interior could be settled and its commerce extended.

As with much of the law governing property in the colony, the procedures to be followed in establishing a new road were based on those in effect in the Mother Country. Landowners who wanted a public road in their area petitioned the local court for an order directing its creation. The court conducted such hearings as it deemed necessary, and if it determined that the petition had merit, "viewers" of the proposed new road were appointed to lay out its route and report back. Viewers naturally tried to use existing private roads wherever possible, both to keep construction costs down and to avoid upsetting the already-established pattern of travel in the area. If the viewers' report was accepted, then an "overseer" (sometimes called a "surveyor") of the road was appointed to attend to its construction and maintenance.

An important step in the road building and maintenance process was an identification of all the "laboring male tithables" on the properties to be served by the road, since those persons constituted the construction and maintenance work force. In the colonial era, a tax, or tithe, was assessed on certain defined persons, and any person who met the definition was a "tithable." "Laboring male tithables" were typically able-bodied males sixteen years of age or older, whether slave, indentured, or free. For all slave and indentured tithables, it was the duty of the master to present the individual or a substitute at the time when their labor on a road was required.

Each tithable was required by the court to labor a certain number of days per year on the road (usually six), bringing all the tools and wagons or ox carts, with teams, needed to do the work. In this manner it was expected that county public roads could be built and maintained at no cost to the public treasury. For larger, more complicated projects, such as bridges or ferries, the court would appoint special commissioners to enter into construction contracts on behalf of the county. Later, in the nineteenth century, Virginia created a Board of Public Works to coordinate the development of multi-county projects such as railroads, canals and turnpikes.

Slaves were often substituted for all the actual tithables due from a large landowner; however, masters were routinely loath to take workers out of the fields, whether slave or free. The combination of foot-dragging landowners and frustrated overseers often resulted in petitions to the court to order performance. On the other side of that coin, users of a poorly maintained road often petitioned the court to discipline or discharge its overseer.

Records dealing with roads, known in historic research circles as "county road orders," are a rich source of information about a county's early history. They can be found in places as diverse as Acts of Assembly or vestry minutes, but the primary source is always the local court records. Not only do road orders identify roads, along with their associated overseers, they also often identify the nearby farms and plantations, including their owners, and describe landmarks, terrain, streams, and intersection points with other roads.[5] Many times that information exists nowhere else. Orange County is fortunate to have complete public records all the way from its date of formation. The county is also one of the handful in Virginia for which some tithables lists survive, specifically the lists for 1736-39, 1752-55, and 1782.[6]

Orange County is especially indebted to Ann Miller for employing her research and writing talents to produce *Orange County Road Orders, 1734-1749,* and *Orange County Road Orders, 1750-1800.* The Orange County Historical Society assisted in the sponsorship of that first work and in so doing became the first private organization in Virginia to become involved in publishing county road orders. Ann had acquired her interest and skills by working with Nathaniel Mason Pawlett, who had earlier produced a compilation of Spotsylvania County road orders. Combining Mr. Pawlett's

---

[5] A sample from County Order Book #5, dated November 24, 1749: "Ordered that the Male Labouring Tithables belonging to the Reverend Robert Rose, Mrs. Susanna Taliaferro, Mr. William Hunter, John Moran, Benjamin Porter, Nicholas Porter & John Seayres do work under John Marr who is an Overseer of a Road in this County and that they clear the Road from the Island Ford to the main Road by Simms."

[6] Counties whose early records are missing or incomplete are typically called "burn" counties, since a fire was almost always the cause.

work with Ms. Miller's gives us road orders for all of this part of Virginia from 1720 to 1749, and thereafter for Orange and Greene counties until 1800, an enormous and valuable resource for historical researchers.

Now, having an understanding of how things were supposed to go, we learn that the first of Orange County's roads turned out to be an exception to the rule. That first road was the one built from Fredericksburg to Fort Germanna in 1714. Lieutenant Governor Spotswood argued that the colony's need for the outpost at Germanna, plus the absence of both land-owners and tithables in that frontier region, dictated that the road to the fort should be built with public funds. The Burgesses and Council prob-ably had no trouble understanding that such a road would also benefit pri-vate commercial interests, especially those of their Lieutenant Governor, but everyone was still getting along famously at the time, and the road project was funded. Such a proposal would have met stiff resistance just a year or two later when Spotswood was often at odds with his legislators.

Typical exceptions to the usual road-creating process were the "moun-tain roads" created by counties whose western settlements had reached the Piedmont frontier. Some of those roads, such as the Goochland mountain road, or "three notch'd road" as it became known, ultimately extended to or beyond the Blue Ridge. Others simply penetrated into the back country for a ways before fading out or connecting with another mountain road.

Orange County was particularly benefited by the construction of moun-tain roads. Remember that the lands going to make up the eastern portion of Orange County were the western extensions of Essex, King and Queen, and King William counties. All three of those counties had mountain roads. When those roads were initially being extended by stages into the back country, there were probably never more than a handful of tithables living out ahead of them, and some public funding was necessary. The expecta-tion was that settlement would follow quickly, and the roads could then be maintained in the normal way. Also, during the 1730s the Valley began to be settled from the north, which both accelerated the demand for the ex-tension of at least some mountain roads across the Blue Ridge and pro-duced tithables to help with the work.

The primary mountain road through Orange County was known as the Spotsylvania County mountain road and is referred to in many documents simply as "the mountain road." Its origins were the old Essex County moun-tain road, which generally followed a trace just south of the Rappahannock River until it got to Fredericksburg. The road built to Germanna in 1714 actually served as an extension of the Essex mountain road. (The Ger-manna site was initially in Essex County.) Beyond Germanna it turned northwest towards the present-day town of Orange. Later extensions of that road were made by Spotsylvania County, hence the name it bore by the time Orange County was formed. Ultimately that mountain road extended to Harrisonburg via Swift Run Gap. The many versions of Routes 3, 20, and 641 have in places tended to follow the corridor of the Spotsylvania County mountain road through Orange County, though their actual roadbeds are probably rarely lying directly on its trace. There are, however, local historians who suspect that the heavily worn section of Route 641 west of Orange between Liberty Mills and Montford is a portion of the old original mountain road, still in use today.

The King and Queen mountain road ran generally through central Spotsylvania County, joining the Spotsylvania road in Orange County in the vicinity of today's New Verdiersville. Today's Routes 621 and 608 probably come close to tracing that old route. The King William mountain road skirted along the northeast edge of today's Lake Anna before coming cross-country to a point just east of the Town of Orange, where it joined the Spotsylvania road. Portions of Route 612 look as though they might possibly qualify, but no modern road is a clear successor to the King William mountain road.

As anticipated, settlement and commerce followed the roads, and those roads with the most commerce were the ones that provided connections to ocean shipping. In the mid-eighteenth century there were deep-water docks all along the Rappahannock, and there wasn't a bigger port city in our part of the world than Fredericksburg. Roads fanning out from the Rappahannock docks supported the development of Orange and surrounding counties and in turn made Fredericksburg one of Virginia's most prominent commercial centers in the early colonial period.[7]

Intersecting the Spotsylvania mountain road at what would become the town of Orange was a north-south road which crossed the Rapidan at a ford that rivaled Germanna in width, shallowness, firmness of river bottom, and ease of approaches: today's Barnett's Ford at Madison Mills. The intersection, therefore, attracted such commercial traffic as there was in the region, and those roads became widely-known travelways. In 1766 the Single Sisters, a band of 18 Moravian women, passed through Orange on their 500-mile walk from Bethlehem PA to Bethabara NC. In North Carolina they joined forces and lives with a band of men who had made the same trip earlier, and together they founded what is today Salem Women's

---

[7] The colonial government directed Col. Henry Willis and a committee to lay off the town of Fredericksburg in 1727. The future great inland port cities of Richmond and Alexandria were not laid off until 1737 and 1749 respectively.

College in Winston-Salem NC.[8] Around 1800, a young Davey Crockett, his frontier adventure days and his heroic stand at the Alamo yet to come, came through Orange with a herd of cattle. Crockett's employer was a cattle drover from the Kentucky-Tennessee region.[9]

The arrival of railroads in our part of Virginia in the 1840s and 50s replaced roads as the major factor in controlling local settlement and commerce for nearly a century. The arrival of the railroads actually brought on a flurry of road building, but those roads — the Rockingham and Blue Ridge turnpikes and the Orange Plank Road — were built as a reaction to the arrival of railroads and not as unrelated avenues of commerce. Following World War II and the emergence of cars and trucks as the primary movers of people and goods, roads, or "highways" as we tend to call them today, resumed their dominance over local commerce and development.

As the twentieth century approached, the state government became increasingly interested in local roads. The tithable system, a museum piece from the colonial era, was struck down by the courts in 1894. By then, "road gangs" of state and local prisoners were doing that type of work anyway. In 1906, and again more thoroughly in 1918, state legislators organized a state highway department and incorporated major county roads into a state road system. Orange County wound up with several numbered "state highways," but they were not the numbers by which we know them today. Today's Route 33 was Route 17, Route 15 was Route 32, Route 20 was Route 374 (part county, part state), and Route 3 was Route 37. On a 1925 highway map, that single-lane Route 37 was shown as "non-hard surfaced." It was, however, listed as "improved," meaning that it had been widened to the impressive, modern width of eighteen feet.

Most of the county's roads, however, remained narrow dirt tracks and reflected every imaginable level of maintenance. Counties, with state financial assistance, were also expected to maintain the state roads within their borders, meaning that even the condition of state roads varied widely across Virginia. For a time in Orange County, individual magisterial districts were responsible for maintaining the roads within their boundaries. The late R. Monroe Waugh often spoke proudly of the time when

---

[8] The October 18, 2001, *Orange County Review* reported on the visit of Erika Barnett, a Salem College senior who was repeating that walk as her senior honors project.

[9] Crockett, *A Narrative of the life of Davey Crockett of the State of Tennessee,* 1834.

Post card published by Ricketts Drug Store, showing Madison Road in the very early 1900s. The laundry house for the hotel operating in the T. A. Robinson house is in the right foreground. The 1859 court house is across the street to the left, just out of the picture. Courtesy of R. Duff Green.

Gordon District floated its own road bonds — and had the best roads anywhere around.

During the Great Depression the combined demand for a statewide road system of uniform good quality and the threadbare finances of most counties led the state government to move. The Byrd Road Act was adopted in 1932, and almost all of Orange's roads were taken into a statewide roads system in which the roads were to be maintained by a department of the state government.

In closing, take with you two pieces of Orange County road trivia which are obvious but sometimes overlooked. One, if you wish to stay dry, the only way you can cross the northern border of Orange County is on a bridge. There are five of them at present.[10] Two, the only major east-west corridor through the county as of this writing is Route 20.

---

[10] As of this writing, local historian and author Patricia Hurst is working on a publication that will present local history associated with the Rapidan and will describe the many bridges that have spanned it over the years.

## C. Smoke Stacks in the Wilderness

In the early 1720s when his Tubal furnace went into blast on the banks of the Rappahannock, Alexander Spotswood placed himself and our part of Virginia at the forefront of the Industrial Revolution in America. Investors were soon building additional furnaces in the region (six in all were built), and Spotswood was not shy about proclaiming that he and his fellow iron producers deserved all the credit for converting American iron production from a local subsistence enterprise into a major colonial export industry.[11] Spotswood played a pivotal role in that effort, for it was he who got the Lords Board of Trade and Plantations to indicate that while they could not expressly authorize such colonial "manufacture," they would not be inclined to order such operations shut down. Spotswood was so confident that the Lords would take that position that his furnace was already producing iron in Virginia while he was in London seeking permission to operate it.

The focal point of a typical smelting operation was a heavily-built stone chimney, or "stack," some 30-50' tall, built near a stream and at the foot of a hill or ridge. A water wheel driven by the stream operated air bellows, and the air flow was directed into the stack a short distance above its base. A hot fire was built in the stack, the air blast started, then coke (similar to charcoal), iron ore, and lime (usually in the form of oyster shells in this part of Virginia) were wheeled in barrows from a charging house on the ridge, across a platform, and dumped into the stack. The furnace was "in blast" at that point, and the goal was to keep it in blast for as long as possible. The white-hot coke melted the iron out of the ore, and the molten iron sank to the bottom of the stack. The waste and impurities combined with the lime and floated on top of the iron as "slag."

There was a tap hole at the bottom of the stack which was plugged with clay. Extending out on the ground in front of the tap hole was a bed of sand, which had been leveled, and then channeled. There was a center channel extending from the tap hole the length of the bed. At intervals on each side of the center channel, short side channels were created. When the person in charge thought enough molten iron had accumulated in the stack, he ordered the clay plug to be broken, or "tapped." The molten iron flowed down the center channel and overflowed into the side channels.

---

[11] There had been earlier isolated blast furnace operations elsewhere. (One furnace in Massachusetts had been struggling along since the mid-1600s.) The significance of their output was nominal and their commercial viability suspect.

The slag, which came out behind the iron, was diverted to one side, and a new clay plug was installed. The heat hardened the clay quickly, and charging was resumed.

The iron in the sand bed was allowed to cool into what were called "bars" of "cast iron," and then it was removed. The center bar was called the "sow" bar, and the shorter side bars were called "pigs." The cast iron bars were then hauled to Fredericksburg and other Rappahannock docks for transport to England.

Spotswood, as usual, added his own twists to the process. First, his Tubal furnace was a twin stack unit, capable of producing enormous amounts of iron. Second, at his private docks at Massaponax, he had an "air furnace," which remelted and purified a little of the pig iron for the production of some household and farm items. Both practices probably went against the spirit of his understanding with the Lords Board of Trade, but Spotswood seemed to believe firmly in a principle that forgiveness is easier to obtain than permission.

The enormous fuel needs of the furnaces required clear-cutting vast areas of the centuries-old timber standing on the poor soils in the region. What timber was initially missed or able to regrow was later cut for plank roads and the steam engines of the gold mines. The stunted, dense re-growth that became known as "the Wilderness" was already a century old by the time of the Civil War. Spell it with a capital "W," because it was man-made.

Catharine Furnace. Located in western Spotsylvania County in the Chancellorsville Battlefield Park. One of the six furnaces whose enormous demand for wood was a primary cause for the creation of the Wilderness. The Catharine was in operation during the 1863 Chancellorsville fighting, but the Federals damaged it beyond repair. The stack was later partially rebuilt by the National Park Service. Photo by Bernice Walker. Reproduced with permission.

By the 1800s, larger and more efficient furnaces were in operation elsewhere, and the production of Wilderness iron declined. There was a brief resurgence at the start of the Civil War, when all operable furnaces went back into production to supply iron for the Confederacy. Federal forces, however, destroyed furnaces whenever they gained access to them, and by the end of the war, iron producing operations in the Virginia Wilderness had been stilled

Interest in high quality Virginia iron ore, however, did not disappear entirely. The Fredericksburg *Virginia Star* of December 21, 1881, reported that Maj. Erasmus Taylor of Meadowfarm had contracted to deliver 3,000 tons of iron ore per month to a buyer in Pennsylvania. Taylor's mine was "on his farm near Orange Courthouse," and a spur line was to be built from Madison Run railroad station to the mine to get the ore cars out to the main line. A tremendous amount of iron ore is still all around us, but it is questionable whether we will ever do any more with it.

## D. Mills and Stores Dot the Countryside

Virtually all grains have to be cracked or ground to make them useful as human or animal food, a process we call "milling." While the Virginia colonists initially had to use the hand or animal-powered mills associated with earlier times, they remembered the large water-powered mills of their homeland, and they began to build them in America as soon as they could. By the time Orange County was settled, both the construction and the operation of sophisticated water driven mills were significant commercial activities.

While the description which follows refers to grain-grinding, or "grist" mills, there were many other types of mills built to take advantage of harnessed water power. As examples, there were "land plaster" mills, grinding limestone for soil application; "saw" mills, producing lumber; and "fulling" mills, producing cloth.

A watercourse of some sort was first dammed to create a small lake, usually called a "mill pond." There were apparently few Orange County streams deemed inadequate for the purpose. Grymes mill was located on one of the small streams near today's Orange airport. During the winter of 1863-64, Confederate soldiers in the vicinity of Sleets Shop dammed up what some called a trickle and were able to run a small mill. There was of course a cost in efficiency from relying on small streams. The Grymes mill, for example, routinely took ten hours to produce 25-30 bushels of corn meal. During dry times, the output dropped drastically, and droughts shut the mill down completely.

Damming a major river like the Rapidan guaranteed plenty of water but brought with it a special set of problems. Court permission had to be sought to block such streams, and in the case of the Rapidan after 1749, petitioners found themselves having to satisfy the requirements of two county courts instead of one. Then there were the risks associated with being on a river bank when the floods came. Whole mills were sometimes washed away, but what happened most often was that the dam went out.

Dam-building was an expensive and sometimes risky undertaking, and what made it frustrating was that the mill sat idle and unprofitable until the job was finished. Typically, large wooden cribs were built and set on a line across the stream. The cribs were then filled with stones. Heavy wooden beams were next installed to connect the cribs and create a frame for the dam face. Finally, a dam facing of boards was installed on a slant from the top crib beams to a point in the river bed upstream of the cribs. Hard, sometimes dangerous work in the middle of a river which could rise again at any time and wash everything away before it was completed.

From the mill pond created by the dam, a man-made stream, called a "mill race," was tapped off and channeled to the mill. The mill was located at a point downstream, well below the level of the dam, and the mill race channel limited the slope, or "fall," of its water on the way to the mill. The mill race water then fell into the "buckets" of a water wheel, actually a series of watertight pockets built along the face of the wheel. The wheel turned in response to the weight of the water, allowing the water in the buckets at the bottom of the wheel to escape downstream via a "tail race" as the upper buckets were being refilled from the mill race. The water wheel drove a complex system of gears, shafts, and pulleys, all of which in turn drove the mill machinery.[12]

Most grist mills had two sets of mill stones. A small set produced finely-ground products, such as wheat flour for bread. The large set produced cracked corn and other coarsely-ground items. One stone of each pair was fixed in place while the other turned against it. In the early days of the Virginia colony, imported French quartz stones were thought to be the best.

Initially, only the locally wealthy invested in the necessary machinery and hired millwrights to build mills. Over time, as more people settled the

---

[12] Resourceful and imaginative millwrights actually built innumerable variations from the common "overshot" water wheel described above. Popular variations were the "undershot" water wheel and the turbine. In Colonial Williamsburg, there was a wind-driven mill.

county and the apparent profitability of milling operations attracted investors, many more mills were built.[13] As a way of speeding up the return on the investment, mill operators typically served all comers. The absence of ready cash, however, meant that millers often took a portion, or "share," of the grain being ground as payment. If a fire or flood wiped out the miller's private stocks before he could get them sold, he could be out of business.

Mill owners also typically set up stores nearby to sell such necessities as pins and plows, sugar and saddlebags, window glass and whiskey. Mills, therefore, became local commercial and social centers in Orange County. People in a particular locality would all tend to go to a certain mill. While waiting for their "orders" to be ground, the locals could attend to a great deal of other business: dealing at the store, arranging among themselves for other needed goods and services, and sharing information on every subject under the sun.

The evolution of Orange County's stores, like its mills, initially involved the locally wealthy. Plantation owners with good commercial connections across the Atlantic and an eye for business opportunities at home routinely used their agents, or "factors," in London and elsewhere to sell the plantation's tobacco or grain and make purchases of goods, some of which were actually for neighbors or for sale at a store. Chief among such persons in the early days of Orange County was James Madison, Sr. Later, full-time storekeeper/merchants began to move into Orange County and set up stores. One of the earlier of those was Robert Stringfellow, whose store was at Raccoon Ford. Before opening his store at the ford, Stringfellow had operated stores at both Fredericksburg and Stanardsville and had been involved in a number of local business ventures. As a well-known and experienced merchant, Stringfellow built up an enormous business, and in the process made Raccoon Ford a commercial center in Orange County's pre-railroad era. Local attorney and former Orange County Historical Society President Atwell Somerville has one of Stringfellow's Raccoon Ford store ledgers, the first entry in which is dated 1826. The entries reveal the tremendous variety of items Stringfellow stocked and sold; for example, caskets. Orange County also attracted its full share of that era's traveling salesmen. Numerous peddlers, or "drummers" as they were sometimes called, traveled the county's roads to offer their goods and services.

---

[13] The profitability may have been more apparent than real. In 1820 there were 21 flour/grist mills in Orange and Greene Counties combined, 47 in 1840, but only 24 by 1860. Schlotterbeck, *Plantation and Farm*, p. 275.

## E. GOLD!!!

In 1782, Thomas Jefferson reported the discovery of a four-pound chunk of gold ore on the north bank of the Rappahannock four miles downstream of Fredericksburg. The ore yielded poorly though and news of the isolated discovery was overshadowed by the closing events of the Revolution. When wash deposits of gold were found on the White farm in western Spotsylvania County in 1806, the response was still relatively muted, even though the Whitehall mines became well-known locally. By contrast, in 1826, when some children on their way home from church kicked up a huge nugget on Ellwood, the William Jones farm in Orange County, gold fever (sometimes called "Mexican Measles") broke out unchecked.[14]

Jones and his son-in-law, Spotsylvania County Judge John Coalter, began leasing mining sites on the farm for a share of the find. In one three-year period, a single miner paid them between $3,000 and $4,000 each year. Huge money at a time when Virginia's economy was flagging. Additional strikes were reported in the Wilderness, then came the sure signs of a gold rush: New York investors, flim-flam artists, and con men.

With all the hoopla that continues to accompany Orange County's gold mining era, one might think that the local mining operations were outrageously profitable and made a monumental impact on the county economy. Initially, as easily accessible "placer deposits," or washed-out surface deposits, were being worked, that seemed likely. The miners used any of several simple, inexpensive washing techniques to separate the gold from the loose ore. The gold was collected, and it was off to the bank. That kind of fun, however, didn't last long.

It was almost 1830 before Orange County deposits were being systematically worked, and by 1850, all the easily mined Orange County gold was gone. From then on, large initial investments of capital were required to build the facilities to mine the "lode deposits," the hard-rock ore veins, and to then separate the gold from it. Once built, those facilities were expensive to operate and maintain. Mine operators soon learned that it was more profitable to mine the investors than it was to mine the ground.

Fifteen large mine sites were known to exist in the county, and they were worked at various times by over twenty different mining companies. In addition, there were a host of smaller operations. Some of the names of the better known mines were the Ambler, Chicago-Virginia, Coulter's,

---

[14] This is the same Ellwood owned by J. Horace Lacy at the time of the Civil War. The gold fields by then had been sold off.

Dickey, Grasty, Greenwood, Grymes, Jones, Melville, Orange Grove, Partridge, Randolph, Rapidan, Saunders, Seldon, Stuart, Vaucluse ("vawcluse"), Wilderness, Woodville, and Young.

The Virginia Mining Company of New York was the first of the corporate mining ventures in Orange County. Formed in 1831, it started working both the Grasty mine on Mine Run and the Vaucluse in the Wilderness. A few of the other companies that tried their luck here over the years were: the Liberty Mining Company of London, the Rapidan Gold Company of New York, the Central Virginia Mining and Milling Corporation, the Piedmont Mining and Metallurgical Corporation, the Melba Mining Company, the Orange Grove Mining Company, and the V-M Corporation.

The Grasty, the Chicago-Virginia, and the Dickey mines were unusual in that while they were well-known operations, they were all located along Mine Run, west of what evolved as the gold mining district of the county. The gold fields of Orange County are usually thought of as being in that area of the Wilderness east of Locust Grove, with the largest concentration of good producing mines being between today's Route 3 and the Rapidan River. The gold-pyrite belt which was being mined actually yields workable deposits in a large number of places from Maryland through North Carolina, with some traces of it appearing as far south as Alabama.

The peak year for Virginia gold production turned out to be 1849. In that year just a little under $130 thousand in gold came into U. S. mints from Virginia. That was the same year, however, in which those mints received a staggering $5 million plus in gold from California. Production in Orange County and in all of Virginia declined in the years following 1849, as California's large and easily processed gold deposits lured investors and workers away. Everything pretty much shut down during the Civil War, and only a few of the better mines were reopened after it. Fewer still lasted into the Great Depression. The last of the large Orange County mines, the Melville and the Vaucluse, were worked off and on until 1937.

A clearer picture of how difficult and expensive mining gold in Orange County had become emerges with the employment of the Todd brothers by the Melville mine in the early 1930s. James T. Todd is best known for the 32 years he spent working for Orange County, 12 of those as its Deputy Treasurer and 20 as its Treasurer. As a youngster, however, possessing both a strong back and a bookkeeper's certificate, he spent a few years in both the shafts and the offices of the Melville mine. His brother, Thomas D. Todd, worked in the mines longer, and after he left to go to college, he wrote an essay entitled, "A History of the Vaucluse Gold Mine,"

The Vaucluse Gold Mine's 120hp Cornish steam engine and its boilers, photographed in 1929 just before their removal to Henry Ford's Michigan museum. The mine operators had long ago switched to other sources of power, and such shelters as there had been for this abandoned equipment had disappeared. Photograph from the Orange County Historical Society files.

a work which remains the basic reference document on Orange County gold mining.[15]

James's recollections were less extensive than his brother's, but they did not lack for drama: "When I joined the miners, they were in the process of sinking and rebuilding the old shaft at the Melville mine site. They had gone to the bottom of the shaft, a depth of about sixty feet. There a cross-cut led to numerous tunnels which were all clogged up with debris of all kinds, mainly broken timber and rock falls — and foul air. . . . If

---

[15] The writings of the Todd brothers, plus much more on gold mining in the Wilderness, are on file at the Orange County Historical Society's Research Center. See also Orene Todd's *Dear Cousins*, which provides additional information on gold mining, on life in the Wilderness, and on the Todd family generally.

there were any mine inspectors, I never saw one. . . . I had the nerve to work at the bottom of the shaft one night from 6 p.m. to 6 a.m. all by myself, when the only company I had were the flickering figures dancing on the wall reflecting from my miner's light, and sometimes this would go out from the foul air coming out of the cross-cut."[16] For this, he was being paid the princely sum of $2 per day.

The Melville bought the neighboring Vaucluse, and James began to spend more and more time handling accounts in the office while Thomas helped to bring the Vaucluse back into production. Operating six shafts, at least one down to 300 feet, the Vaucluse had the richer ore of the two. At an earlier time the Vaucluse surface facilities had resembled a small town, complete with an in-house physician to attend to the some 150 resident employees and their families. The mine had run into financial trouble, however, and in 1929, automobile tycoon Henry Ford bought it. Ford's reason for buying the Vaucluse was not to mine gold, but to strip it of equipment for his museum in Michigan. A particularly desired prize was the mine's 120hp Cornish rocking beam steam engine, believed to have been built in 1830.[17] After Ford had taken what he wanted, he had sold the Vaucluse to the Melville operators.

During the Todd tenure, ore from the Vaucluse was hauled to the Melville's works, where the obvious non-gold bearing rock was hand-sorted out before being put through a crusher. The crushed ore was then run through a ball mill, which reduced it to a very fine, almost mushy, sand. Other mines, including the Vaucluse, had used stamping mills to pound the rock into fine gravel, which was then subjected to additional grindings to reduce it to sand.

In the Todd brothers' day, the gold and other metals were separated off in a chemical flotation process. The floated material was collected, dried, bagged, and sent off to a New Jersey smelter for a final separation. Earlier operations had used mercury to trap the gold, after which the mercury was boiled off for reuse and the gold collected. Some mines used cyanide solutions to dissolve out the gold. No matter how it was done, mining Orange County gold was an expensive proposition, and by today's standards, an environmental disaster. Mine accountant James Todd ruefully noted, "Al-

---

[16] Jim used to say that his accounting responsibilities still had him going down into the mine to collect assay samples.

[17] That engine, which was in Ford's Greenfield Village Museum for years, is now on exhibit at the Western Museum of Mining and Industry in Colorado Springs CO.

though more than a million dollars in gold had been mined, this did not near cover the operating costs." Brother Thomas, for his part, noted one real benefit: "Those of us who lived in the area and worked at the mines, during that time of economic depression, in our Country; will ever be grateful for the job opportunities provided us at the mines."

When torrential rains flooded the Vaucluse in 1937, the owners had seen enough. They walked away, and the era of large-scale commercial gold mining in Orange County was over. It had ended earlier for the Todds. Thomas was in college, and James' accounting skills were in the employ of the county. Left behind is a legacy of open pits, partially collapsed shafts and tunnels, and mounds of waste material — not exactly the best place in Orange County to take a Sunday stroll without a guide.

It has been observed that the current price of gold could make mining in Orange County's Wilderness attractive again. In recent years, two commercial gold mines have received permits and have gone into operation elsewhere in Virginia. Trying to meet the environmental requirements here, however, would probably not make it worth the effort.

## F. Taverns, Inns, Hotels, and the Travel Business

Orange County has been successfully attracting visitors since the colonial era, but the reasons why they appear on our doorstep have changed. Initially, the county's importance as a transportation and commercial center brought people here. Now most of our visitors are tourists. Tourism is Virginia's second largest industry, and the county has been attracting an ever-increasing share of that business. Most are coming to investigate our scenic open and forested spaces, our many beautiful and old buildings, and the evidences of our extensive historic legacy. The present-day existence of those attractions reflects for the most part the fact that they went undisturbed through most of the twentieth century. As we have learned, however, those times were far from boring.

After decades of trying to establish a tourism services industry in the county, things are finally happening. There are any number of reasons for past failures and present successes, but the opening of Montpelier as a tourist destination in 1987 by the National Trust for Historic Preservation is a major contributor to the successes. Also, the growth of the Virginia wine industry has had a significant impact locally. (Virginia is poised to become one of the top ten wine grape producers in America, with Orange County already one of the top three in grape acreage in the state.) Coming ever so slowly now is a private and public tourism infrastructure which will allow Orange County to both present and protect its attractions. The creation of a county Department of Tourism and the operation of its Visitors' Center, plus the visitors' services available at privately owned destinations, such as Montpelier, the wineries, the bed & breakfasts, etc., all serve to enhance visitor experiences and spread the word about Orange County.

Fundamental to a local travel/tourism industry is the availability of lodging places, and the story of their evolution in Orange County tracks the evolution of the county generally.

INITIALLY, THERE WAS LITTLE WHICH QUALIFIED AS PUBLIC ACCOMMODATIONS here in the Virginia wilderness. As settlement moved west, however, homeowners living near a traveled way were routinely being asked by wayfarers to please take them in for the night. As a rule, they were not refused, and the self-invited guest would often be served food and drink as well. At the end of the stay, the host would be given something of value for his trouble. Cash money was the most appreciated, since there was so little of that highly prized article around.

On major travel ways, some homeowners eventually decided to go into the business of accommodating travelers. A number of these new businesses consisted of the setting aside of a room or two in a private home. That practice survived as the local "tourist homes" of the 1940s and 50s, and the "bed & breakfasts" of the 90s. A twenty-first century term for rural versions of the latter is apparently going to be "country inn," which harkens back to origins of that type of enterprise.

Other homeowners added "public wings" to their houses, allowing them to both handle a large number of travelers and do it in a way that might keep the host family from being overrun. These became the commercial taverns of the era. The lower level of the residence section was typically open to the public wing during business hours, and the preparation and serving of food and drink was done there. Also, that would be where the money transactions were handled. At a time set by the host, the travelers would be dismissed to the public wing, and the host family would reclaim their home, albeit briefly. It would be decades before tavern operations began to resemble anything like our modern hotels and motels, but the beginnings were there.

A fully-developed tavern facility would also have a "wagon yard," a place where teamsters could pull off the main road and park. Taverns on major travelways, such as the Orange Turnpike could have wagon yards covering more than an acre. In and around the yard there would be pens to hold the livestock that was being herded along the road. The drovers could run their herds or flocks into the pens for the night, paying pen rent to the tavern-keeper. Also, in the yard there would be places to buy hay, grain, and fodder for all the kinds of livestock present. There would be stables for rent to the riders and drivers who did not want to leave their animals out in the weather. In the midst of all this would be one or more blacksmith shops, wheelwrights shops, harnessmakers shops, and carpenter shops; their proprietors sometimes working through the night to have their customers ready to roll in the morning.

Fully-developed tavern facilities were the full-service truck stops of their day. Many were called a "-ville," such as "Chancellorsville" or "Maddensville," even when there were no houses other than the tavern keeper's and one or two for family members. When things were busy, those taverns neighed, mooed, cackled, honked, rattled, banged, clanked, smoked, and stank, but all of that sounded and smelled like money to the tavern keepers. If a tavern was part of a larger settlement the wagon yard might have to be moved to its edge to keep peace with the neighbors. Orange's wagon yard wound up in the area now roughly outlined by the C&O railroad tracks, the Route 20 bypass, and Walker and Grasty streets, an area which later became part of the Orange Horse Show grounds.

Because travelers would usually not know of other available, competing accommodations, there was the possibility that hosts might unfairly take advantage of their guests. To help create a sense of fair play among hosts and confidence among the traveling public, the County Fathers not only got into the business of licensing taverns, but also started setting prices for many of the services they offered. The county order books contain numerous orders permitting various persons to operate inns and taverns, and setting prices for various sleeping arrangements, whiskies, ales, regular and "small" beer, hot and cold "dyets" (meals), etc. It is clear that the provision of travelers' services was an important and closely regulated commercial activity in early Orange County. As history is repeating itself this time around, Orange County is again dealing with the problems and opportunities presented by a rapidly growing influx of visitors, but providing access to and control of sites and venues is today's challenge, not the pricing of small beer.

In the town of Orange, court houses replaced the two most prominent pre-railroad taverns, Crosthwait's and Bell's. During and after the Civil War, railroads came to dominate the hotel industry, and it was not until after World War II that significant accommodations catering primarily to highway travelers resurfaced.

OF THE POST-RAILROAD HOTELS, THREE WILL BE DISCUSSED. THEY WERE THE
Orange Hotel (touching on several which used that popular name), the
Hotel Coleman, and the James Madison Hotel/President Madison Inn.
Unfortunately, none of these businesses enjoyed extended periods of prosperity. With the 1950s came intense competition from the convenient and
modern "motels," while the construction of bypasses and interstates steered
the traveling public away from most small-town hotels. Those hotel operations in Orange and elsewhere eventually closed down.

Orange has had at least three other "Orange Hotels" in addition to
Paul Verdier's. The April 25, 1861, issue of the *Orange Chronicle* carried
an ad for "William Graham's Orange Hotel." By that time, the court house
was standing on the Verdier/Hiden/Rawlings Orange Hotel site, so this
had to be a different structure. Then the April 20, 1900, *Orange Observer*
carried an ad for an "Orange Hotel," stating that it was located across the
street from the Court House. The ad also announced that D. P. Coleman
was its proprietor. It is tempting to imagine that the structure was both
Graham's old Orange Hotel building and the nucleus of what would become the Hotel Coleman. As of this writing no connection had been found.

A 1935 snapshot of the 1859 court house. A WWI cannon is in the side lawn.
WPA workers are widening Route 15 through town, and to do so, had to
move the Confederate sentinel statue. They encountered the ruins of the
William Bell tavern and the Orange Hotel, which in their times also occupied
that site. Picture taken by J. W. Green and reproduced with permission of his
son, R. Duff Green, both in their day editors of the *Orange Review*.

Another Orange Hotel, the one which operated in the post-railroad era, was located on East Main Street, east of today's 7-Eleven. There is currently a vacant lot where it used to stand. That particular Orange Hotel had its origins in a 1910 transfer of a town lot to Mabel and R. H. Wells.[18] The deed recited that the transfer included the residence of the late Mary O. Fry, which probably became the core of that particular Orange Hotel. Unfortunately, the Wellses could not survive the war-induced travel slump, and in 1943 they defaulted on a note secured by the property. The property was then sold in foreclosure.[19]

It isn't clear how long that particular Orange Hotel property operated as a hotel after Mr. & Mrs. Wells lost it. Locally, old hotels tended to fade into residential apartment housing while retaining the "hotel" name, making it difficult to spot the moment when they were no longer really hotels. It was clearly all over for this property, however, when it was sold in 1973. The deed description calls it the old hotel property, but also states that the hotel building had been "substantially destroyed."[20] Richard Sanford, who was at one time connected with the ownership of the property, recalls that the hotel was also known locally as "Wells' Hotel."

THE HOTEL COLEMAN WAS LOCATED DIRECTLY ACROSS MAIN STREET FROM the historic 1859 Court House. The hotel lot was east of today's county office building lot and shared a common boundary with it.[21] David P. Coleman acquired that tract of land with Main Street frontage in 1903, and if he wasn't already running a hotel there, he soon was. There were only a handful of cars around at the time, so Coleman's focus initially had to be on rail passengers. Motorists were not long in finding him, however. Following David Coleman's death, Josephine Coleman acquired his property, combined it with some adjacent property she already owned, and continued the hotel business. In 1954, the heirs of Josephine Coleman sold the property to the Orange Investment and Development Corporation. Shortly thereafter, the hotel was closed, and the building pulled down. The old hotel lot was then subivided and sold.

---

[18] 93 OCDB 11.

[19] 121 OCDB 182.

[20] 269 OCDB 769.

[21] See plat recorded at 162 OCDB 318.

THE PRESIDENT MADISON INN STILL STANDS ON CAROLINE STREET ACROSS from St. Thomas' Church, but it has not been operated as an hotel for years. It was the first hotel in Orange built specifically to serve a driving public and was the only one of that type locally until the DeVivi Motel went into business on the south edge of town.

The President Madison Inn had its beginnings in the transfer of lots 16 and 17 of the May-Brooking Subdivision to Maddux, Marshall, Moss & Mallory, Inc., on December 15, 1926. An examination of the plat of the subdivision reveals that most if not all of lot 16 is the parking lot behind today's President Madison Inn building.

The "Four M's" organized the James Madison Hotel Company and built the hotel. Hard times in the form of the Great Depression soon arrived as a most unwelcome guest. In 1935 the property was sold in a fore-closure auction for $13,000, with the new owner, Mr. Percy Faulconer of Charlottesville, continuing the hotel operation.

Competition in the years following World War II was brutal, but the President Madison Hotel continued to struggle along. By 1958, however, Mr. Faulconer was dead, and the hotel was closed. Local businessmen and brothers, Welford and Fred Sherman, decided to try to revive the business. They formed the President Madison Inn Corporation, which in February 1958, bought the hotel property. Following extensive renovation and re-modeling, the inn was opened to the public.

Success was hard to come by in the small town hotel business, but the Shermans stuck with it long after most hotels in other rural Virginia towns had closed their doors. When the construction of the Madison Road extension through town took Route 15 away from the front door of the inn, the Shermans decided that enough was enough. Its Route 20 exposure had been lost years earlier to another bypass. On February 28, 1977, the President Madison Inn property was sold and the building converted to other uses.

THERE WERE MANY MORE TAVERNS AND HOTELS IN ORANGE COUNTY THAN those covered in this subchapter, and subsequent research may find ones with even more histories that those described here. For example, there were three railroad-era hotels in Gordonsville: the Exchange Hotel, the Magnolia House, and the St. Johns Hotel. The Exchange Hotel's Civil War hospital role is particularly interesting.

The town of Orange also had an Exchange Hotel at one time. It was located on Main Street about midway between the 1859 court house and Belleview Avenue, and it was in operation during the Civil War. Possibly it had a pre-railroad era name of "Lafayette Hotel," since a description for the location of a hotel by that name in the 1830s puts it "up the street" from Rawlings' Orange Hotel.

"Exchange" in a hotel name usually meant that it was anticipated that most of the facility's guests would be in a layover status, awaiting transfer from one public carrier to another. At the time, however, only the Orange & Alexandria served the town, plus a stage line or two. That said, there is a copy of a letter from a Confederate soldier to his mother, describing his eating meals at the Exchange Hotel in Orange before and after his visit to Montpelier. (Civil War soldiers, both Confederate and Federal, were <u>great</u> tourists.) Also, the April 25, 1861, issue of the *Orange Chronicle* advertised the accommodations of the Yates & Cullen Exchange Hotel. Finally, a note in the May 14, 1926, Orange *Observer* recalls that the town post office was at one time in the old Exchange Hotel.

Also in the 1830s, Mr. James G. Blakey had a hotel in Orange. At the time, Mr. Blakey's establishment, along with the Lafayette, and Rawlings' Orange Hotel were considered the "big three" in the town. By the 1870s, the Virginia Hotel, owned and operated by E. M. Coleman, had become the prominent establishment in Orange. It was the hotel in which U. S. President Rutherford B. Hayes was entertained when he came to Orange in 1878 to visit Montpelier.

Courtney McIntosh remembers hearing of a Stevens's Hotel on Main Street during the very late 1800s. By the time McIntosh was a youngster, however, it was already gone. That seems to be typical. It apparently took an exceptional tavern or hotel operation to survive longer than twenty years.

WHEN IT COMES TO ORANGE COUNTY HOTELS, SPECIAL NOTICE HAS TO BE taken of the extended saga of the T. A. Robinson house. For this writer, it began with the fourth quarter 1997 *O-M-C News,* a publication of the Orange-Madison farmers' cooperative. A feature story in that publication described the John William Tatum family of Madison County, people around whom and with whom this writer grew up and worked during his farming days. The article brought back to mind a time when John Tatum spoke of his family home having once been a hotel in the town of Orange, and that when he was a youngster, some of the rooms in that old house still had numbers on the doors. It was time to find out more.

The search involved the Orange County land records, old town maps, and equally old newspaper articles. A number of possible candidates for the Tatum house surfaced, and several leads were followed before the right one was found. The entire process was interesting, and the following is the reconstructed story of that building.

By deed dated July 1, 1856, James and Jane Shepherd conveyed a lot in the town of Orange to a Mr. Thomas A. Robinson. The Shepherds were living in Mobile, Alabama, and Robinson was local. Among the many words of description for the property being conveyed were the following: " . . . [A] certain lot at Orange Courthouse, upon which is a tanyard and other buildings and improvements now in the occupancy of Alexander Daley, and is the same tanyard lot which was allocated in the estate of the late James Shepherd . . . "[22]

The James Shepherds of Mobile were thus conveying property that Mr. Shepherd had inherited from his father of the same name. The elder James Shepherd had in turn been a son of the very successful and well known Scot merchant, Andrew Shepherd, whose house and store had been located roughly where today's 7-Eleven stands. The tanyard, with its mess and smells, was located on the next hill to the west. Probably still too close.

The Alexander Daley noted as occupying the tanyard lot was in his day a shaker and mover in Orange. One of his larger projects was the construction of the Star Building on Railroad Avenue, a structure which Mr. and Mrs. Emil Levy later made famous with their retail establishment known as "Levy's Busy Corner." That building was in the southwest corner of the Main Street/Railroad Avenue intersection, and after the Great Fire of 1908 the Levys quickly rebuilt it.

As the new owner of the tanyard lot, Thomas Robinson proceeded to build his home there, right in the northeast corner of the intersection of Main Street and the road leading to Barnett's Ford (Madison Road), almost exactly where a present-day building stands. In 1859, the Court House was completed across the Barnett's Ford Road from the Robinson house, and the intersection began to become a commercial center. The April 25, 1861, edition of the *Orange Chronicle* carried an advertisement placed by Robinson, offering dry goods, shoes, china, and groceries for sale. He had become a storekeeper. But the Civil War was about to change everything.

On the morning of August 2, 1862, Federal cavalry stormed into Orange from the east. The initial fighting took place in Main Street, and its narrow width allowed the vastly outnumbered Confederates to hold their own and buy time until help arrived. The Federal advance in fact bogged down right in the front yard of the Robinson house. That was about when William "Grumble" Jones and the rest of his 7th Virginia Cavalry arrived.

---

[22] 44 OCDB 133. Also see 10 OCWB 213.

Jones hit the Federals on the front and flank and initially routed them back out of town.[23] Once in the open, however, the Federals were able to reorganize, and the fact that they held vastly superior numbers was obvious. By this time they had also figured out the layout of the town and were not restricted to fighting in Main Street alone. The Confederates were promptly hustled through and out the other side of Orange, whereupon the Federals broke off their pursuit and busied themselves with poking around the town and generally terrorizing its residents. Before dark, the enemy was gone. Diarist Fanny Page Hume reported in part for that day: "A sharp fight took place in the Village; a Yankee Colonel or Major was killed just before Mr. Robinson's door & many were wounded on both sides."[24]

The Civil War tended to produce more hard times than battle excitements, and as the Robinsons learned, the hard times tended to continue long after the shooting had stopped. By deed dated July 11, 1868, Thomas and Evangeline Robinson conveyed a portion of their Main Street property to a trustee overseeing Mr. Robinson's bankruptcy.[25] But the Robinsons were at least able to hang on to that corner house lot for the rest of their days.

In 1884 and 1885, the heirs of the Thomas Robinsons conveyed their interests in the corner house lot to Mary O. Fry,[26] who in turn by deed dated April 1, 1901, conveyed it to the American Bank of Orange. The deed description states in part: " . . .[U]pon which is situated the dwelling occupied as a hotel and a bank . . .."[27]

So now the former T. A. Robinson residence and store had become both a hotel and a bank And that's not all of the uses to which it would be put while it remained in town. For example, the *Orange Observer* of May 14, 1926, notes that for a time, the town post office was located in the old Robinson Building on the corner lot.

---

[23] Leading the charge up the tracks into the Federal flank was Major Thomas Marshall, a grandson of the late Chief Justice.

[24] Grymes, *Hume Diary,* p. 129. In their after-action reports, neither Colonel Jones (Confederate) nor Colonel Tompkins (Federal) mention such a high ranking casualty.

[25] 46 OCDB 363.

[26] 51 OCDB 556, and 52 OCDB 225. The latter transfer also involved the chancery suit of Willis v. Fry.

[27] 59 OCDB 339. This involved only a portion of Robinson property bought by Mrs. Fry.

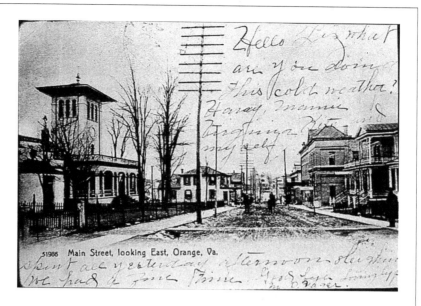

The T. A. Robinson house, on the left side of Main Street Orange just east of the court house. Removed to make room for Ricketts' Drug Store, the old house continues to serve as a family home in Madison County. From a post card in the Orange County Historical Society collection. Reproduced with permission.

The combination of a hotel and bank in the Robinson house could have been convenient for folks who might have wanted to stay near their money, which they ought to have done in that particular case. Shortly after the bank became the owner of the Robinson property, its president ran off with the deposits, and the bank went under.

The court awarded the Robinson property to the trustees for the creditors of the now-defunct American Bank, and they proceeded to try to auction it off. The auction fell through, but J. L. Fray of Culpeper came forward and offered to buy a small lot which would include the old residence/store/hotel/bank/post office building. The trustees surveyed off that lot and conveyed it to Mr. Fray on August 1, 1904.[28]

Mr. Fray didn't choose to enjoy his purchase for long. On November 11, 1904, he conveyed his Main Street, Orange, property to L. S. Ricketts.[29]

---

[28] 62 OCDB 431.

Dr. Ricketts was a druggist who had a thriving pharmacy business in the Gaines Building, located across the tracks and just a few yards south of today's train station, adjacent to Levy's Busy Corner. Railroad Avenue was clearly Orange's main commercial center of that day, but possibly Dr. Ricketts had already sensed that the automobile was likely to make Main Street the place to be in the years to come. His actions after the Great Fire of 1908 would tend to indicate that.

When the Great Fire wiped out most of Railroad Avenue, including Dr. Ricketts' store, almost all of the business people who had been burnt out committed themselves to immediately recreating the avenue and reestablishing their businesses, as though nothing had happened. Not Dr. Ricketts. The *Orange Observer* of November 13, 1908, reported that Dr. Ricketts had reestablished his business on Railroad Avenue but that "he will later build a two-story brick building on his Main Street lot — after he gets rid of the Yeager Building." A 1905 map of the town identifies the structure at the Main Street/Barnett's Ford Road intersection as the "Yeager Hotel," presumably the business of a tenant of Dr. Ricketts. Also during a part of the time remaining to the Robinson house in its town of Orange location, a portion of the structure housed the Greiner & Ricketts hardware store. A very busy building.

The *Orange Review* of April 20, 1912, carried a picture of Dr. Ricketts' new building, noting that it had been built in 1908-09, after he had sold the old frame building which had stood on that corner "to the junk man." Never has it been truer that one man's junk is another man's treasure. No bill of sale has been found, giving a date, names, and a documented connection to the Tatum family, but the common knowledge of that day was that the old T. A. Robinson house had been cut into sections and sold to "someone in Madison County." And how many Madison homes had numbers on their doors at one time and a history of having once been a hotel in Orange.

The sale produced one additional adventure for the old house. It had to be transported across the Rapidan River. There was a bridge at Madison Mills by 1908, but sections of a house would have probably had trouble fitting inside its structure. Old Barnett's Ford was still accessible, and people used it for years to wash cars, water horses, and tighten wagon wheels. It was also probably the scene of the T. A. Robinson house, in pieces, crossing the Rapidan.

---

[29] 62 OCDB 522.

The old Thomas A. Robinson residence/store/hotel/bank/post office/ hardware store building still stands some seven miles from where it was built, serving usefully to this day as the Tatum family residence. Whether the Tatums bought the house directly from Dr. Ricketts or whether they did indeed buy it from "the junk man," they got themselves an ante-bellum home with an extensive history, a <u>very</u> extensive history.

As was true most everywhere, railroads were the dominant factor for hotels built and operated in the Orange area from the time of the Civil War until the early 1920s. If a hotel was not right at the railroad station, quick transportation to it needed to be at hand, and it wouldn't hurt if the ride was free. Three Orange "railroad hotels" of that era were the Morris, Barbee, and Piedmont hotels. All three share some common connections, and they will be considered together.

The story begins with Mr. G. T. Barbee, who was a truly persistent, if not always successful, Orange businessman. On July 31, 1894, Mr. Barbee gave a mortgage to John E. Morris to secure a loan paying overdue rent. The mortgage recites that a portion of the property securing the loan is the property of the Hotel Barbee.[30] The "John E. Morris" noted in the mortgage is almost certainly John E. Morris, Sr., who by that time was in competition with Mr. Barbee.

Unfortunately, not all of Mr. Barbee's financial worries were behind him. On March 28, 1895, he gave another mortgage, pledging all the property of the Hotel Barbee, including the hotel lease, as security for a loan from W. R. Barbee.[31] The late Mr. Russell Barbee said that he really didn't remember grandfather G. T. Barbee, who died when he was very young; however, he did remember W. R. (William Randolph) Barbee, his "Uncle Bill," who was G. T.'s son.

Presumably W. R. Barbee's loan to his father had paid off John Morris, thus freeing the property to be re-pledged. By this time, however, Mr. Morris' own hotel business was going full swing, and we leave Mr. Barbee for a moment to pick up the Hotel Morris story.

On February 15, 1889, P. P. Barbour, Esq., a local attorney acting as a Special Commissioner of the Court in the matter of <u>Helwig v. Helwig's Trustee,</u> had conveyed to John E. Morris a town lot standing in the name of Mrs. S. E. Helwig. The lot is described as lying along the margin of Church

---

[30] 55 OCDB 375.

[31] 55 OCDB 558.

Street, "east to the lands of the Charlottesville & Rapidan Railroad Co."[32] The Charlottesville & Rapidan Railroad was the initial developer of a right of way which it shared with the Washington City, Virginia Midland, and Great Southern Railroad (of Fat Nancy wreck fame). It is now of course the Norfolk Southern right of way which, just south of the Church Street crossing, curves south and west behind today's Satchells' Funeral Home and the Not the Same Old Grind buildings.[33]

An undated map of the town of Orange, prepared by O. M. Gray & Sons, shows the Mrs. S. E. Helwig lot at a time before the Charlottesville & Rapidan tracks were laid. There is what was probably the Helwig residence in the northwest corner of the lot, but no building is shown on the lot where the Hotel Morris later stood. There is a hotel shown on the Railroad Avenue/Church Street corner, just across from the Helwig lot. Possibly that unidentified hotel was the Hotel Barbee. In any event, John Morris was going to establish his own competing hotel almost directly across the street from it.

On November 27, 1901, J. E. Morris joined in a boundary line agreement with the Charlottesville & Rapidan Railroad Co. and the Southern Railway Company.[34] The agreement recites that the parties all "agree that the said line of division running through the property used as a yard and garden of the said J. E. Morris, and attached to his hotel in the county and town of Orange [etc.] . . . ." So the hotel is there by 1901.

A 1905 town map prepared by the Sanborn Map Co. identifies the hotel at that location as the Hotel Morris It stood roughly where the Orange Farm and Garden building is today, with the Not the Same Old Grind building shown as its adjacent livery stable. This hotel would not be in operation long, but it would occupy a secure niche in the Orange business community while it lasted, thanks in large part to its owner.

According to J. E. "Jack" Morris, Jr., his grandfather, John E. Morris, Sr., was a town policeman for over 40 years, and for some of those years,

---

[32] 53 OCDB 55.

[33] The P. P. Barbour who made the conveyance to John Morris for the Court was the grandson and namesake of the late U. S. Supreme Court Justice Philip Pendleton Barbour, whose 1823 manor house, Frascati, still stands on Route 231 south of Somerset. Young Barbour practiced law from an office located on the grounds of the Gordon Tavern. That office was later moved a short distance down the street, and stands in Gordonsville today by the name of the "Spencer House."

[34] 60 OCDB 152. Plat at 60 OCDB 155.

one of the only two policeman for the town. Officer Morris was a large—no, huge — person. Jack Morris recalls calling his grandfather "Big Man" and estimates that Big Man must have weighed over 300 pounds, and it wasn't fat. Mr. Russell Barbee worked for years at Crafton & Sparks, a men's clothing store on East Main Street, and he also remembered Morris. Mr. Barbee's favorite mental picture of Morris was one of seeing him easing that large frame onto a ledge at the front of the store building in order to give his tired, aching feet a few minutes' rest.

John Morris' size probably went a long way in explaining why only one man was needed when he was on duty; however, the law enforcement work load of those days was also not usually an every-minute-of-the-day job. In fact, while his hotel was in operation, Morris oversaw its operations while continuing to serve in his law enforcement capacity. One supposes that the Hotel Morris clientele were an orderly, law-abiding crowd, despite the fact that the hotel bar was a popular local watering hole, selling "take out" whiskey by the bottle. The bar in the Hotel Morris wasn't anything unusual, in fact it would have been unusual for a hotel of that time not to have one.

Bars in Old Orange were so numerous as to be almost underfoot. Historian Paul Slayton advises that in his review of old county newspapers from the early 1900s, he discovered that in 1905 there were eight or nine

Looking southwest along Main Street Orange following the November 1908 Great Fire. The structure shell is the old Orange Baptist Church at the Main Street/Short Street intersection. A short distance behind it are the railroad tracks. Railroad Avenue was the town's commercial center of the day, and the burned-out area was quickly rebuilt. The town soon closed its bars and started a fire company, the presence of the former and the absence of the latter seen as contributing to the disaster. Photograph courtesy of R. Duff Green.

bars in Orange busily serving thirsty locals. The most famous was George Gaines' on Railroad Avenue, immortalized by Towles Terrill as "The Halls of the Montezumas." Within easy staggering distance, however, were the Hotel Morris bar, the "Nuf' Said Bar" at the back of the railroad passenger station, and the Barbee Restaurant bar. Mr. Barbee was apparently out of the hotel business at the time, but he hadn't gone away. Other popular bars were C. P. Dillard's, a/k/a "Hickey's Bar," and the ones in the Hotel Coleman, in Mrs. Reed's Oyster House, and in the Yeager Hotel, the latter occupying the T. A. Robinson building.

On March 24, 1899, the *Observer* carried a Hotel Morris bar ad offering the public "pure Irish whiskey" for a mere $0.63/quart. For years, local banker Ed Woodward collected bottles used by Orange County businesses in selling their products, and some years ago he finally obtained a Hotel Morris whiskey bottle. Recently, John Faulconer acquired Ed's collection, and he kindly showed that bottle to this writer. Unfortunately, it was empty.

At this point, the story takes another turn. The October 12, 1905, *Orange Observer* announced that the Piedmont Hotel will soon be opening. We are told that this hotel is located on Railroad Avenue near the passenger station. Keep in mind that in 1905 the passenger station was on the west side of the tracks and very near the Church Street crossing.

The ad goes on to state that Mr. G. T. Barbee is to be the manager of the Piedmont Hotel. Note "manager," not "proprietor" or "owner." Also, the 1905 town map shows no hotel on the north side of Church Street. Mr. Barbee was apparently out of the hotel business and running a restaurant by then. Did he keep the restaurant going while he ran the Hotel Piedmont? Also, is the Hotel Piedmont a renamed Hotel Morris? Mr. Barbee's situation remains a mystery, but there is evidence to indicate the renaming of the Hotel Morris.

By deed dated June 30, 1906, John Morris conveyed his hotel property to John B. Parrott of Monroe County, West Virginia. [35] Parrott paid $5,500 for the hotel property—and for the scare of his life. On November 8, 1908, most of Railroad Avenue burned during the Great Fire of Orange. The flames reached and consumed the passenger station just across the street, along with all of the other buildings between it and Main Street, but they did not cross Church Street. The fires of Hell dared not cross the Holy Highway. The hotel survived, but Mr. Parrott had seen enough.

---

[35] 64 OC DB 292.

By deed dated March 15, 1909, Parrott conveyed the hotel property to Clifford B. Maddox. The property being conveyed was described as including the furniture, fixtures, gas plant, water engine, etc., of the Piedmont Hotel. So it seems that the Hotel Morris had indeed become the Piedmont Hotel.[36]

It is not certain that Mr. G. T. Barbee hung on through all of these changes in ownership. We do know that for a time he was running a store in a building owned by Mrs. Julia Perry. On March 3, 1907, he gave a mortgage, securing a loan with the store property.[37] Barbee's store is thought to have been on the corner of Byrd and Church streets, at the present site of The Country Mouse. (Mr. Russell Barbee told me that he still had a coffee can from the old G. T. Barbee store.) True, he could have run the hotel, the restaurant, and the store simultaneously, but we don't know exactly what his situation was when the Hotel Morris/Hotel Piedmont story came to a sudden, disappointing end.

On March 17, 1910, almost a year to the day from when he bought the hotel lot, Mr. Maddox and his wife conveyed its title to a trustee to secure a $1,000 loan. The description states in part: ". . . that certain lot in the Town of Orange upon which the Piedmont Hotel formerly stood."[38] So the hotel is gone — poof — just like that. A fire? Probably.

Sadly, there is an additional marginal note in the deed book beside that 1910 conveyance, stating that the Maddoxes defaulted on the note and the property was sold at auction. The county land books indicate that Mr. and Mrs. Maddox remained active in the business of the town for years after that auction, but they must have been going through a bad patch when they lost the hotel. So, all three hotels, the Barbee, the Morris, and the Piedmont, all interrelated, are all gone. A disappointing way to have to end a long story.

## G. Planes, Trains, and Automobiles

THE FIRST TIME MY FATHER SAW AN AIRPLANE UP CLOSE AND PERSONAL WAS around 1919. A WWI vintage machine landed in a field near Orange, and its pilot, a "barnstormer" as they were called, was offering rides for a price. Father recalled that the plane's engine was smoking and appeared to be

---

[36] 67 OCDB 392.

[37] 65 OCDB 93.

[38] 69 OCDB 64.

leaking oil. He declined to purchase a ride, which may account for my being here to write this.

While the Gordonsville Airport was the first commercial airstrip in the county, the Orange County Airport has been the one to receive the greatest attention and support. It is county-owned and is seen as more favorably situated insofar as future airport expansion and surrounding commercial development is concerned. The appearance of the flying Holladay brothers to manage the Orange airport right after WWII also did much to focus local interest on that facility and its commercial possibilities. As is typical with small rural airports, however, the ones in Orange County serve as a vital aids to local commerce, not as a major employment or profit centers in themselves.

Probably the best known airplane-related incident in the county occurred in 1935 and involved a commercial airliner whose pilots had determined that they would have to land here. The plane was on a scheduled flight to Cleveland, but the appearance of an in-flight problem required that the plane be brought down as soon as possible.

As the pilots slowly circled the Orange area at low altitude, trying to pick out a landing spot, some of the locals guessed that it was coming down. Getting into their cars, they began to follow the plane as best they could on county roads. Finally the pilots put the plane down in a barely-adequate field just east of Montpelier, and some of its pursuers arrived just as it crunched into the fence row at the far-end of the field. After a few minutes, the door of the plane opened. A woman wearing a magnificent full-length fur coat stepped to the door, looked out over the rural landscape with its excited spectators, and asked, "Is this Cleveland?" The locals loved it.

After the plane's passengers were safely on their way via ground transportation, matters took a more utilitarian turn. The farmer who owned the field said that the plane wasn't going anywhere until he was paid some money. This was during the Depression, and opportunities to bring in a few extra dollars were few. Negotiations ensued, and the farmer received an agreed sum. The wings of the plane were then removed, and the plane was towed down the highway to a point where it could be reassembled, inspected, serviced, and flown away.

RAILROADS WERE A DOMINANT NON-FARM INDUSTRY IN ORANGE COUNTY ALmost from the moment of the arrival of the Louisa Railroad at Gordonsville in 1841until shortly after World War II. In the late 1930s local people wanting to travel had their choice of some eleven passenger trains that regularly stopped at Orange. Those late Depression years, plus the WWII years, saw railroading activity at its peak locally. During the early months of WWII, trains passed through Orange on the average of one every ten minutes. Following the war, however, railroads went into a decline. A passenger train last stopped at Orange in 1970, although there is now talk of establishing a commuter stop in the foreseeable future.

The Chesapeake & Ohio, a/k/a "Chessie System" and The Southern were and are the major lines through the county. Orange County has a long association with the C&O, since the Louisa Railroad was first renamed "The Virginia Central," and then in 1867, "The Chesapeake and Ohio." The entire Chessie System grew from those modest beginnings.[39] The C&O was still busy building overpasses in the county as late as the 1950s; however, it was simultaneously seeking to phase out passenger service. Freight hauling was and is where the money is made. In 1948, local business interests prevailed in retaining passenger service at Gordonsville, but it was only a matter of time. Eventually the the railroad had its way and a wrecking crew knocked Gordonsville's station down before many of the town's citizens knew it was happening.

The Southern right of way, initially developed in the 1880s, was double tracked around 1915 and remained so through WWII. During the 1950s, however, nearly all of the second set was taken up.

FOR A TIME, TWO ADDITIONAL RAILROADS WERE OPERATING IN ORANGE County, the Rapidan Railroad and the Potomac, Fredericksburg, & Piedmont. Both were dwarfed by the operations of the C&O and Southern, but they did do their bit for the county's commerce and left some interesting stories behind when their days were done.

The Rapidan Railroad began running in 1920 to serve logging camps being operated by the West Virginia Timber Company along the Conway and Rapidan River watersheds in Madison County. The timber company had invested in the railroad with the expectation of bringing out large numbers of blight-killed Chestnut logs and other hardwoods from the mountains. Local folks labeled it the "dinky railroad," for the dinky, or switch, engines being used to assemble the trains at Graves' Mill and Wolftown.[40] A comparatively larger Shay engine then made the pull to Orange.

---

[39] For more on that interesting railroad, see: "The Louisa Railroad" by Chas. W. Turner in the Winter 1980 number of *Virginia Cavalcade*.

[40] An early name for today's settlement of Wolftown was "Rapidan," providing an additional reason for giving that name to the railroad operation.

The railroad crossed the Rapidan into Orange County at Spicer's Mill, and the concrete abutments for that bridge are still visible just upstream of the Rapidan/Poplar Run junction. The road bed then generally followed the line of Spicer's Mill Road into Orange. Coming into town, the railroad was on the north side of Spicer's Mill Road, the town portion of which was then being called Vanderhoff Street. Near the present-day Spicer's Mill Road/ Madison Road intersection, the tracks turned south across Spicer's Mill Road and brought the log trains to a station and rail yard in the area currently occupied by a gas station and a used equipment sales lot.

After the trains arrived at the Orange depot, the logs were dumped into a shallow pond covering a part of the area now occupied by the silk mill building on the east side of Madison Road. At the far end of the pond were the extensive sawmill and lumber handling facilities of the West Virginia Timber Company, the site now occupied by American Woodmark.

Unfortunately, neither the volume nor the quality of the timber coming out of the mountains met the expectations of the timber company, and the railroad was taken out of operation in 1928. The tracks and other equipment were sold, and the right of way was deeded back to the adjacent landowners. Much of the cut-over area in the mountains was subsequently incorporated into the Shenandoah National Park. The Orange depot, however, continued to stand in the hollow across from the Silk Mill until the first of a series of restaurants was built on the site. Our only reminders of the Rapidan Railroad today are the few traces of the old right of way that remain on the land in Orange and Madison counties and the railroad bridge abutments at Spicer's Mill.

For as long as it ran, the Dinky Railroad hauled not only logs, but also passengers and freight for local businesses along its route. The tracks were laid in narrow gauge on a roadbed which deteriorated over time. Also, the run to Orange required extensive braking, which could tax the ability of the Shay engine to maintain the necessary steam pressure. Some of those trips, then, were on the slightly dangerous side of exciting, but fortunately the railroad left us no tales of major catastrophes.

THE IDEA TO CREATE THE POTOMAC, FREDERICKSBURG, & PIEDMONT Railroad came from the Fredericksburg business community, which was seeing its commercial ties with north-central Virginia slip away. Things hadn't been the same since the combination of the Rappahannock silting up and the construction of ever-larger ships had served to eliminate Fredericksburg as an international port of entry following the Revolution. More and more commerce began to flow north-south between Richmond and Alexandria instead of east-west to Fredericksburg.

Fredericksburg commercial interests had already sponsored the construction of a turnpike and a plank road to Orange, as well as a canal running along the north bank of the Rappahannock well up into Fauquier County. None of that seemed to be helping much. But what about a railroad? That was the wave of the future in the 1850s. By the time the railroad actually went into operation, however, that particular future had already become the past.

Talk about a railroad connecting Fredericksburg to the west started as early as the 1830s, but it was not until 1853 that things began to get serious. That year a rail company charter was granted by the Virginia General Assembly. The requirements were that the company was to have its funding completed in three years and the railroad in operation in another ten. That schedule set everything on a collision course with the Civil War, and the railroad never really recovered from that particular wreck.

By the time of the Civil War the right of way had been secured, and in most places it was graded and ready for the laying of tracks. That is the condition in which the railroad went through the war, and the road bed became immortalized as the "unfinished railroad" in the thousands of accounts of local Civil War actions. At the end of the fighting, the railroad was disorganized and destitute, but its promoters wouldn't give up.

Construction of the railroad from the Fredericksburg end was underway again by 1869. By 1876, the tracks still hadn't quite reached Orange, and the company had already reorganized several times.[41] One of the early company presidents was Carter Braxton, the former commander of the Fredericksburg Artillery. Early in 1865, Braxton had married local diarist Fanny Page Hume, only to lose her to an illness a few months later. Each reorganization gave the railroad a different name, and the Potomac, Fredericksburg, & Piedmont was the name under which its equipment finally rolled into Orange in 1877.

The railroad's rolling stock mirrored its operations. With very limited funds, the management had looked for something cheap and immediately available. The equipment built and used at the just-closed 1876 Centennial Celebration in Philadelphia fit the bill. It was narrow gauge, but beggars couldn't be choosers. Then cinders from the smokestack of the train hauling that just-purchased equipment to Orange burnt some of it up, just another sign of how snakebit this little railroad was. One of the engines was

---

[41] A couple of the interim names for the railroad were the Fredericksburg & Gordonsville Railroad and the Fredericksburg, Orange & Charlottesville Railroad, both reflecting the changing plans of its promoters.

so small that a man could shine virtually all of its brasswork while standing on the ground. There was so much brass on that engine that folks thought it looked like a yellow Daffodil, and it was accordingly christened "Daffy." The other, less attractive engine was called "Mogul."

The operations of the Potomac, Fredericksburg and Piedmont were so obviously threadbare that folks began calling it the "poor folks & preachers railroad," and it became the target of many unflattering stories and jokes. A salesman traveling on it on one occasion reported being thrown around violently in his passenger car, at the same time loose items were being being hurled from the freight cars behind him. In 1881, a state senator and a California millionaire chartered the PF&P for a trip to inspect the local gold mines. The engine broke down, and the men had to hike out. Pointed remarks were made to the locals about the railroad, after which the men, and their potential investment, left via other transportation.

Then there is the story of a man who had gotten tired of waiting for the train and had started walking along the right of way to his destination. Eventually, in the distance behind him, he heard the train, working its way through the fifteen scheduled stops between Orange and Fredericksburg. When the engine finally caught up with him, the engineer leaned out as he went hissing and clanking by and hollered over the noise, "WANT US TO STOP AND PICK YOU UP?" The exasperated pedestrian hollered back, "NO, THANKS. I'M IN A HURRY."

In 1926 financier Langbourne Williams bought the railroad, beginning its over fifty-year association with his family. He renamed it the Virginia Central, the old Virgina Central having long ago become the C&O. It was also rebuilt to standard gauge, requiring the corresponding investment in equipment, and a freight station was built in Orange which still stands on Church Street. (The old narrow gauge passenger station also still stands on Byrd Street.) Langbourne Williams, Jr., succeeded his father as president. He also bought Retreat Farm in Rapidan, but his duties elsewhere required that other, local family members run things. The last Williams to serve as president of the railroad was George D. Williams of Rapidan.

The newly-reorganized railroad also requested and was granted permission by the State Corporation Commission to change the names of some of its stations. Screamerville became Chancellor, New Hope became Gold Dale, Tinder became Mine Run, Reynolds became St. Just, Lafayette became Rhoadesville, Mine Road became Mellon, and Verdiersville became Nolting.

The operations of the "new" PF&P struggled to compete against the growing number of local automobiles and trucks; then came the Great Depression. Toward the end, the railroad consisted of a single gas-engine powered car, referred to as a "doodlebug." There was a turntable just west of the narrow gauge station, and one of the local amusements accompanying the arrival of the doodlebug was to help turn it around and aim it back towards Fredericksburg. Finally, on January 1, 1938, the PF&P/Virginia Central made a final run to Orange. Photographs were taken, memories shared, and the doodlebug departed, never to return.

The Doodlebug derailed. Symbolic of the fortunes of the Potomac, Fredericksburg and Piedmont, renamed the Virginia Central, the single gas-engine powered car awaits help. It made its last fifteen-station run from Orange to Fredericksburg on January 1, 1938. Picture reproduced courtesy of R. Duff Green.

WHILE THE OPERATIONS OF THE RAPIDAN RAILROAD AND THE PF&P WOULD seem to be prime sources of train mishaps, it actually turns out that the C&O/Southern main line operations are the ones which have given Orange County its most memorable wrecks. The first actually occurred on the old Orange & Alexandria, a predecessor of the C&O.

Writing in her diary under the date of May 25, 1861, Fanny Page Hume reported breathlessly, "A terrible accident occurred on the railroad just in front of Aunt Sarah's, two or three men are killed and eight or nine wounded." Fanny is referring to the derailment and wreck of the lead train of a convoy of three Confederate troop trains headed to Manassas.

"Aunt Sarah's" was already known as Rebel Hall, which still stands at the May-Fray Street rail crossing. The recently widowed Sarah Dade Taliaferro Bull had moved in with her five daughters shortly before the war started. She also took in Fanny's sister, who needed a place to stay. All of that femininity in one place had lonely soldiers hanging about the residence like bees around an apple tree in bloom. Many were away from home, fireside, and family for the first time in their lives, and just the sight of a female in a domestic setting did them wonders. The name "Rebel Hall" was a natural.

Sabotage was suspected. The combination of overworked people operating worn-out equipment on a deteriorated road bed certainly couldn't have had anything to do with it, now could it? That was for others to resolve anyway. The "wounded" needed attention.

Fanny reported further: "We girls walked up to Aunt Sarah's after dinner. Her house had been turned into a hospital. They seemed tired and excited and firmly believed it a planned thing. The people all dined the soldiers, who expressed themselves delighted with the accommodations. A basket of provisions, milk & etc., went up from here." Delighted? Probably ecstatic.

IN THE WEE HOURS OF THE MORNING OF JULY 12, 1888, TRAIN NO. 52 OF THE Washington City, Virginia Midland & Great Southern Railroad eased out of Orange, bound for Somerset, Barboursville and beyond. It wasn't going to pick up much speed because it had to negotiate the Fat Nancy trestle about two miles out of town. In those days, the tracks ran on the high ridge on the north side of Route 20, above Graham Cemetery. A little west of the cemetery the ridge was interrupted by a hollow with a small stream meandering through it. Trestles were simple, low wooden bridges used by railroads to span such places. The Fat Nancy trestle was some 487 feet long, and at the point of maximum clearance, the ground was 44 feet below the tracks.

The trestle was named for a black lady who lived beside it. She took in wash for a living and was known to the train crews as the woman who waved to them as they went by. The crews responded by throwing out a shovelfull or two of coal. Nancy would gather up the coal for her wash fires. She may have even been a "trestle watcher," receiving a few dollars from the railroad company in return for reporting any problems with the trestle. We don't have any pictures or even a last name to tell us more about Nancy, but evidently she was substantial.

It was already known that the trestle was becoming unstable, and orders were to cross it at minimum speed, something like 5mph. An earth fill

The Fat Nancy trestle, approximately two miles west of Orange. In the far background is the road which later became Route 20. In the 1880s railroad publications were warning of the instability of these trestles, and the Fat Nancy was being replaced with an earth fill at the time it collapsed in July 1888. A photograph from the Green family newspaper files. Reproduced courtesy of R. Duff Green.

to replace the trestle was already under construction, and Cornelius Cox, the person in charge of that work, was actually on Train No. 52, headed home for a brief visit. The engine rocked and swayed its way across the trestle, then cars behind it began derailing. There was a splintering crash, and about 190 feet of the trestle collapsed, carrying almost all of the train down with it.

Mr. A. C. Nicholson of Baltimore provided the account of the wreck that is most often quoted: "It was in the dead of night. We had got nearly across the bridge when it gave way without warning. The engine had just reached the other side but was pulled down by the falling baggage car. The only car left on the track was a sleeper for White Sulphur Springs which had been coupled onto the end of the train so it could be dropped off at Charlottesville.

"The mail car and the smoker were totally demolished. I was in the sleeper that went down. Don't know how I escaped, but it gave me a fright to find myself looking out of a car that was hoisted in the air over the ruins of broken coaches.

"As soon as we passengers could extricate ourselves from the precarious position and work our way gingerly down to safety, we did what we could to rescue the injured. There wasn't much we could do for the night was pitch black. Luckily, our engine had dropped pilot [front] foremost and thus her fire was not thrown back into the cars.[42] Nor were flames added to the horrors of the night, as the dim oil lamps in the cars had been extinguished by the abrupt fall. Shrieks of the victims, shouts of wildly excited passengers, and the hissing of steam from the engine were terrible to hear."[43]

The engineer, slightly injured, walked to town and had the Orange station agent telegraph the railroad's Washington headquarters. Probably arriving about the same time with news of the wreck were one or more residents of Oakley, the Browning home overlooking the trestle. Other Oakley residents went down to do what they could at the wreck scene. A special train from Washington, carrying a hastily assembled team of physicians and nurses with their medical supplies and equipment, and accompanied by the railroad's General Manager, soon arrived in Orange.

The wreck claimed the lives of eight men and one woman. An additional 26 were sufficiently injured to be named in the issue of the *Orange Observer* which reported on the wreck. The mail car had been crushed, and two postal clerks were killed with four others badly injured. One or two of the dead were Confederate veterans returning from a 25th commemoration of the Battle of Gettysburg. Former Confederate General James Longstreet was reported to have been on the sleeper which stayed on the tracks. Ironically, one of the dead was Cornelius Cox, the railroad employee in charge of replacing the Fat Nancy trestle, and his name is carved into the keystone of the culvert located under the earth fill. The culvert can be seen from Route 20 today in the hollow just east of the Oakley house. Several of the dead are buried in the old part of Graham Cemetery, beside the Confederate cemetery section.

That 1888 wreck at the Fat Nancy remains one of Virginia's larger rail disasters; however, we have never been able to interest a banjo-toting poet or some such person to immortalize it. Probably too much of a challenge to get anything to rhyme with "Fat Nancy," but it's never too late for someone to try.

---

[42] Photographs indicate that Mr. Nicholson was apparently mistaken about how the engine fell.

[43] See *The Railroad Journal* issue for January-February 1960, p. 16, *et seq.*

ON OCTOBER 17, 1917, THERE WAS A FATAL TRAIN WRECK AT HATCHERS CUT near Spotswood Station. That station was between Orange and Rapidan, just a bit north of today's railroad bridge over State Route 632. For some reason, three trains were all arriving at that stretch of track at about the same time, one headed south, two north. One train was shunted onto a side track, but a head-on collision was inevitable. There was some talk about a switch failing to operate properly, but there were too many trains for that section of track anyway. Unfortunately, engineer Frank Lammond and his fireman were killed.

At the time of his death, Lammond was a senior engineer for his rail line. His home was in the town of Orange, and many locals knew him. They could spot his engine by the shiny brass eagle he had mounted on its front, and waves would be exchanged as he went by. Lammond's widow continued to live in Orange after his death.

A WRECK THAT RIVALS THE FAT NANCY IN DRAMA, BUT FORTUNATELY NOT IN fatalities, was the wreck which took place in the town of Orange on the evening of February 1, 1965. The weather was very cold, and snow was forecast. It was a little after 5 p.m., and the station master had just closed the station for the evening. He was making his way home as a 140-car Southern freight train rolled into town from the south. The engines pulled smoothly around the long sweeping curve to the Church Street crossing, rumbled past the station, and headed out of town. The cars of the train clattered uneventfully across the various crossings in town until its last four flat cars approached the Church Street crossing.

On those last four flat cars were truck trailers loaded with steel bar joists, a type of metal framing typically used under floors and flat roofs. One or more of the tie-downs holding joists on a trailer had failed, and as the cars rounded the curve at the Church Street crossing, the joists began sliding off the front of their trailer and swinging out towards the station. When the joists plowed into the ground and then the station, they derailed the car carrying the trailer, causing additional cars to derail and more trailer loads of joists to burst free.

The ground reportedly shook up to five blocks away as roughly 100 tons of the steel joists were strewn through town. Some speared through the walls of the just-closed station and landed in Short Street on the other side. A large tangled pile of them blocked Main Street. Steel seemed to be everywhere.

Fortunately, no one was hurt. Lindsay Boxley was standing at the station and ducked behind a concrete wall just before the steel reached him. Martha Joyner, stopped at the May-Fray crossing, was too busy keeping her head down to see the derailed cars as they were dragged through the crossing in front of her, followed by the caboose which was sliding on its side. She, and probably everyone else in Orange, couldn't miss hearing it.

Locals, and then railroad crews, began gathering at the wreck site, and they worked through the night in a light snow. Before long, something over 40 trains were backed up north and south of Orange, and time was money. During the next day, the tracks were cleared and repaired. Trains were soon rolling through town as the traffic jam began to clear. The great wreck of 1965 was already starting to become the property of memories. It would still be a while, however, before the last of the steel was hauled away and the gaping holes in the station walls repaired.

THERE WERE ONLY A FEW AUTOMOBILES IN VIRGINIA AT THE BEGINNING OF the 1900s, and those machines were largely confined to the cities. People living in the country tended to be more conservative and to have less money to invest in fads than their city cousins. Also, there were fewer good roads out in the country. By 1906 there were at least enough autos in Virginia to cause the legislature to consider regulating their ownership and use. That year it was thought that some 600 cars were bumping along Virginia's roads somewhere.[44] Orange County wound up playing a role in the early development of Virginia's auto economy that greatly exceeded what might have been expected of a small rural county. Much of that can be attributed to the fact that the county got into the automobile business early.

In February 1909 the *Orange Observer* announced to the world that "Professor J. Carter Walker of Woodberry Forest School has just purchased a very handsome and costly automobile in which he is taking his family out for a daily spin." Front page news. The story in the family and around the school was that brother Joe Walker had talked Carter, the acknowledged "deep pocket" of the six Walker brothers, into buying the car, but that it was really for Joe's use. What the paper missed was the even earlier interest of Carter's brother, Joe, in automobiles. For Joe, that machine was an answer to his prayers.

Joe Walker had early on become the business manager for the school and farm operations at Woodberry Forest in neighboring Madison County. While he could be somewhat less than tactful, he had good business sense and stayed on top of things. The farm part of his job was especially diffi-

---

[44] The *Virginia Stastical Abstract* reports that by 1977 there were 5.7 million motor vehicles registered in Virginia, almost one for every state citizen.

cult, though, because he was violently allergic to horses. Because of Joe, Woodberry became primarily a mule-powered operation, but some contact with horses still couldn't be avoided. As one of the youngest brothers, my father was periodically detailed to drive Joe around the farm. The conveyance was a one-horse surrey containing a glass-enclosed riding compartment in which Joe sat. My father, as driver, sat outside of the compartment and had to respond to constant, insistent rappings on the glass and frustrated pointings of the directions to drive. There were days, my father recalled, when he could have cheerfully shot brother Joe.

Joe was one of the very first buyers of an automobile in this area, and in those days, buying an auto was an invitation to other business possibilities. Auto manufacturers routinely offered rural buyers a chance to represent them as commission salesmen, and Joe was not one to ignore opportunities. In fact, he quickly developed that particular opportunity into a serious business venture.

In November 1910, the Orange Automobile Club was organized, with Joseph G. Walker as president and James A. Hill as treasurer and salesman. The "club" designation may have reflected the prevalent early attitude towards driving automobiles as something of a hobby or sport. That attitude did not last long. In February 1913, the Orange Automobile Company was organized to replace the club. The garage was located in the northwest corner of Church and Chapman streets, and from it Ford, Buick, and REO automobiles were sold and serviced.

Among the offerings of the company were: (1) a 28hp. six-passenger Buick touring car with electric lights and starter for $1,300.00; (2) a Buick roadster for $930.00, and (3) the famous Ford two-door runabout with its

Woodberry students posing with Headmaster J. Carter Walker's EMF automobile. The EMF was built by the Studebaker Wagon Company, a well-known maker of horse-drawn farm and freight wagons which went on to manufacture automobiles for the greater part of the twentieth century. Photo courtesy of Woodberry Forest School.

"rumble seat" (sometimes called a "mother-in-law seat"), a steal at $500.00. You couldn't go wrong buying a car from Joe Walker. In the last ten months of 1913 the Orange Automobile Company delivered 33 cars to local buyers, and in so doing nearly quadrupled the number of cars in Orange County.

1913 was a landmark year for automobiles in Orange County for a number of reasons. Around noon on a day in May that year, three carloads of tourists from Fredericksburg thundered into Orange. They had left home around 9:00 a.m., heading for Charlottesville. After a bit of refreshment, the hardy travelers continued on. By 8:00 p.m. they were back in Orange, headed home. Awesome speed! In July, Dr. Chauncey Dovell married Miss Estelle Eddins, the couple standing in the back of Mr. J. R. Smith's automobile, which had been pulled into the Robinson River ford on the road to Culpeper. Minister and guests stood on the river bank. Local farmers were using their flivvers to pull plows, operate wood saws, and power feed mills. The machine was quickly being adopted into our culture – and just as quickly was changing it.

Even in 1913, our relationship with the automobile was not a totally happy one. Garrett A. Waugh had his arm broken cranking a car. Goree Waugh had become a dealer almost as soon as Joe Walker, and possibly it was one of his cars that nailed a relative. A car ran out of control on East Main Street and ran up onto the porch of Mrs. Fry's house. Three porch posts were broken, but no one was hurt. Later that year we had our first fatal auto wreck. Paul Oddenino was killed by a train at a railroad crossing just on the south edge of town. Paul had been operating a taxi service, somewhat against his family's wishes. He evidently felt very comfortable operating a car, and the story was that he had been racing that train all the way from Winston in Culpeper County.

Some time prior to 1915, Joe Walker's company opened a dealership in Gordonsville. The auto business was booming, but Joe had growing family business demands at Woodberry which had first call on his time. In late 1914 or early 1915, William C. Graham and Company took over the Orange Automobile Company, and Joe Walker stepped down. He had already begun to make Orange into an automobile town, though, and that legacy continued without him.

In 1914 the Bates Brothers Dodge dealership went into business on Chapman Street, a door or two up from Joe Walker and his Fords. In 1919, they added the Nash automobile line. By the 1930s Bates Brothers had become the local Chrysler-Plymouth dealer. Messrs. Macon and Carter started an Overland dealership in 1915. Ware Chevrolet started up in a building that stood directly behind today's Virginia National Bank building, then they moved right next door to the Orange Motor Company, the

Autos ply Orange's spacious Main Street in the 1930s. Behind the tree on the right is the Coleman Hotel, across from the court house. In the far distance is Mayor Perry's home, deliberately built out into Main Street.

new Ford dealership at the same old Chapman Street location. William Graham left the Ford dealership in the early 1920s and started a Hudson-Dodge dealership at "the foot of court house hill" in the old skating rink building. Powell Motor Company was formed to sell Nash and Star autos in today's James Madison Museum building, and C. D. Quisenberry began selling Indian motorcycles from his Main Street jewelry store. Orange was a Motor City.

Orange County was so deep into the automobile business that in 1930 the total retail value of automobiles and related parts, accessories, and supplies sold in the county amounted to roughly $700,000. In that same year, groceries and related foodstuffs rang up just a little under $525,000. A rural, gardening county never spent much on groceries, but the comparison was surely a Chamber of Commerce talking point. Small wonder, then, that Chapman Street, the heart of the local auto business, became known as Wall Street. Even the post office delivered to that address.

A 1922 auto parts catalog on file in the Orange County Historical Society offered parts for fifty different manufacturers of automobiles. If there wasn't a local dealer for the car or its part, somebody would find a way to get it for you. Take your pick.

| | | |
|---|---|---|
| Apperson | Hudson | Overland |
| Auburn | Hupmobile | Packard |
| Briscoe | Jordan | Paige |
| Buick | King | Peerless |
| Cadillac | Lafayette | Pierce-Arrow |
| Case | Liberty | REO |
| Chalmers | Locomobile | Saxon |
| Chandler | Marmon | Scripps Booth |
| Chevrolet | Maxwell | Standard |
| Cole | Mercer | Stearns |
| Crow Elkhart | Mitchell | Studebaker |
| Cunningham | Moon | Stutz |
| Dodge | Nash | Velie |
| Dort | National | Wescott |
| Essex | Oakland | White |
| Franklin | Oldsmobile | Willys-Knight |
| Haynes | | Winton |

Wanna buy a car?

## H. Hail, Mighty Gordonsville

In 1728, Col. Henry Willis, an acknowledged shaker and mover who later helped create Orange County, patented 10,000 acres in what would be the southwestern part of that county. A plat of his patent on a county map shows a long, narrow rectangle of land lying along the southern boundaries of patents that had been earlier granted to Col. James Taylor II, Ambrose Madison, Thomas Chew, Col. David Bray, William Todd, and John Baylor. Those earlier patents had taken up almost all of the best farming land in the area, and Col. Willis may have been trying to lay his patent in a way as to pick up such scraps of good soil as might have escaped his neighbors.

Col. Willis was ever ready to turn a profit on his investments, and he soon sold a portion of his 10,000 acres to Ambrose Madison, grandfather of the President. This included the tract the Madisons called "Black Level." In 1787, descendants of Ambrose sold 1,350 acres of that land to Nathaniel Gordon, a Scot merchant and one of the many Gordons who have called this region home, both then and now. Gordon had an eye for a good business location, and his purchase got for him the land around the intersection of "the Fredericksburg Great Road" and the Richmond Road, for all practical purposes the present routes 15/33/231 traffic circle intersection in today's Gordonsville. By 1793, Gordon had built his residence and a tavern at the crossroads, and his reputation as an excellent tavern keeper was growing.

Among the many notables who partook of Gordon's hospitality were Thomas Jefferson, Henry Clay, John Randolph of Roanoke, and James Monroe. Jefferson took to recommending Gordon's establishment as a "good house" to southern legislators who were looking for a stopover on their way to attend Congress. By 1813, the tavern and crossroads had already attracted a fair-sized settlement, and Gordon decided to apply for a permit to operate a post office. Gordon had been calling the settlement "Newville," but with history looking him square in the eye, he seized the moment and his application was for a post office at "Gordonsville." Can't fault the man for that.

Gordon was dead by the time the Marquis de Lafayette revisited Orange County in 1824, but the tavern operation was still such that it was selected as the site of a reception for that beloved hero of the Revolution. From a tavern porch, a much-aged Marquis addressed the crowd of well-wishers who had come to pay their respects. By 1830 the tavern was no longer in operation, and the structure was then used at various times as a residence, a boys' school, and then a girls' school.

In the 1940s, the building was deemed obsolete and in the way of modern commercial development. The tavern had entered that architectural never-never land, where it is too old to be useful and too young to be revered and preserved. Most structures do not survive that period, and the Gordon Tavern was no exception. A brief note in a 1947 number of the *Orange County Review* advised readers that the old tavern building was going to be pulled down soon "to make room for progress." Even before the building came down, however, a memorial marker to it had already been placed nearby. That marker still stands on the southeast side of the Gordonsville traffic circle.

Business as usual in the Gordonsville community suddenly became Big Business when the Louisa Railroad received permission in 1840 to extend its lines into the Gordonsville area of Orange County. By 1841, the railroad facilities were established some two-thirds of a mile south of Gordonsville, and a settlement calling itself "Gordonsville Depot" began to grow up around it. With the construction of the Rockingham and the Blue Ridge turnpikes and the arrival of the Orange & Alexandria Railroad from

The Gordon Tavern. The "good house" of Jefferson's description once stood adjacent to the Routes 15/33/231 traffic circle in today's Gordonsville. It was a popular stopover for many colonial-era notables, including Lafayette on his 1824-25 return visit to America. A monument commemorating its existence stands there now. Pen and ink sketch by local artist B. Edwin Talley. Reproduced with permission.

the north, all in the 1850s, Gordonsville was the unchallenged commercial center of the county.

By the 1850s a son-in-law of Nathaniel Gordon, Dr. Charles Beale, owned the land between the two Gordonsville settlements. Dr. Beale envisioned a prosperous Piedmont town coming into being on his land, and he began to plan for its creation. Unfortunately, the doctor's untimely death kept him from personally realizing his dream, but his plans were carried out through the instructions left in his will. Streets and building lots were laid off on the late Doctor's land, and the lots were sold for the benefit of his widow. The lots were then quickly built upon, and the Gordonsville tavern and depot settlements merged into a single proud and prosperous community.

As Virginia entered the Civil War, Gordonsville held obvious strategic importance. Its railroad facilities were essential to the maintenance of any significant Confederate military presence in north-central Virginia and would have to be held at all costs, or in the military parlance of the day, "at all hazards." In the late winter of 1861-62, when the decision was made to pull the Confederate army out of Northern Virginia, Gordonsville and Fredericksburg became the rail hubs for what evolved into the Rapidan and Rappahannock defensive lines. The arrival at Gordonsville of the Moore Hospital from Manassas confirmed the resolve of the Confederacy to defend its possession of the town. Then, for a handful of days in August 1862, Gordonsville became that community in Virginia whose importance to the overall Confederate effort was probably only surpassed by the capital city of Richmond itself.

Stonewall Jackson had arrived in late July 1862 and on August 9 had defeated the Federal Army of Virginia in the Battle of Cedar Mountain in Culpeper County. Jackson had then pulled back behind the Rapidan line and camped in the meadow adjacent to Woodley, south of the town of Orange. By mid-August Robert E. Lee and virtually all the rest of the Confederate Army of Northern Virginia headed to Gordonsville to join up with Jackson. The town was strained to its limits to support the massive buildup surrounding it, a buildup which led to the Second Manassas/ Antietam Campaign. For the people of Gordonsville, those times had to be both exhilarating and exhausting.

The single-track Virginia Central, successor to the Louisa Railroad, was called upon to bring in the troops and all the supplies and equipment their presence required. Many units actually marched part or all of the way to Orange County from Richmond in order to ease the burden on the railroad. With so many of the soldiers suffering from diseases caught in the swamps east of Richmond, that was a brutal hike in the hot August sun. No matter how bad they felt, the sight of all the activity they found at Gordonsville had to be exciting. Clearly, big events were close at hand.

Long wagon trains and large drives of all kinds of livestock were coming in on the turnpikes from the Valley. The local roads around Gordonsville were equally crowded, as military and civilian wagons rolled in and out of town, servicing the needs of the innumerable camps in the county. The wagon parks around the town were filled to overflowing, and the nearby pens and pastures crowded with animals. The rail yards and shops for the Virginia Central and the Orange & Alexandria pounded, clanked and hissed on an endless list of jobs, many of which demanded around-the-clock work. The blacksmith shops, wheelwrights' shops, harness makers' shops, taverns, stables, etc., were all busy beyond imagining.

The streets were teeming with newly-arrived soldiers and civilians, many probably looking for a place to stay until they could catch up with their unit or return to the road. Locals were bustling about, trying to find an open spot to put up one more boarder and surveying the passing wagon trains for supplies of fresh food available for civilian purchase. The throngs had to part to allow military units to tramp or clatter by, but then the streets would refill in their wake.

In addition to contributing heavily to the small mountains of supplies and equipment in and around Gordonsville, the railroad was also providing transportation for the hospital, bringing in the items it needed and removing sick and wounded to more distant and surely quieter hospitals. Some of those sick soldiers who had come from Richmond were now too ill to continue, and their appearance at the hospital added to the already heavy burden created by the Cedar Mountain fighting. The churches were full, the grave diggers busy — there wasn't much in Gordonsville that wasn't tasked to the breaking point.

The people of Gordonsville had to sense that the eyes of the entire nation were on them and their community. They had one of the finest armies the world had ever known in their midst. Its leader, Robert E. Lee, in his performance in the battles around Richmond, had finally shown the ability that had long been claimed for him. That international legend, Stonewall Jackson, was with Lee, as well as the flamboyant Stuart and a whole host of other Confederate military notables. Great, momentous events were bound to happen. Gordonsville and its citizens were supplying and caring for this huge army as though it were a Richmond or an Atlanta. Hail, Mighty Gordonsville!

In late August, Lee and his army left Orange County on what became the Second Manassas/Antietam Campaign. A tremendous amount of material continued to pass through Gordonsville up the Orange & Alexandria to the army, and a tremendous number of casualties arrived on the return runs, but it was still relatively quieter than before. The following year, when the army returned to Orange County from Gettysburg for the winter of 1863-64, things got busy again, but this time there were fewer supplies to handle, and a lot of that went directly to Orange, the headquarters town for that particular stay in the county. No, Gordonsville seemed destined to never again be quite so busy or so important as it was in August 1862. One, however, learns to never say "never."

Following the Civil War, Gordonsville remained the commercial center of Orange County for a while longer. Then in 1880 the Charlottesville & Rapidan Railroad Company, in combination with the Washington City, Virginia Midland & Great Southern Railroad, secured a right of way from Charlottesville to Orange that bypassed Gordonsville. One still occasionally hears whispers that the Virginia Central and Orange & Alexandria convinced the Gordonsville town fathers to keep the competing railroad out of town, but it's not certain. The only thing for sure is that Gordonsville has never been the same since.

Where the new railroad crossed the Rockingham and Blue Ridge Turnpikes at Barboursville and Somerset respectively, those communities blossomed, as turnpike traffic stopped there instead of going on to Gordonsville. Also, with Orange now the junction point for two major railroads, more and more rail traffic continued on through Gordonsville without stopping. Orange's rise as a commercial center was accompanied by Gordonsville's decline. The general decline in rail based commerce after WWII added insult to injury, and thanks in great measure to Joe Walker's allergy to horses, Orange moved more quickly than Gordonsville to become an automobile town.

Gordonsville did not go down quietly, however. Its commerce supported a number of local businesses well into the twentieth century. As late as 1930, the Jones Hardware was advertising that it was the oldest continuously operating hardware business in a four-state area, and many other Gordonsville businesses were still going strong. In 1937, the history class at Gordonsville High School compiled the following list of Gordonsville businesses:

*Communication Facilities*
  1 post office, 3rd class
  1 R. F. D. mail route
  1 star mail route
  1 telephone exchange
  1 telegraph station
  1 newspaper (weekly)

*Transportation*
  1 railroad (C. &: 0.)
  1 bus line (Virginia Stage)
  5 truck lines
  2 taxi cabs
  1 airport

*Miscellaneous Business*
  3 general stores
  3 local grocery stores
  1 produce & feed store

4 garages, 3 with auto sales
3 gasoline-station stores
2 gasoline station restaurants
1 blacksmith shop
1 lumber yard
2 coal and wood firms
1 farm machinery/hardware store
1 undertaking firm
3 insurance agencies
1 real estate firm
1 men's and ladies' clothing store
1 ten-cent and novelty store
2 drug stores
1 florist shop
2 barber shops
1 billiard/pool room
1 shoe repair shop
1 laundry
1 radio shop and jewelry store

1 bank

2 hotels

1 tourist home

1 boarding house

4 restaurants and cafes

*Professional Persons & Tradesman*

7 school teachers

8 clergymen

5 trained nurses

6 insurance men

2 contractors

5 stone and brick masons

2 electricians

1 jeweler

6 auto mechanics

1 aviator

1 music teacher, white

5 physicians

2 dentists

1 druggist

3 undertakers

20 (approx.) carpenters

1 plumber

2 dressmakers

1 radio repairman

2 barbers

*Churches*

4 Baptist

1 Catholic

2 Episcopal

1 Methodist

1 Presbyterian

1 Christian

*Schools*

1 high

2 grade

There were probably a few additional small businesses and a private school or two the class missed. All mostly gone now. Remaining, in addition to the historic public buildings is a collection of interesting and picturesque Piedmont small-town homes. Mr. Ferol Briggs has contributed his collection of Orange County photographs to the Orange County Historical Society. A number are of the old Town of Gordonsville buildings which survived to the mid- and late-twentieth century but are now gone. The notes accompanying the photos are a Gordonsville history lesson in themselves.

In sum, today's Gordonsville is only a shadow of the community that ruled Orange County during the forty plus years which followed the arrival of the Louisa Railroad. Some say that the memory of that lost prominence still haunts Gordonsville in the way that the loss of the Civil War still haunts some Southerners and Southern institutions. Clearly the competition between Orange and Gordonsville on any subject of mutual interest is often spirited and sometimes spirited in the extreme. At the close of the twentieth century, the town had attracted prominent supporters, and there are now signs of growth. As long as the sun rises, there's hope.

## I. Orange County Seeks Revenue to Pay its Bills

If you hate to pay taxes, you would not have found living in early Orange County much fun. In the same way we are required to support the federal, state, and local governments today, early Orange County citizens were called upon to support not only the royal, colonial, and local governments, but also the colony's Anglican Church. There was a "head tax" on tithables to support the colonial government, quitrents of two shillings per hundred acres assessed against landowners for the royal government, import duties on slaves and other valuable property for both the royal and colonial governments, and export duties of two shillings per hogshead of tobacco going to the colonial governor's discretionary fund. Locally, there were parish levies and county levies to pay. The court system also produced some fine revenue, and there was an extensive governmental fee-for-service structure, which for some county employees was their sole source of income.

While public monies were calculated in English pounds, shillings, and pence "sterling" (based on the value of silver), hard currency on the early frontier was virtually nonexistent. The most popular medium of exchange was tobacco, valued at so much per hundredweight. Even parish priests' salaries were routinely paid in tobacco, ultimately leading to the famous Parson's Cause lawsuit that propelled Patrick Henry into the revolutionary spotlight. By the time of the Revolution, several types of money were circulating in Orange County. English pounds sterling of course, but also colonial currencies created by individual colonies and valued at some percentage of the pound sterling. There were also tobacco warehouse receipts and locally valued scrip issued by merchants and millers, a stray French coin or two, and Spanish currency in dollars, doubloons, pistereens, and pieces of eight.

As the Revolution wound to a close in 1782, the Virginia General Assembly enacted an overhaul of the state's hodgepodge of tax laws, substituting an income tax and a uniform system of real property and personal property value assessment, with a tax imposed as a percentage of that assessment. Old habits die hard however, and those taxes were still calculated in pounds sterling until 1810.

Up until the 20th century, wealth in Orange County tended to follow land ownership. For all of their moaning and poor-mouthing, farmers and planters were usually realizing at least some income from their operations. The county was allowed to tax real property (land and buildings, with their fixtures and attachments) and personal property (equipment, furnishings, livestock, inventory) as its primary sources of revenue, while the state and federal governments taxed virtually everything else.

AGRICULTURE DOMINATED THE LOCAL ECONOMY FOR OVER TWO HUNDRED years, but by the time WWI ended (1918) there were signs of a major change taking place. As an industry, agriculture was peaking. Almost all the land that could be farmed profitably was in production, and new advances in farm equipment and farming practices promised fewer, not more, farm jobs. Young people were abandoning the county's spartan rural life and flocking to the higher paying jobs and better living conditions of the cities, leaving their parents and grandparents to support the county. It was also becoming clear that the costs of local public services, the largest item of which had become public education, were headed beyond what an agriculturally-based property tax could be called upon to support. The answer to both the jobs and revenue problems lay in non-farm manufacturing, and the county leaders redoubled their efforts to attract industry to the county.

In 1924 the Orange County Chamber of Commerce was founded. The fledgling Chamber saw the creation of new jobs for county citizens as its first priority. In 1929 the Chamber played a major role in getting the American Silk Mills Company to locate in Orange. A more timely result of its efforts could not have been imagined. The Great Depression was getting a grip on America's economic jugular as this new Orange County employer (350 jobs) started operating. In 1931, the Chamber reported that the county's housing stock remained full and that unemployment was low. At one time the largest processor of raw silk in America, the mill adapted to the disappearance of Asian silk at the onset of WWII and emerged from the war with the capability to handle synthetic fibers.

Also in the late 1930s, with war clouds gathering, the Adrian-Snead Aircraft Corporation completed its relocation to Orange County from New Jersey. Originally envisioned as an aircraft parts manufacturer, the company had developed an internationally recognized expertise in building and installing metal book stacks, elaborate library conveyor systems, and steel door and frame products. The company won War Department contracts to build pontoons for floating bridges, and it buckled down to work. By 1942, there were close to 1,200 people on the payroll. After the war, the company returned to its old lines of business, changing its name to Virginia Metal Products, then to Virginia Metal Industries.

Among the smaller industries, the "velvet mill" on Spicer's Mill Road operated in various names and formats for decades. Probably its best known product was indeed a velvet used in funeral caskets. Clark Manufacturing was a small metal shapes producer which made parts for munitions during

WWII and went on to produce both metal items for the furniture industry and cabinets for the local construction market. When the founder of Clark Manufacturing died, he left the company to his employees.

Some time around the mid-1950s there began a gradual refocusing of the county's economic development efforts. More and larger employment centers were evolving outside of the county, and county residents were starting to commute to them. A wide variety of jobs could be found in Charlottesville, Manassas, Fredericksburg, or Richmond, and attracting a few employers to the county wasn't going to stop worker migration. At the same time, the need to expand the county's nonfarm tax base had never been greater. Growing the tax base, rather than job creation, started to become the county's goal.

In the 1960s Clarostat-Virginia Corporation, a manufacturer of specialized electrical components, opened its doors in the town of Orange. In 1971, Blue Bell, a work clothes manufacturer gave people jobs at an East Byrd Street plant, and in 1973, the Doubleday publishing corporation built a large book printing plant just off of Route 15 between Orange and Gordonsville. Orange County's largest employer and the largest non-agricultural source of tax revenue in the late twentieth century was Liberty Fabrics, based in Gordonsville.

There is one similarity between all of the companies noted above; they are all gone. It points out just how difficult it is to maintain the county's industrial tax base. The Chamber of Commerce and its former Industrial Development sub-committee, now the independent Economic Development Corporation, work hard and receive help from the county Office of Economic Development and the county's Industrial Development Authority, but it still isn't easy. The assessed value of all Orange County commercial and industrial real estate in 1998 amounted to slightly less than 8% of the total. Those entities, however, did produce a critical 20% of the county's personal property tax revenue. We can't do without them.

FOR A TIME DURING THE MID-TWENTIETH CENTURY, IT WAS TOUTED THAT THE way to enhance local tax revenue was to encourage residential development. Residential real estate is assessed at a much higher rate than open farm land, the argument went, therefore local tax revenues will be significantly enhanced. By observing nearby counties, Orange County did get a chance to see what extensive residential development could do to a rural county.

In nearby Prince William County, the Dale City residential development started up. Its promoters chanted the mantra that this conversion of low value farm land to higher value residential property was an economic bonanza for the county. The Virginia Farm Bureau was not convinced and commissioned a study of the economic impact of Dale City. The study revealed that when the additional public services and infrastructure burdens (roads, schools, law enforcement, fire, rescue, trash, etc.) were factored in, every time a house was built and occupied in Dale City, it cost Prince William County more than it received in taxes. That study, and the innumerable ones like it, have become accepted reality.

Most counties experiencing residential development are now trying various strategies to offset the added costs of development, but none seem to be able to keep property taxes from climbing. Enough court cases have been decided to make it clear that short of some very real health or safety issue, a county cannot stop development totally. Another element of the problem is that development does tend to produce very real short-term benefits for the politicians and business people who authorize and service it in their locality. By the time the long-term permanent problems arise, those people can be out of office, retired, moved away, or otherwise insulated from the public they have burdened. The temptations and pressures to act irresponsibly are enormous, and men and women of strong principles and high character remain — as they always have been — the public's only hope.

With the exception of Lake of the Woods subdivision in the mid-1960s, Orange County escaped extensive residential development through most of the twentieth century, and the tax burden to service its population remained relatively low. That is now changing with a vengeance. Between the 1990 and 2000 censuses, Orange County grew 20.8%, and there are close to 5,000 building lots currently available for sale in the eastern end of the county alone. The 1998 assessment of Orange County real estate shows that over 68% of the total assessed value of county land now comes from property in residential uses, with only 24% from farm tracts of 20 acres or more. And property tax rates are starting to rise.

One of the earliest moves to recognize and protect the architectural and cultural significance of a section of the county came with the formation of the Rapidan Foundation in 1967. In 1987 the Foundation secured the listing of the historic village of Rapidan in the Virginia Landmarks Register and in the National Register of Historic Places. In 1990, the huge 32,500 acre Madison-Barbour Rural Historic District was similarly listed to focus attention on the historic structures and significant viewsheds of virtually all of Orange County north of Route 15. In 1998 the town of Orange secured a listing for its downtown commercial historic district.

Some Orange County land owners, recognizing that public land-use controls can only delay, but not deny, development, are placing permanent development restrictions on their land. The most common practice is to grant easements, which convey away some or all of their land's development potential, to an organization authorized by the state to accept and hold those easements. There are often tax benefits; but many owners are simply acting out of a love for the land. As of this writing, 20,000 acres of Orange County's privately owned land has been so protected, out of the county's approximately 227,000 total acres.

Civil War battlefields present an opportunity for the double benefit of historic site and open space preservation. Preservation groups are buying such battlefield tracts as they can afford and placing development restrictions on them. Where the land is within a military park boundary, the preservation group will usually offer to resell the land to the park. Once the park has completed its cumbersome bureaucratic purchasing process, the preservation group can recover at least a part of its outlay for reuse in additional purchases. In the case of the huge Mine Run Campaign area in eastern Orange County, the Piedmont Environmental Council and the Civil War Preservation Trust combined their resources and efforts to purchase almost 700 acres, including the virtually undisturbed Payne's Farm battlefield. That land is not within a park, and portions of it will be permanently held while other portions may be offered for sale after the restrictive easements have been placed on it.

DURING THE TWENTIETH CENTURY, THE TAX ON AUTOMOBILES GREW INTO THE largest single source of personal property tax revenue for Orange County. Those funds helped greatly in dealing with "unfunded mandates," laws enacted in Richmond that require counties to provide additional public services, but for which Richmond does not contribute state funds to pay for them. Like all Virginia counties, Orange has always scratched and scraped to raise the additional funds and postponed tax rate increases until they were inevitable. Then in 1998 the state passed the Personal Property Tax Relief Act. The act provided for the elimination of the local "car tax" and for the state treasury to replace the revenue counties would lose as a result. The state government had given itself an absolutely enormous unfunded mandate. There has been little opportunity to gloat, however, since the mandate's effect has coincided with a general economic downturn which has drastically reduced state revenues. Unlike the federal government, Virginia is restricted in its ability to use debt financing, and as of this writing the economic pain is still spreading. For years a county income tax has been discussed as a supplement or replacement for the local property tax, and possibly its time has come.

## J. Getting the Word Out:
## Letters, Newspapers, and Telephones

Just behind roads in contributing to the initial development of the county's economy were its various information distribution services. If buyers and sellers were going to transact business in any other way but face to face, the speed of the deal hinged on how fast offers, counter-offers, terms and conditions, etc., could move between the parties. Long before the appearance of today's sophisticated equipment and services, smart minds were working on the problem.

The earliest mail was literally "posted," that is, attached in some weather-resistant manner to a post or tree, usually at a crossroads. Presumably every literate passer-by read as much as he wanted, and one who was going in the direction of the person addressed could take the message along, in anticipation of being rewarded for his trouble upon delivery. As areas settled, more traditional mail handling systems quickly followed. The Virginia colony, however, refused for years to enter into the organized postal system serving the colonies.

It was not until former Lieutenant Governor Alexander Spotswood became the Deputy Postmaster for the colonies in 1729 that Virginia dropped its objections. Spotswood set up his offices at New Post in Spotsylvania County, and ran the colonial postal system from there. One particularly bright young man by the name of Benjamin Franklin caught Spotswood's eye, and he ultimately appointed Franklin Postmaster of Philadelphia. That was no act of generosity, because Philadelphia was becoming one of the most important cities in the British Empire. By the time of the Revolution, it was larger than every English-speaking city in the world except London. Philadelphia needed a highly competent postmaster, and Spotswood knew ability when he saw it.

By 1796 a post office had been established at Orange Court House, and on April 1 of that year, Postmaster Andrew Shepherd submitted the first report for that office. (It was not until January 1890 that "Orange Court House" was changed to simply "Orange.") Shepherd was one of the most prominent businessmen in the settlement of Orange in 1796, and that turns out to be almost an automatic qualification for early local postmasters.

By the time of the Civil War, Henry Hiden, the owner of Peliso, was the Postmaster for Orange Court House. At the onset of hostilities, Fanny Hume was still engaged to an officer in the Federal navy, a carryover from her pre-war days as a resident of Alexandria. Apparently Mr. Hiden took exception to Fanny's letters to her fiancé. In any event, he soon had troubles of his own. By August 1862 the Confederate government had commandeered his house for use as a hospital and as the headquarters for the 7th Virginia Cavalry. In addition, the soldiers had dug a cannon pit in his front yard.

In August, 1865, John F. Almond became Orange's Postmaster and served until September 1871. Mr. Almond was soon reappointed to the post; however, in a few months he was replaced by Miss Ann E. Almond, who then served for eleven years. As of this writing, Anne Almond is the only Postmistress the town of Orange has ever had.

As the seat of government for the county, Orange was well ahead of most local communities in getting a post office. By contrast, Nathaniel Gordon did not seek a post office for his community until 1813. Thornhill was granted a post office permit in 1829, Liberty Mills (Somerset) in 1837, and Unionville in 1852. For those wishing to pursue this line of interest, the Virginia Postal History Society is an excellent source of information on both the state's postal services and its post offices.

NOT ONLY DID NEWSPAPERS CARRY STORIES ABOUT ISSUES AND EVENTS OF local interest, they also carried offers to transact business in the form of notices and advertisements. This greatly speeded up the contract-forming process. Even before newspapers achieved circulation on the Virginia frontier, local court houses could usually be identified by the flyers and leaflets with which they were plastered. Newspapers never totally replaced those more basic communications, but a newspaper had wider circulation and was almost certain to be more legible than what one might find flapping on the court house door.

Initially, newspapers from long-established commercial centers held sway in the county. Purdie's *Virginia Gazette* out of Williamsburg and newspapers from neighboring colonies held the attention of Orange County's early readers. Later, competition from the *Virginia Herald* and *Fredericksburg Advertiser* and the *Virginia Independent Chronicle* left little entry room for a locally produced paper.

Finally in 1830, the county court records contain a reference to a local paper called the Orange *Record*. As of this writing, nothing else is known about that publication, but apparently it was Orange County's first newspaper. If the *Record* was a typical publication for its day, it would have been a weekly publication consisting of a single sheet of paper, folded to create four pages. The first and last pages would have been filled with advertising and columns either submitted by guest writers or copied directly from other newspapers. Page two was reserved for the editor to say his or her piece, and local news was the province of page three. While the gentlemen were likely to be the closest scanners of the ads, the far and away most popular section of the paper for the ladies was the social column. Who was traveling where to visit whom. Who had held teas or receptions. Who was the guest of honor or who poured. Who was engaged or married, etc. Critical stuff for a society in which travel and opportunities to socialize were limited.

Over the years, a veritable flood of local newspapers followed in the path of the *Record*. Locals have been able to read about themselves and other almost as interesting subjects in the *Gordonsville Gazette*, the *Orange County News and Virginian*, the *Native Virginian*, the *Orange County News*, the *Southern Chronicle, The Orange Expositor,* the *Orange Democrat* ("Principles-Not Men"), the *Orange Press*, the *Orange Observer*, ("We labor for the best interests of the people—and our pocketbook"), and the *Orange County Review*. Very likely there were other local newspapers which appeared and then disappeared in years past. Any reader who has knowledge or evidence of any such publication, kindly please get that information into the files of the Orange County Historical Society.

There have also been a few publications employing a newspaper format and dealing with special areas of interest in the county. The *Orange County Americana* was published in the 1960s by Richard H. "Dick" Matthews and dealt primarily with county history. *The Patriot* appeared in 1975 and focused primarily on land-use and county growth issues. *The Orange Express,* distributed primarily in eastern Orange County, is the only currently existing example of a newspaper directed to a specific region or interest area within the county. A short-lived publication of the same general format was the *Orange Bullet*, published in the 1990s.

Two of Orange County's longest running newspapers were family operations, which in turn probably helps explain their longevity. The *Orange Observer* was a work product of the Robinson family, holding forth in Orange County from the early 1880s until the mid-1930s. The particular *Observer* editor whose memory still fires the imaginations of some of the long time county residents is Miss Bertha Gray Robinson. Back in the early days of female reporters, there was a term which was applied to some, not without a touch of respect: "news hen." Miss Bertha was apparently a combination of news hen and blood hound. Curiosity and tenacity were her hallmarks. Also, she had an impish sense of humor that truly blossomed when romance was the subject. On such occasions, Miss Bertha would sometimes launch into verse, and while the poetry was often less than a technical masterpiece, there was no doubting her sincerity.

The Green family produced the *Orange Review* locally from the early 1900s until they sold the paper to a Charlottesville based publisher in the

1970s. They hit the local version of the big time when the *Orange Press* was merged into their paper in 1912. The key to a local paper's success seems to have been for at least one of its top management to be a character. In the case of the *Review*, if there ever was a Green who was not at least something of a character, the family successfully kept him/her out of sight. The paper is still published and distributed in the county at the time of this writing, albeit without the Green touch. The memory and files of former editor and staff photographer Duff Green are a fabulous storehouse of Orange County history.

Soon after the civil war, the widely-known Virginia humorist Dr. George W. Bagby took up residence in Litchfield, a house on property which had once belonged to Frances Taylor Madison Rose, the youngest sister of the President. Litchfield is now a part of the Thomas Lee Industrial Park on Route 15. From those quarters, Dr. Bagby saw to the publishing of the *Native Virginian*, first in Orange, then moving his operations to Gordonsville in 1870. There, he launched the *Gordonsville Gazette*, which ran from roughly 1873 to 1917. Some of Bagby's work in the black dialect and white slang of the day has been appropriately filed away as relics of a past era. Other portions of his work, however, are worth a present-day look for their lively humor in the midst of the rather bleak Reconstruction era. Gustavus Judson "Jud" Browning of Oakley, adjacent to the Fat Nancy trestle, was immortalized as the uninhibited narrator in several of Bagby's stories. Browning was a distinguished Civil War veteran, a businessman, an 1866-67 delegate to the General Assembly, and he was not famous for having a sense of humor. He must have had one, however, because he tolerated Bagby's characterization of him without a murmur. Most likely he joined many in Orange County who missed Bagby when that entertaining editor left for Richmond to assume the post of State Librarian.

TELEPHONES BROUGHT WITH THEM THE ENTIRE WORLD OF ELECTRONIC communications. The beginnings, however, were modest in the extreme. A patent for the first telephone was granted in 1876, but it was some 20 years before the first one appeared in Orange County.

The first telephone in Orange County is thought to have been the one installed in Dr. Ricketts' drug store on Railroad Avenue in the town of Orange. Dr. Ricketts had arranged with the Culpeper Telephone Company to string a line from Culpeper to Orange via Locust Dale. As best as we can tell, the year was 1896. In 1899, Gordonsville druggist J. H. Stratton got the Louisa Telephone Company to string a line to his Main Street store. Tradition holds that Walter George Newman of Mount Athos was also one of the earliest in the county to have a phone installed. Keep in mind that the installation of a telephone in the early 1900s was usually instant fodder for chat circles and a hot item for the local newspaper.

The growth of Dr. Ricketts' telephone business was typical for most. As additional telephones were installed in the town and their lines strung to his store, he installed a switchboard to route the calls between the local phones and to send long distance calls out onto the "trunk line" to other switchboards. By default Dr. Ricketts became Orange's first switchboard operator. Both the Ricketts and Stratton phone operations had local doctors as their earliest customers. For some, the phone might be a toy, but for these doctors and druggists it was a solid business proposition.

In 1903, the Culpeper Telephone Company bought out the Orange system of 57 phones. Dr. Ricketts had just moved the switchboard out of his drug store into the Perry home, located where the Post Office currently stands. The first of a long line of female operators was Miss Bessie Perry who was trained by Dr. Ricketts.

In 1920 the switchboard was moved across Belleview Avenue into the home of Mrs. M. A. Barbee. When the Main Street fire house was to be built on that site in 1938, the Barbee house was moved to the adjoining lot, with the operators remaining inside and running the switchboard as the building moved. Eventually a space was designed and built at the rear of the fire house to house the expanded switching facilities.

Small local and regional telephone companies quickly followed the lead of individual investors, and the 1920s saw a number of them doing business in Orange County. In addition to the Culpeper and Louisa companies, there was the Pamunkey Mutual Telephone Company, the Orange-Fredericksburg Telephone Company, the Rapidan Telephone Company, and the Wilderness Telephone Company. One of the original investors in the Wilderness company was a local black man, but no one seems to have recorded his name anywhere.

Getting phone service out into the rural areas of the county produced a subhistory all its own. To cover installation and maintenance costs, several phones would be installed on a single line, called a "party line." There was a ring code which was intended to let the parties know who was being called: two longs and a short for the Johnsons, three longs for the Smiths, etc. And of course nobody ever picked up on anybody else's ring and "listened in." Believe that, and you will believe anything. Those old radio soap operas couldn't hold a candle to a party line.

As phone operations grew, the requirement for greater capital investments and more specialized services became more than most small operations wanted to deal with, and the systems were sold to larger companies. In 1929, the Chesapeake & Potomac Telephone Company (C&P) bought the Culpeper Telephone Company and became the major system in the county. It would be years, however, before most of the old system inter-connect problems were resolved.

In 1930, the ten telephone Barboursville exchange sought the assis-tance of the Orange County Chamber of Commerce to help it get toll-free calling to Orange. They persevered and finally succeeded—in 1961. In eastern Orange, Flat Run was the dividing line between the C&P and Con-tinental telephone systems. When Flat Run was dammed and the Lake of the Woods community built around the resulting lake, the residents learned that it was an extra charge, long distance call to talk to people they were looking at across the lake. It was a howling headache until the two compa-nies finally worked out a fix for the problem.

The years following the Second World War saw the start of an explo-sive growth in telecommunications which seems to have no end. The C&P company figured that from the time the telephone was invented until 1950, a bit over seventy years, 500,000 units were installed in its service area. The second 500,000 were installed in the next ten years. On top of all that has come television, computers, and the whole modern world of wired and wireless communications. Orange County has come a long, long way from flyers nailed to the court house door.[44]

## K. One Last Story

This chapter could go on for heaven knows how much longer, but it is time to end this effort and leave the reporting of the additional vast history of Orange County to others. Almost nothing has been said about the build-ing trades, fire companies, vineyards, rescue squads, schools, electric utili-ties, etc. The histories for some of those worthy public and private enter-prises are already on file at the Orange County Historical Society. Others beg to be written. Virtually nothing has been said about banks and related financial institutions, but I do want to get in one last story, and it is sort of a bank story.

My father was president of the National Bank of Orange at the time the long shadows of the Great Depression began to fall across America.

---

[44] My particular thanks to Daniel F. "Dan" Sale, a member of the Telephone Pioneers whose decades of working for the C&P Telephone Company led him to research and present a paper on the subject to the Orange County Historical Society. That paper and the other related notes on file at the Society were liberally consulted for this subchapter.

The first sign of serious trouble close at hand arrived one morning in a message waiting for him when he got home from the barn. A quick drive to town confirmed the message: President Roosevelt had declared a national "bank holiday," and the bank was closed. <u>All</u> banks were closed. The economy was crumbling by the hour, and Americans were being locked away from their money.

Father suspected that the major depositors and stockholders of the bank would be directly across the street at Rickett's Drug Store, and sure enough, there they were, sitting at the tables and talking in subdued tones. Father started going from table to table, trying to bolster spirits, when suddenly Barclay Taliaferro burst through the door. Taliaferro did not qualify as a major depositor or stockholder, in fact his finances were usually pretty threadbare. But he knew everybody and everybody knew him. Taliaferro started moving towards the group, loudly calling out greetings to any and all. His hearers finally succeeded in getting his attention.

"Barclay, Barclay. Didn't you see? The bank is closed."

"YES—AND I'M OVERDRAWN."

# Selected Bibliography

Alexander, Edward Porter, ed., *The Journal of John Fontaine (An Irish Huguenot Son in Spain and Virginia, 1710-1719)*. Williamsburg VA: The Colonial Williamsburg Foundation, 1972.

Audibert, Philip. *Local Folks: A collection of Stories about People from the Files of the Orange County Review.* Orange VA: Orange County Review, 1989.

Benson, T. Lloyd. "The Plain Folk of Orange: Land, Work, and Society on the eve of the Civil War." *The Edge of the South*, eds., Edward L. Ayres and John C. Willis, pp. 56-78. Charlottesville: University Press of Virginia, 1991.

Brown, Stuart E., Jr. *Virginia Baron: The Story of Thomas, 6th Lord Fairfax.* Berryville VA: Chesapeake Book Co., 1965.

Bushnell, David I., Jr. *The Manahoac Tribes in Virginia, 1608*. Washington DC: Smithsonian Institution, Smithsonian Miscellaneous Collections 94(8), 1935.

Cannan, John. *The Wilderness Campaign, May 1864*. Conshohocken PA: Combined Books, 1993.

Carter, J. B., J. W. Wills and W. E. Cummings. *Soil Survey of Orange County, Virginia*. Washington DC: U. S. Government Printing Office, 1971.

Clark, Kenneth M. and Edward T. Moore. "Burials in Graham Cemetery to 1994." Orange County Historical Society, Inc., 1996. Copies available at the Society's Research Center, 130 Caroline Street, Orange VA 22960. Periodically updated.

Cortada, James W., ed. *1861 Diary of Miss Fanny Page Hume*. Orange VA: Orange County Historical Society, Inc., 1983.

Davis, Margaret G. *Madison County, Virginia: A Revised History*. Madison VA: Board of Supervisors of Madison County, 1977.

Dame, William Meade. *From the Rapidan to Richmond and the Spotsylvania Campaign*. Baltimore MD: Green-Lucas Co., 1920.

Des Cognets, Louis, Jr. *English Duplicates of Lost Virginia Records*. Baltimore MD: Genealogical Publishing Co., 1981.

Dodson, Leonidas. *Alexander Spotswood, Governor of Virginia*. Philadelphia: University of Pennsylvania Press, 1932.

Dowdey, Clifford and Louis Manarin, eds. *The Wartime Papers of Robert E. Lee*. New York: Da Capo Press, [1991] c1961.

Ellis, Joseph J. *Founding Brothers*. New York: Alfred A. Knopf, 2000.

Fall, Ralph E., Rev. *Hidden Village: Port Royal, Virginia, 1774-1981*. Verona VA: McClure Printing, 1982.

Fitzgerald, Ruth C. *A Different Story: A Black History of Fredericksburg, Stafford, and Spotsylvania, Virginia*. Greensboro NC: Unicorn Press, 1979.

Flood, Charles B. *Lee-The Last Years*. Boston: Houghton Mifflin, 1981.

Ferguson, Ernest B. *Chancellorsville, 1863: The Souls of the Brave*. New York: Alfred A. Knopf, 1992.

Graham, Martin F. and George F. Skoch. *Mine Run: A Campaign of Lost Opportunities, October 21, 1863–May 1, 1864*. 2nd Edition. Lynchburg VA: H. E. Howard, 1987.

Griffith, Tarisa. Untitled Summer Intern Research Report on the Activities of the Freedman's Bureau in Gordonsville. Historic Gordonsville, Inc., 2000. On file with Historic Gordonsville, Inc., 400 S. Main Street, Gordonsville VA and Mary Washington College, Fredericksburg VA.

Grymes, J. Randolph, Jr., ed. *The Fanny Hume Diary of 1862: A Year in WartimeOrange, Virginia*. Orange County Historical Society, Inc., 1994.

——————— *The Octonia Grant*. Orange VA: Orange County Historical Society, Inc., [1999] c1977.

Harrison, Noel G. "Atop an Anvil: The Civilians' War in Fairfax and Alexandria Counties, April 1861-April 1862." *The Virginia Magazine of History and Biography* 106, no. 2, (Spring 1998): pp.133-164.

Havighurst, Walter. *Alexander Spotswood: Portrait of a Governor*. Williamsburg VA: Colonial Williamsburg Foundation, 1967.

Hendrickson, B. H. *Soil Survey of Orange County, Virginia*. Washington DC: U. S. Government Printing Office, 1927. (Bureau of Chemistry and Soils Bulletin #6, Series 1927).

*Hening's Statutes*. See Swem, this listing.

Hunt-Jones, Conover. *Dolley and the "Great Little Madison."* Washington DC: American Institute of Architects Foundation, 1977.

Holland, C. G., Sandra D. Speiden, and David van Roijen. *The Rapidan Mound Revisited*. Occasional Papers #4. Orange VA: Orange County Historical Society, Inc., 1982.

Hurst, Patricia J. *Soldiers, Stories, Sites and Fights: Orange County, Virginia, 1861-1865, and the Aftermath*. Published by the author, 1998.

———— *The History and People of Clark Mountain, Orange County, Virginia*. Published by the author, 1989.

Jefferson, Thomas. *The Correspondence of Jefferson and Du Pont de Nemours*. Baltimore MD: The Johns Hopkins Press, 1931.

Jennings, Paul. "A Colored Man's Reminiscences of James Madison." *White House History* 1, no. 1 (1983): 46-51.

Joyner, Ulysses P. *Orange County Land Patents*. 2nd Edition. Orange VA: Orange County Historical Society, Inc., [2002] c1999.

———— *The First Settlers of Orange County, Virginia*. Orange VA: Orange County Historical Society, Inc., 1987.

———— Numerous unpublished reference works, including: "Clerks of Orange County," "The Judges of Orange County," "The Village of Orange Court House," "Preachers and Politicians," "Trinity Methodist Church at the Millennium," and "The Methodists of Orange County," all of which he plans to publish as one or more reference works at some future date. They are presently on file at the Orange County Historical Society's Research Center, 130 Caroline Street, Orange VA.

Ketcham, Ralph. *James Madison: A Biography*. Charlottesville: University Press of Virginia, 1990.

Krick, Robert K. *Stonewall Jackson at Cedar Mountain*. Chapel Hill: University of North Carolina Press, 1990.

Langguth, A. J. *Patriots: The Men Who Started the American Revolution.* New York: Simon and Schuster, 1988.

Luvaas, Jay and Wilbur S. Nye. "The Campaign That History Forgot." [Mine Run]. *Civil War Times Illustrated,* November 1969: 12-41.

Mack, Tinsley. *Characteristics of the Everona Formation in Virginia.* Information Circular #10. Charlottesville: Virginia Division of Mineral Resources, 1965.

Marten, James. *The Children's Civil War.* Chapel Hill: University of North Carolina Press, 1998.

Mattern, David B. and Holly C. Shulman, eds. *The Selected Letters of Dolley Payne Madison.* Charlottesville: University of Virginia Press, 2003.

McIllwaine, H. R., ed. *Journals of the House of Burgesses of Virginia.* Bowie MD: Heritage Books. Of special interest are the following volumes, identified by dates: 1727-1734 and 1736-1740; 1712-1714, 1715; 1718, 1720-1711, 1723-1725.

————— *Executive Journals of the Council of Colonial Virginia.* Richmond: Virginia State Library, 1925-1966 [multiple volumes published during those years].

McPherson, James M. *For Cause and Comrade: Why Men Fought in the Civil War.* New York: Oxford University Prerss, 1997.

————— *Battle Cry of Freedom.* New York: Oxford University Press, 1988.

————— *The Abolitionist Legacy: From Reconstruction to the NAACP.* Princeton NJ: Princeton University Press, 1975.

————— *The Struggle for Equality: Abolitionists and the Negro in the Civil War and Reconstruction.* Princeton NJ: Princeton University Press, 1964.

Meima, Ralph C., *Spotswood's Iron*, Revised Edition. Fredericksburg VA: Chancellor Village Press, 1993.

Miller, Ann L. *Antebellum Orange. The Pre-Civil War Homes, Public Buildings, and Historic Sites of Orange County, Virginia.* Orange VA: Orange County Historical Society, Inc., 1988.

———————— *The Short Life and Strange Death of Ambrose Madison*. Orange VA: Orange County Historical Society, Inc., 2001.

———————— "Historic Structures Report: Montpelier, Orange County, Virginia; Phase II: Documentary Evidence Regarding the Montpelier House." Prepared for the National Trust for Historic Preservation, Washington DC, 1990. Unpublished manuscript on file at Montpelier, P. O. Box 67, Montpelier Station VA, updated 2002

Miller, Ann [L.] Brush and Nathaniel Mason Pawlett. *Orange County Road Orders, 1734-1749*. Charlottesville: Virginia Highway & Transportation Research Council, 1984. Reprinted with permission by the Orange County Historical Society, Inc., Orange VA.

———————— *Orange County Road Orders, 1750-1800*. Charlottesville: Virginia Highway & Transportation Research Council, August 1989.

Miller, William Lee. *The Business of May Next: James Madison and the Founding*. Charlottesville: University Press of Virginia, 1992.

Morton, Virginia B. *Marching Through Culpeper.* Orange VA: Edgehill Press, 2001.

Musick, Michael P. *6th Virginia Cavalry*. Lynchburg VA: H. E. Howard, 1990

Norfleet, Elizabeth Copeland. *Woodberry Forest: The Extended View*. Orange VA: Green Publishers, 1979.

"Orange County, Virginia, Comprehensive Plan." Adopted September 14, 1999. County Administrator's Office, Orange VA.

O'Reilly, Francis Augustine. *The Fredericksburg Campaign: Winter War on the Rappahannock*. Baton Rouge: Louisiana State University Press, 2003.

Madison, James. *The Papers of James Madison*. A Congressional series of 17 volumes covering his production up to 1801, a Secretary of State series of 5 volumes (out of a projected 12), a Presidential Series of 4 volumes (out of a projected 12), and a Retirement Series, whose first volume is expected soon. The first 10 volumes were published by the University of Chicago Press, the remainder by the University Press of Virginia.

Pfanz, Donald C. *Richard Ewell: A Soldier's Life*. Chapel Hill: University of North Carolina Press, 1998.

Purdue, Charles L., Thomas L. Barden, and Robert K. Phillips, eds. *Weevils in the Wheat.* Charlottesville: University Press of Virginia, 1976.

Rakove, Jack N. *James Madison and the Creation of the American Republic.* Edited by Oscar Handlin. New York: Addison Wesley Longman, 1990.

Rakove, Jack N., ed. *James Madison: Writings.* New York: Library Classics of the United States, 1999.

Rhea, Gordon C. *The Battle of the Wilderness, May 5-6, 1864.* Baton Rouge: Louisiana State University Press, 1994.

——————— *The Battles for Spotsylvania Court House and the Road to Yellow Tavern, May 7-12, 1864.* Baton Rouge: Louisiana State University Press, 2000.

Rosengarten, Theodore, ed. *Tombee.* New York: William Morrow & Co., 1986.

Rowe, Joseph Y. *The Greatest Generation of Orange.* Orange VA: Hammond Printing, 2001.

Salmon, Emily J. and Edward D. C. Campbell, Jr., eds. *The Hornbook of Virginia History: A Ready-Reference Guide to the Old Dominion's People, Places, and Past.* Richmond: Library of Virginia, 1994.

Schlotterbeck, John T. "Plantation and Farm: Social and Economic Changes in Orange and Greene Counties, 1716 to 1860." Ph.D. diss., Johns Hopkins University, 1982.

Scott, W. W. *A History of Orange County, Virginia.* Richmond, VA: Everette Waddy, 1907. (This work has been reprinted several times by various other printers.)

Steere, Edward. *The Wilderness Campaign: The Meeting of Grant and Lee.* Mechanicsburg PA: Stackpole Books, 1960 and 1994.

Sutherland, Daniel P. *Seasons of War.* New York: Simon & Schuster, 1995.

Swem, E. G. [Earl Gregg], ed. Virginia Historical Index. Gloucester MA: Peter Smith, 1965. Reprinted by permission of the Virginia Historical Society. [this is a detailed index to: (1) *Virginia Magazine of History and Biography*, Vols. 1-38 (1839-1930); (2) *William & Mary Quarterly Historical Magazine* Series #1, Vols. 1-27 (1892-1919) and Series #2, Vols. 1-

10 (1921-1930); (3) *Tyler's Historical and Genealogical Quarterly*, Vols. 1-10 (1919-1929); (4) *Virginia Historical Register*, Vols. 1-6 (1848-1853); (5) *Lower Norfolk Antiquary*, Vols. 1-5 (1895-1906); (6) Calendar of Virginia State Papers, Vols. 1-11 (1652-1869); and (7) *Hening's Statutes of Virginia*, Vols 1-13 (1619-1792). A monumental resource!]

Taylor, Francis. "The Diary of Francis Taylor, Orange County, Virginia, 1786-1799." Original in the Archives and Records Division of the Library of Virginia, Richmond. Transcribed from microfilm by Gunston Hall Plantation, Lorton VA.

Thomas, William H. B. *Gordonsville, Virginia; Historic Crossroads Town.* Verona VA: McClure Printing, 1971.

———————— *Orange, Virginia; Story of a Courthouse Town.* Verona VA: McClure Printing, 1972.

———————— *Patriots of the Upcountry.* Orange VA: Green Publishers, 1976.

Todd, Orene D. *Dear Cousins: An Intimate Visit With Five Generations of Todds.* Baltimore MD: Gateway Press, 2001.

United States War Dept. *The War of the Rebellion: A Compilation of the Official Records of the Union and Confederate Armies.* 128 volumes. Washington DC: U. S. Government Printing Office, 1880-1901.

*Virginia Cavalcade,* Published quarterly from 1951 to 2002 by the Library of Virginia, Richmond. Compiled table of contents online at www.lva.lib.va.us/whatwedo/pubs/cavalcade/volumes/index.htm

*Virginia Magazine of History and Biography,* a quarterly publication of the Virginia Historical Society. See Swem, this listing.

Whitfield, Theodore M. *Slavery Agitation in Virginia 1829-1832.* Baltimore MD: Johns Hopkins Press, 1930.

Woodward, Harold R., Jr. *Major General James Lawson Kemper, C.S.A.: The Confederacy's Forgotten Son.* Natural Bridge Station VA: Rockbridge Publishing Co., 1993.

# *About the Author*

Frank Stringfellow Walker, Jr. was born and raised in Madison County, Virginia, just across the Rapidan River that divides Madison and Orange counties. He was the fourth generation of Walkers to live at Rosni, the dairy farm that had been in the family since it was purchased in 1805 from the heirs of Francis Madison, brother of the President. Although history was not an everyday topic of conversation in his childhood home, the family was steeped in history. On his mother's side Mr. Walker can trace his lineage to Thomas Jefferson; and on his father's side to Robert Stringfellow Walker, a Confederate cavalry captain with Mosby's Rangers. When the Civil War was over, Captain Walker married and had six sons, and together with his wife and sister established Woodberry Forest School, a nationally renowned college preparatory school for boys in Madison County.

Mr. Walker was educated at Woodberry Forest, Virginia Tech (BS in agronomy) and the University of Virginia (MBA & JD). After a couple of decades as a farmer, followed by over a decade practicing law, Mr. Walker decided in 1994 to pursue yet another profession. His growing knowledge of local history became a calling. Looking around where he had lived all his life, he saw significant heritage at every turn. At the same time he observed that many people knew little of that rich heritage, while growth and development threatened to overshadow, if not erase, the evidences of it. Mr. Walker established Tourguide, Ltd., and as a freelance tour guide, speaker and writer, began sharing his accumulated knowledge of the region with both locals and visitors. He is motivated by the belief that as more people become aware of Orange's heritage, they will join in the effort to promote and protect it for the next generation, even in the face of inevitable growth and development.

Mr. Walker lives in Orange County, just across the Rapidan River from where he grew up. He is married and has two adult daughters and two granddaughters.

# Index

Numbers in italics refer to footnotes and numbers in boldface refer to captions.

# Notes

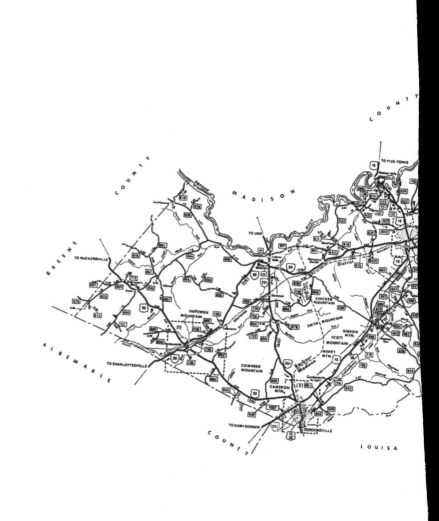